Napoleon Bonaparte occupied a central place in the consciousness of many British writers of the Romantic period. He was a profound shaping influence on their thinking and writing, and a powerful symbolic and mythic figure whom they used to legitimize and discredit a wide range of political and aesthetic positions. In this first ever full-length study of Romantic writers' obsession with Napoleon, Simon Bainbridge focuses on the writings of the Lake poets Wordsworth, Coleridge and Southey, and of Byron and Hazlitt. Combining detailed analyses of specific texts with broader historical and theoretical approaches, and illustrating his argument with the visual evidence of contemporary cartoons, Bainbridge shows how Romantic writers constructed, appropriated and contested different Napoleons as a crucial part of their sustained and partisan engagement in the political and cultural debates of the day.

CAMBRIDGE STUDIES IN ROMANTICISM

This series aims to foster the best new work in one of the most challenging fields within English literary studies. From the early 1780s to the early 1830s a formidable array of talented men and women took to literary composition, not just in poetry, which some of them famously transformed, but in many modes of writing. The expansion of publishing created new opportunities for writers, and the political stakes of what they wrote were raised again and again by what Wordsworth called those 'great national events' that were 'almost daily taking place': the French Revolution, the Napoleonic and American wars, urbanization, industrialization, religious revival, an expanded empire abroad and the reform movement at home. This was an enormous ambition, even when it pretended otherwise. The relations between science, philosophy, religion and literature were reworked in texts such as *Frankenstein* and *Biographia Literaria*; gender relations in *A Vindication of the Rights of Woman* and *Don Juan*; journalism by Cobbett and Hazlitt; poetic form, content and style by the Lake School and the Cockney School. Outside Shakespeare studies, probably no body of writing has produced such a wealth of response or done so much to shape the responses of modern criticism. This indeed is the period that saw the emergence of those notions of 'literature' and of literary history, especially national literary history, on which modern scholarship in English has been founded.

The categories produced by Romanticism have also been challenged by recent historicist arguments. The task of the series is to engage both with a challenging corpus of Romantic writings and with the changing field of criticism they have helped to shape. As with other literary series published by Cambridge, this one will represent the work of both younger and more established scholars, on either side of the Atlantic and elsewhere.

For a complete list of titles published see p. 260.

NAPOLEON AND ENGLISH ROMANTICISM

George Cruikshank, *The Modern Prometheus, or Downfall of Tyranny* (London 1814).

NAPOLEON AND ENGLISH ROMANTICISM

SIMON BAINBRIDGE

University of Keele

Published by the Press Syndicate of the University of Cambridge
The Pitt Building, Trumpington Street, Cambridge CB2 1RP
40 West 20th Street, New York, NY 10011-4211, USA
10 Stamford Road, Oakleigh, Melbourne 3166, Australia

First published 1995

Printed in Great Britain at the University Press, Cambridge

A catalogue record for this book is available from the British Library

Library of Congress cataloguing in publication data

Bainbridge, Simon.
Napoleon and English Romanticism / Simon Bainbridge.
p. cm. – (Cambridge Studies in Romanticism)
Includes bibliographical references and index.
ISBN 0 521 47336 5 (hardback)
1. English literature – 19th century – History and criticism.
2. Politics and literature – Great Britain – History – 19th century.
3. Napoleon I, Emperor of the French, 1769–1821 – Influence.
4. English literature – French influences. 5. Kings and rulers in literature. 6. Romanticism – Great Britain. I. Title. II. Series.
PR457.B25 1995
821'.709351 – dc20 95-713 CIP

ISBN 0 521 47336 5 hardback

For
my parents
John and Rosemary
and for
Anne-Julie

Contents

Illustrations

Acknowledgements

I would like to thank the many people who have helped me throughout the writing of this book. Tim Webb encouraged me to undertake the project and provided stimulating advice during its early stages. Hugh Haughton's generous commentary on individual chapters, his enthusiastic suggestions and his supportive friendship have been invaluable. Steven Matthews, John Birtwhistle and Marilyn Butler, as well as two anonymous readers at Cambridge University Press, read versions of the manuscript and made many valuable recommendations which have sharpened the critical focus of the book. Thanks are also due to Alan Marshall, David Duff, Jim Mays and Jack Donovan for their various suggestions, Jaques Berthoud, Gerald Hammond and Anthea Trodd for their support and Simon Newbronner for technical advice during the final stages of the writing of this book. Josie Dixon at Cambridge University Press has given me encouragement and advice since I first proposed the book to her and has been of great help in seeing it through the various stages of production. My parents have been supportive throughout. My greatest debt is to Anne-Julie Crozier who has not only sustained and encouraged me through the project but has read and commented on numerous draft chapters.

A version of the final part of chapter 5 has appeared in *Romanticism*, 1,1,1995. Illustrations are reproduced with the permission of the Trustees of the British Museum. Leigh Hunt's unpublished letter of 2 April 1814 to Lord Byron, quoted on pages 150–1, is reproduced with the kind permission of John Murray (Publishers) Ltd.

Abbreviations

BL Samuel Taylor Coleridge, *Biographia Literaria or Biographical Sketches of my Literary Life and Opinions*. 2 vols. ed. James Engell and W. Jackson Bate. Bollingen Series. London: Routledge and Princeton University Press, 1983.

BLJ *Byron's Letters and Journals*. 12 vols. ed. Leslie Marchand. London: John Murray, 1973–82.

CL *Collected Letters Of Samuel Taylor Coleridge*. 6 vols. ed. E. L. Griggs. Oxford: Clarendon Press, 1956–71. Cited by volume and letter number.

CNB *The Notebooks of Samuel Taylor Coleridge*. 6 vols. ed. Kathleen Coburn. New York: Pantheon Books, 1957–73. Cited by volume and entry number.

CoC *The Convention of Cintra* (full title: *Concerning the Relations of Great Britain, Spain, and Portugal, to Each Other, and to the Common Enemy, at this Crisis; and Specifically As Affected by the Convention of Cintra: The Whole brought to the test of those Principles, by which alone the Independence and Freedom of Nations can be Preserved and Recovered*), in vol. 1 of *The Prose Works of William Wordsworth*. 3 vols. ed. W. J. Owen and Jane Worthington Smyser. Oxford: Clarendon Press, 1984.

CPW *The Poetical Works of Samuel Taylor Coleridge*. 2 vols. ed. Ernest Hartley Coleridge. Oxford University Press, 1912 rpt 1983.

EoT Samuel Taylor Coleridge, *Essays On His Times – in The Morning Post and the Courier*. 3 vols. ed. David V. Erdman. Bollingen Series. London: Routledge and Princeton University Press, 1978.

EY *Letters Of William And Dorothy Wordsworth, The Early Years, 1787–1805*. ed. E. de Selincourt, 2nd ed., revised Chester L. Shaver. Oxford: Clarendon Press, 1967.

F Samuel Taylor Coleridge, *The Friend*. 2 vols. ed. Barbara E.

Rooke. Bollingen Series. London: Routledge and Princeton University Press, 1969.

HCW — *The Complete Works of William Hazlitt.* 21 vols. ed. P. P. Howe. London: J. M. Dent, 1930–4.

LoL — Samuel Taylor Coleridge, *Lectures 1808–1819 on Literature.* 2 vols. ed. R. A. Foakes. Bollingen Series. London: Routledge and Princeton University Press, 1987.

LS — Samuel Taylor Coleridge, *Lay Sermons.* ed. R. J. White. Bollingen Series. London: Routledge and Princeton University Press, 1972.

MLR — *Modern Language Review*

MY I — *Letters of William and Dorothy Wordsworth, The Middle Years, Part I, 1806–1811.* ed. E. de Selincourt, 2nd ed., revised by Mary Moorman. Oxford: Clarendon Press, 1967.

MY II — *Letters of William and Dorothy Wordsworth, The Middle Years, Part II, 1812–1820.* ed. E. de Selincourt, 2nd ed., revised by Mary Moorman and Alan G. Hill. Oxford: Clarendon Press, 1967.

SiR — *Studies in Romanticism*

SL — *The Life and Correspondence of the Late Robert Southey.* 6 vols. ed. Rev. Charles Cuthbert Southey. London: Longman, Brown, Green & Longmans, 1850.

SNL — *New Letters of Robert Southey.* 2 vols. ed. Kenneth Curry. New York and London: Columbia University Press, 1965.

TWC — *The Wordsworth Circle*

Introduction: the poets and the conqueror

> When Buonaparte fell, an English editor (of virulent memory) exhausted a great number of the finest passages in *Paradise Lost* in applying them to his ill-fated ambition. This was an equal compliment to the poet and the conqueror: to the last, for having realised a conception of himself in the mind of his enemies on a par with the most stupendous creations of the imagination; to the first, for having embodied in fiction what bore so strong a resemblance to, and was constantly brought to mind by, the fearful and imposing reality!
>
> Hazlitt, 'On Means and Ends' (*HCW* XVII, 22)

This book is concerned with the response of several British writers of the Romantic period to the career of Napoleon and to the political and aesthetic challenges it came to represent. It focuses on the writings of the three Lake poets – Wordsworth, Coleridge and Southey – and of two of their most vehement antagonists, Byron and Hazlitt. These writers constructed, appropriated and contested different Napoleons as a crucial part of their sustained and partisan engagement in the political and cultural debates of the day. To use terms I have drawn from Richard Whately's pamphlet of 1819, *Historic Doubts Relative to Napoleon Bonaparte,*[1] Napoleon became an 'imaginary' figure for them, a 'fabrication' created to embody their political and personal hopes and fears. Yet these writers also saw Napoleon as occupying a place in the public 'imagination' which reinforced his hold on power. Depending on their political orientations, they sought through their representations of him to consolidate his place in this vital arena or to drive him out of it.

If there was a contest among these writers over the representation of Napoleon, however, there was also a series of contests between them and the figure of Napoleon himself, between the poets and the conqueror. Napoleon became crucial to their thinking about their own roles and their acts of self-conception. They both identified with him, appropriating him as a figure of power, and used him as an *Other* against which they could define themselves. Napoleon was the supreme embodiment of the hero in an age in which the artist was increasingly seen as heroic,[2] but his career raised numerous questions about the nature of heroism itself. The dilemma of how to respond to the fascinatingly ambivalent figure of Napoleon prompted these writers to evaluate themselves in Napoleonic terms, even to conceive of themselves along Napoleonic lines. Keats, who argued that Napoleon 'had done more harm to the life of Liberty than any one else could have done',[3] nonetheless seems to have adopted 'Little Boney' on at least one occasion as a figure whose successful career, despite his class and height, provided an important role model for an ambitious, yet diminutive, 'Cockney' poet. In his long letter of 14 February to 3 May 1819 he wrote to George and Georgiana Keats:

> I heard that Mr L[ewis] Said a thing I am not at all contented with – Says he 'O, he is quite the little Poet' now this is abominable – You might as well say Buonaparte is quite the little soldier – You see what it is to be under six foot and not a Lord – . . .[4]

The leading poetic Lord of the day, Byron, acted out a life-long identification with Napoleon, hailing himself in *Don Juan* as 'the grand Napoleon of the realms of rhyme' (XI, 55).[5] But the tag was an ambiguous one, both in its judgement of Napoleon and its attempt to reconcile the world of 'action' with that of 'rhyme'. What these writers regarded as Napoleon's genius, energy, imagination and daring, qualities which they saw as central to their own work, made him a powerful role model. Yet Napoleon's staggeringly successful career in the world of political and military affairs, be it for good or bad, dynamically called into question the value of their own roles as writers or poets. What, as Wordsworth asked himself in 'October, 1803', was the poet to do when confronted by 'one Man, of Men the Meanest too! / Raised up to sway the World, to do, undo, . . .'? (lines 2–3).[6] His response was to pit himself, both as a poet and a Grasmere Volunteer, against Napoleon, and it is testimony to the importance of this struggle that it can be argued that he achieves some of his greatest realizations of the 'Imagination' when 'in opposition set / Against an enemy' (*The Prelude* XIII, 30–1[7]).

Wordsworth's combative response to Napoleon certainly involved an element of rivalry. Byron conducted his own contest more explicitly and controversially. In one memorable exchange of 1816, he pointedly refused to except even Napoleon when he declared himself 'the greatest man existing'.[8] William Hazlitt, the greatest antagonist of the Lakers, provocatively suggests in *The Life of Napoleon Buonaparte* that it was dread of Napoleon as a 'rival' and a sense of 'jealousy' that prompted the Lake poets' hatred of him:

They had no great objection to what he was doing – but they could not bear to think that he had done more than they had ever dreamt of. While they were building castles in the air, he gave law to Europe. He carved out with the sword, what they had only traced with the pen. 'Never', says Mr. Landor, 'had been such good laws administered over a considerable portion of Europe. The services he rendered to society were great, manifold, extensive'. But these services were hateful in their eyes – because he aggrandised himself in performing them. The power he wielded, the situation he occupied, excited their envy, much more than the stand he made against the common enemy, their gratitude. They were ready enough at times to pull down kings, but they hated him worse who trampled, by his own might on their necks – as more rivals to themselves, as running in the same race, and going further in it. (*HCW* XVI, 245)

Pointedly ignoring the Lakers' 'apostasy' – the usual subject of his attacks – Hazlitt figures Napoleon as enacting with the 'sword' what the 'levelling' Muse of Wordsworth and the other 'Jacobin poets' sought to bring about with the 'pen'.[9] His comments seek to trivialize the Lakers' later criticisms of Napoleon while incorporating their writing within his own radical polemic. Yet Hazlitt's comic exploration of the Lake poets' 'envy' of Napoleon as a man of action, and his critique of their 'building castles in the air' while Napoleon gave 'laws to Europe', suggest one of the crucial Romantic debates – the relationship of poetical to political power; a relationship memorably explored by Coleridge in 'Kubla Khan', a poem which juxtaposes the law-giver Khan's decree with the poet's desire to 'build that dome in air',[10] and by Wordsworth in his sonnets of 1802–4 in which he measures himself against 'young Buonaparte'.[11]

HISTORIC DOUBTS

> What, then, are we to believe? If we are disposed to credit all that is told us, we must believe in the existence not only of one, but of two or three Bonapartes; if we admit nothing but what is well-authenticated, we shall be compelled to doubt of the existence of any. (Richard Whately, *Historic Doubts Relative to Napoleon Bonaparte*, p. 20.)

The centrality and importance of the figure of Napoleon to Romantic culture and politics is powerfully, if somewhat paradoxically, illustrated by Richard Whately's brilliant piece of mock-scepticism, *Historic Doubts*

Relative to Napoleon Bonaparte, published in 1819, four years after the battle of Waterloo and two before the death of Napoleon in captivity on St Helena. Taking as his starting-point the contemporary British obsession with Napoleon – 'we may safely say that no subject was ever found so inexhaustibly interesting' (p. 15) – Whately ironically juxtaposes the different accounts of Napoleon's career and, confronted by their polarity, declares him a 'fabrication' of the circulation-conscious newspapers and the warring political parties (p. 18). Whether presented by the Tory government as a nursery bogeyman and 'political bugbear' to reinforce their ideological control (pp. 15–16), or by the Whig party as a 'hero', Napoleon, Whately concludes, was an 'imaginary' figure (pp. 20–1).

Whately's argument is, of course, an extended exercise in irony and parody. His aim is to produce a *reductio ad absurdum* of Hume's *Essay on Miracles* and so discredit his argument against believing in miracles on human testimony. In an earlier essay 'Of Scepticism' of 1818, which, as Whately's modern editor Ralph Pomeroy has suggested, stimulated the first draft of *Historic Doubts*, Whately describes his intention as being to show 'the folly of boundless scepticism . . . [not] in *abstract terms*, but . . . in the way of illustration . . . by bringing forward plausible arguments against something which no one ever did or can doubt' (p. xxvii). In *Historic Doubts*, the first draft of which followed 'Of Scepticism' in Whately's *Commonplace Book*, Napoleon is chosen as just such an example of 'something which no one ever did or can doubt', providing him with a vehicle for his parody of Hume's conception of testimony. As the *Edinburgh Review* commented in 1861, Whately's aim was to show that 'a piece of well-known history – that of Napoleon, for instance – is as full of apparent inconsistencies and absurdities as the instances you cite from scripture' (p. xvii).

The two sides of Whately's argument provide useful starting-points for thinking about the different ways in which Napoleon is present in the culture of the period as, on the one hand, a real historical personage and, on the other, a 'fabrication' or 'imaginary' figure. Whately's parody is underpinned by a common-sense conviction that the existence of Napoleon cannot be doubted and that history can be 'well known'. Following this line, it can be argued that Napoleon was a 'real' historical personage whose character and actions were the everyday topics of newspapers, caricatures and anecdotes – the media through which the Romantics most frequently perceived him. Then, as now, of course, there was no definitive or stable 'Napoleon' but innumerable and varied accounts of him, themselves available for interpretation. However, taking these mediating factors into account, Napoleon could still be seen as a historical personage whose character and career influenced the thinking and writing of the English Romantics.

Yet Whately's mock presentation of Napoleon as a 'fabrication' and an 'imaginary' hero, and the extensive cultural material he assembles to support his ironic argument do raise important issues about the way in which Napoleon was perceived and represented in the period and anticipate the investigations of more recent critics into the status of historical discourse and knowledge. In his stress on the 'fabricated' or textual nature of historical narrative and his emphasis on the ideological battle that is acted out through the various representations of Napoleon, Whately prefigures the arguments of a number of recent critics that history is not a science – a matter of carefully documented facts giving the reader access to what actually happened – but more of a myth or 'verbal fiction', to use Hayden White's term,[12] shaped according to teleological and often ideological designs.[13] Written history, as Claude Lévi-Strauss has argued in *The Savage Mind*, is 'never history, but history-for'.[14]

Whately's stress on the representation (rather than the presentation) of Napoleon in British culture brings to mind Edward Said's argument that 'in any instance of at least written language, there is no such thing as a delivered presence, but a re-presence or a representation'.[15] Whately presents as futile any attempt to move from representation to presence, from a 'fabricated' Napoleon to the real Napoleon with what he terms 'his true name and authentic history' (p. 22). History, he argues, is ultimately textual and intertextual, with no possibility of returning to an authorizing origin. 'Most persons', he writes, 'would refer to the *newspapers* as the authority from which their knowledge on the subject was observed', but these accounts are either 'copied from other journals, foreign or British (which is usually more than three-fourths of the news published)' or 'refer to the authority of certain "private correspondents" abroad' (pp. 13–14). One signifier leads only to another without ever arriving at the transcendent signified, the real Napoleon Bonaparte. Thus, concludes Whately, 'we find ourselves in the condition of the Hindoos, who are told by their parents that the earth stands on an elephant, and the elephant on a tortoise, but are left to find out for themselves what the tortoise stands on – or whether it stands on anything at all' (pp. 14–15). Given this lack of an authorizing origin for any of the accounts of Napoleon's career, Whately advances his 'important maxim' that '*it is possible for a narrative – however circumstantial – however steadily maintained – however public, and however important, the events it relates – however grave the authority on which it is published – to be nevertheless an entire fabrication!*' (p. 18). His point is not that Napoleon did not exist, but that there is no way of distinguishing the real Napoleon from the numerous fabricated versions of him: 'I do not mean whether there was ever a person bearing that *name*, for that is a question of no consequence, but whether any such person ever performed all the wonderful things attributed to him' (p. 23). We must either believe in 'the existence not only of one, but of two or three Bonapartes' or in none at all (p. 20).

Yet if Napoleon can only be known in these fabricated forms, Whately's argument nonetheless stresses the ideological and economic interest that both individuals and institutions have in maintaining these fabrications within the culture of the period. Napoleon becomes a site of cultural contestation, used to legitimize ideological power and institutional practices. Within the British political system Napoleon functions as 'one common instrument' made use of by both parties (p. 16). For the Tories, he operates as a 'political bugbear', a 'phantom' used to ensure loyalty to their administration and payment of taxes: 'Bonaparte, in short, was the burden of every song; his redoubted name was the charm which always succeeded in unloosing the purse-strings of the nation' (p. 16). For the Whigs, Napoleon is a 'hero' whose cause and character embody their advocacy for liberty and their opposition to the encroachments of monarchical power (pp. 20–1). Similarly, the newspapers have their own investment in certain fabrications of Napoleon, irrespective of historical validity. As Whately asks, 'Have they not a manifest interest in circulating the wonderful accounts of Napoleon Bonaparte and his achievements, whether true or false? Few would read newspapers if they did not sometimes find wonderful or important news in them' (p. 15). Whately presents accounts of Napoleon as operating within a circular economy of investment and interest. Political parties, newspapers and individuals invest in and circulate representations of Napoleon, these representations produce interest – both curiosity and profit – but interest needs to be maintained by the continuation of this process. The maintenance of public interest in Napoleon is inseparable from the economic interest produced. In the penultimate paragraph of his pamphlet, Whately's language implies a parallel between 'fabricated' Napoleons and counterfeit money when he asks those who believe in any account of Napoleon to 'consider through how many, and what very suspicious hands this story has arrived to them . . . and likewise how strong an interest, in every way, those who have hitherto imposed on them have in keeping up the imposture'. Fake Napoleons may be false currency but, as

Whately argues, they can still produce interest 'in every way'.

If the fabrication of Napoleon provides a means of maintaining certain interests, be they political or economic, Whately also suggests that it plays a part in the processes of self-definition and self-validation when he turns to the issue of nationality. Linda Colley, in her book *Britons: Forging the Nation 1707–1837*, has argued that a sense of British national identity was an invention forged above all by the series of wars against France in the eighteenth and early nineteenth centuries. The confrontation with the obviously hostile *Other* encouraged the British to define themselves against it.[16] Whately, though stressing Englishness rather than Britishness, argues that the figure of Napoleon operates in the culture in this way as a hostile *Other*, the hyperbolic definition of whom enables the English to enhance their own sense of national identity and glory:

> There is one more circumstance which I cannot forbear mentioning, because it so much adds to the air of fiction which pervades every part of this marvellous tale; and that is, the nationality of it.
>
> Bonaparte prevailed over all the hostile States in turn, *except England*; in the zenith of his power, his fleets were swept from the sea *by England*; his troops always defeat an equal and frequently even a superior number of those of any other nation, *except the English* – and with them it is just the reverse: twice, and twice only, he is personally engaged against an *English commander and both times he is totally defeated, at Acre and Waterloo; and to crown all, England* finally crushes his tremendous power, which had so long kept the continent in subjection or in alarm; and to the *English* he surrenders himself prisoner! Thoroughly national, to be sure, . . . It would do admirably for an epic poem . . .
>
> Bonaparte's exploits seem magnified in order to enhance the glory of his conquerors – just as Hector is allowed to triumph during the absence of Achilles, merely to give additional splendour to his overthrow by the arm of that invincible hero! (p. 35)

Though written as a parody of Hume, then, and intended as a critique of 'boundless scepticism', Whately's ingenious pamphlet nonetheless reveals just how much is at stake in the representation of Napoleon in the period. The fabrication of Napoleon operates as a way of defining, validating and maintaining certain forms of interests within the culture, be they journalistic, party political or national.

'GREATEST' AND 'MEANEST'

Whately's argument is one that can be used to investigate the various textual representations of Napoleon during the Romantic period.

Wordsworth, Coleridge, Southey, Byron and Hazlitt were all obsessed by the figure of Napoleon, following his career through newspaper reports, anecdotes, essays, and visits to Europe and engaging with him in their public and private writings. The historical figure of Napoleon, what Hazlitt terms 'the fearful and imposing reality' (*HCW* XVII, 22), had a profound impact on their thinking and writing. As Coleridge argued, he was one 'of all those great Men, who in the states or the mind of man had produced great revolutions, the effect of which still remain, and are, more or less distant, causes of the present state of the World' (*CL* III, 818). Coleridge does not state whether Napoleon produced his 'great revolution' in the 'states' or the 'mind of man' but his remark nonetheless gives Napoleon the status of one of the determinants of the period, suggesting that he influenced not only the political history of France and the map of Europe but the consciousness of the age itself.

Yet, for these writers, Napoleon was also important as an 'imaginary' figure, a fabricated embodiment of their political and personal hopes and fears and a site for debating the crucial issues of the day. Like the political parties, the Romantics 'availed themselves of one common instrument', seizing Napoleon as a figure who could be used to serve what Hazlitt terms their 'own purposes', their political and aesthetic ideologies (*HCW* V, 66). Moreover, Napoleon operated for these writers as an *Other* that could be rhetorically conquered through opposition or appropriation, enhancing their own 'glory' and 'splendour'.

As Whately's modern editor, Ralph Pomeroy, has observed, one of the means by which he makes obvious the clash of testimonies regarding Napoleon and hence his 'fabrication' is by opposing the two main modes in which he is represented in contemporary accounts of his career; *hyperbole* and *diminutio* (p. xxxix). On the one hand, Napoleon is described as 'extraordinary', 'gigantic', 'great', 'wonderful', 'marvellous', 'prodigious' and 'tremendous'. On the other, as 'cruel', 'mean', 'merciless', 'perfidious', 'imperious', 'cowardly' and even 'insane'. Similarly, Theresa Kelley has examined the way that Napoleon is represented in contemporary British caricature and writing in either gigantic or miniature forms, as a colossus or as 'little Boney'. Napoleon's exaggerated size, she argues, reveals that his importance for the Romantics was figurative rather than literal. What is at stake 'in the representation of Napoleon is the problem of political representation (or its lack) at home'.[17] These two comments provide a useful starting-point for thinking about the representation of Napoleon during the Romantic period by writers from different positions across the political spectrum. Throughout, a similar polarization operates in the debate over whether Napoleon was the 'greatest' or the 'meanest', a debate which is concerned with much more than the objective assessment of Napoleon's historical status.

When *The Examiner* announced Napoleon's death in 1821, it claimed him as the supreme figure of the Romantic period: 'The age has lost its greatest man. He was far and away from our eyes and our thoughts; but we felt a pervading consciousness that he lived and something of a feeling that he might again appear among us'.[18] But *The Examiner*'s tentatively expressed hope for an almost Christ-like return from exile suggests a political agenda behind its eulogistic elevation of Napoleon. The weekly paper was the mouthpiece for the stridently radical Hunt brothers and its representation of Napoleon as the 'greatest man' of the 'age' was contingent upon his political significance as a figure of symbolic opposition to the restored monarchical system of the post-Waterloo world.[19] Similarly, Byron, who described Napoleon as 'the greatest . . . of men' (*Childe Harold's Pilgrimage*, III, 36), and Hazlitt, the most ardent of the British Bonapartists, who eulogized him as 'the great man', 'the greatest of men', 'the greatest man in modern history' and 'the only great man in modern times' (*HCW* XX, 15; IV, 45; XX, 57; XII, 166), illustrate this important connection between the elevation of Napoleon and the adoption of him as a political symbol.

Yet such hyperbolic claims for Napoleon's supreme position in the age were not uncommon, nor were they made exclusively by writers who adopted him as a symbol of their liberal or radical politics. When Napoleon abdicated in 1814, for example, Lord Burghersh wrote exultingly to the Duke of Wellington: 'Glory to God and to yourself, the great man has fallen',[20] though this comment may again exemplify Whately's satire on the magnification of Napoleon to enhance the 'glory' of his conquerors. Walter Scott, an avowed Tory and author of a hostile biography of Napoleon, could assert boldly that he 'was and will remain the greatest man of his time'.[21] It is worth remembering, however, that Scott had a financial investment in Napoleon's 'greatness' just as Byron, Hazlitt and the Hunts had a political one. He wrote his *Life of Napoleon Bonaparte* with the specific intention of making money after his bankruptcy and his claim for Napoleon's 'greatness' may have been a necessary part of the puffing of this project. Unlike Byron, Hazlitt and the Hunts, however, Scott made his assertion of Napoleon's greatness independent of his judgements of his moral and political character; describing him elsewhere as 'certainly a great man, though far from a good man, and still farther from a good king'.[22]

To some Romantic writers, however, all public claims for Napoleon's greatness were morally and politically reprehensible. From 1802 onwards, Wordsworth, Coleridge and Southey, aware of Napoleon's charismatic appeal, strove to derogate his power over the imagination of their contemporaries. As Wordsworth put it in his Miltonic tract, *The Convention of Cintra*, written during the Spanish Peninsular War, they 'combated for victory in the empire of reason, for strong-holds in the imagination' (*CoC* 261). Their fight necessitated the denial of Napoleon's greatness. Coleridge, for example, was outraged in 1810 by a speech made by the leader of opposition in the Commons, George Ponsonby, in which, as Coleridge noted with amazement, he 'pronounced' Napoleon 'the greatest and wisest human Being that ever existed on Earth!!' (*CNB* III, 3845).[23] Coleridge responded immediately, sketching out an essay in his notebook which undermined Ponsonby's claim and denied Napoleon's greatness (*CNB* III, 3845). In the following year he adopted a different method of response, reminiscent of Fielding's use of 'great' in *Jonathan Wild*, describing Napoleon as 'the greatest proficient in human destruction that has ever lived' (*EoT* II, 276) and so appropriating and inverting the superlative that had so angered him. Wordsworth denies Napoleon's 'greatness' throughout his sonnet sequence of 1802–3, asserting that Revolutionary France has failed to bring forth 'Great Men' comparable to the figures of the English Republican tradition: Sydney, Marvell, Harrington, Vane and Milton.[24] Indeed, in his sonnet 'October 1803' he goes to the opposite extreme and answers hyperbole with *diminutio*, describing Napoleon as 'Of Men the Meanest' (line 2).

This contemporary contesting of Napoleon's status is dramatically illustrated by an anecdote recounted by Southey in a letter to Neville White in which he describes an exchange between himself and Byron some time shortly before Napoleon's first abdication in April 1814. He writes that the 'last time I saw him [Byron] he asked me if I did not think Bonaparte a great man in his villainy. I told him, no, – that he was a mean-minded villain' (*SL* IV, 73). The 'Satanic' Byron, playing devil's advocate and anticipating his later goading of Southey in *The Vision of Judgment*, seeks to shock and taunt the recently appointed Poet Laureate by conferring 'greatness' upon Napoleon. He flaunts his admiration for him symbolically, using it to represent his own anti-establishment heterodoxy, and clearly enjoys the fascinating ambivalence of greatness and villainy in his formulation, and its discomfiting effect on Southey. Southey, who elsewhere described Napoleon as 'in guilt the first, / Pre-eminently bad among the worst',[25] responds in a characteristically flat and one-dimensional way. He not only denies Napoleon's greatness but resorts to the opposite extreme for his judgement, representing him in terms recalling Wordsworth's as a 'mean-minded villain'.

These exchanges, minor skirmishes in the war of words over Napoleon, illustrate both these writers' engagement with him and their fight to establish his status and meaning in the most hyperbolic terms of praise and blame. Whether figured as the 'greatest' or as the 'meanest', Napoleon was a powerful symbolic figure who could be used to legitimize or discredit political or aesthetic positions. The representations of him by these writers often moved away from the factual analysis of history and into the realm of myth or fiction, transforming him into a Messianic or Satanic figure, a romance or epic hero. As Whately points out, contemporary accounts of Napoleon's career always carry 'an air of fiction and romance':

> All the events are great, and splendid, and marvellous: great armies, great victories, great frosts, great reverses, 'hair breadth 'scapes', empires subverted in a few days . . . everything upon that grand scale, so common in Epic Poetry, so rare in real life, and thus calculated to strike the imagination of the vulgar and to remind the sober-thinking few of the Arabian Nights. (pp. 24–5)

Whately's use of the word 'calculated' reveals how much is at stake in the representation of Napoleon's career and the power that can be derived by shaping history through generic forms such as romance, epic or Shakespearean tragedy (the allusion is to *Othello* I. iii. 136). He locates the battlefield of these accounts not in Europe or the colonies but in the popular 'imagination'. The contest over Napoleon is a battle for the imagination, a battle in which these writers feel themselves to be fully engaged.

NAPOLEONIC PLOTS

The point is, of course, that a representation of Napoleon is not simply a public pattern of words or images with which the writer tries to express his own conception of the historical reality of Napoleon Bonaparte. Every representation of him is polemical; it contains an implicit or explicit argument, intended to have an effect on its readers. Ronald Paulson, in his study of the use of aesthetic categories in representations of the French Revolution, makes this point emphatically:

> There is obviously a sense in which images as well as words do not *represent* anything but serve as counters for their users. As Wittgenstein's maxim 'Don't ask

for the meaning, ask for the use' suggests, writers and artists do not use words and images to name a thing so much as to persuade to some end. What they *do* with their words and images is more important than what they represent.[26]

Paulson's argument here is an extreme one; to some extent the Romantic writers *are* trying to name the thing Napoleon, to make comprehensible the nature of the exceptional and extraordinary man of the age. Yet their representations of him are very much part of the post-revolutionary debate and the nationwide propaganda campaign that was waged against Napoleon in pamphlets and caricatures throughout the war. The first generation of Romantic writers saw themselves increasingly as propagandists of the imagination, fighting to undermine the attraction of Napoleon's aura of power and greatness. Byron's and Hazlitt's adoption of Napoleon as a personal idol was an act of political polemic and, to some extent, a reply to the earlier representations and uses of Napoleon, particularly by the Lake poets. In representing Napoleon all these writers made him represent something else, be that a political doctrine, an aesthetic creed or even the writer himself.

Several studies of the literary or textual representation of historical events, both of the French Revolution – such as Paulson's *Representations of Revolution (1789–1820)*, Stephen Prickett's introductory chapter to *England and the French Revolution*, 'Images of Revolution',[27] Marilyn Butler's 'Telling it Like a Story: The French Revolution as Narrative',[28] and Stephen C. Behrendt's 'History, Mythmaking and the Romantic Artist'[29] – and of the two world wars – in Paul Fussell's brilliant studies *The Great War and Modern Memory*[30] and *Wartime*[31] – have examined the way in which seemingly unprecedented historical phenomena were defined in terms of the known and of the models at hand. They have illustrated the ways in which complex and often bewildering events and experiences were conventionalized, narrativized and even mythologized through the use of some externally imposed or derived models of interpretation, be they literary, mythical, biblical, scientific, historical or philosophical. Simultaneously, they have revealed the power that these models possessed as forms of representation, facilitating not only comprehension and assimilation, but a form of prophecy. For example, in her article on the 'plotting' – in both senses – of the French Revolution, Marilyn Butler has written:

In story the revolution was not simply represented but anticipated; narrative forms may represent reality and they may induce it, by making certain futures thinkable . . . Partisans of one side accused the other side of plots, but at a more fundamental level the French Revolution was indeed plotted before it happened. Through the medium of plot it could be discussed, interpreted, received by contemporaries virtually at once, as manifoldly and hugely significant.[32]

Like the French Revolution, Napoleon was often seen in the period as 'extraordinary', to use one of the adjectives Byron applies to him (*BLJ* III, 243). As Whately comments, 'everything relating to this man is *prodigious* and *unprecedented*' and 'in vain will [the judicious man] seek in history for something similar to this wonderful Bonaparte; "nought but himself can be his parallel"' (p. 25). But Napoleon's career was similarly 'plotted' throughout the Romantic period. In seeking to comprehend and assimilate Napoleon, the writers had recourse to a plethora of archetypal historical, literary and mythical figures. They used analogy with these figures to imply a narrative to Napoleon's career, as well as a character judgement. Indeed, the range of figures Napoleon is compared to in the period is bewildering; it includes Alexander the Great,[33] Augustus, Tiberius and Julius Caesar,[34] the Emperor Nepos,[35] Lucius Sulla,[36] Diocletian,[37] Amurath,[38] Dionysius the Younger,[39] Charles V of Spain,[40] Timur and Ghengis Khan,[41] Milo of Crotona,[42] Sesostris,[43] Cambyses,[44] Hannibal,[45] Tamburlaine,[46] Bajazeth,[47] Alva of Belgium,[48] Frederick the Great,[49] Cesare Borgia,[50] Catiline,[51] Charlemagne,[52] Emperor Julian,[53] Charles XII,[54] Attila,[55] Callicles,[56] Ali Pasha,[57] Oliver Cromwell,[58] Marat,[59] George Washington,[60] William Pitt,[61] Spencer Perceval,[62] Wellington,[63] Rob Roy,[64] Macbeth,[65] Richard III,[66] Ulysses,[67] Sir Calidore,[68] Prometheus,[69] Argus,[70] Jupiter,[71] Saturn,[72] Mars,[73] Deucalion,[74] Pisistratus,[75] Goliath,[76] Irus,[77] Gog,[78] Magog,[79] Moloch,[80] Belshazzar,[81] Nebuchadnezzar,[82] Nimrod,[83] and Byron.[84] While this extraordinary list is a testament to the writers' rhetorical and representational range, it can also perhaps be explained by the proposition that the scale and complexity of Napoleon's eventful career not only made him peculiarly available for such a variety of interpretations, but, in fact, compelled the imposition of some interpretative model. Through the use of an analogy Napoleon could be given definite form and meaning.

Moreover, as in Butler's revolutionary 'plots', the writers could exploit the inferred narratives of these analogies in an attempt to anticipate, to make thinkable or to prophesy an ending to Napoleon's career. Analogy with Satan, for example, would not only demonize Napoleon but imply that his career, like Satan's, would end in defeat. Alternatively, to transform Napoleon into a Promethean figure would not only associate him with liberty and grant him qualities of stoicism and defiance but would imply his ultimate triumph. Stephen Behrendt has examined this prophetic practice in general terms in his essay 'History, Mythmaking and the Romantic Artist'. He argues that the Romantics 'envisioned for themselves a crucial role in the shaping of present and future alike'.[85] They achieved this role through the use of what he terms 'myth', a category in which he includes any familiar historical or literary narrative. Their use of 'myth', he writes, functioned by 'arguing by overt or implied analogy in an effort to give shape to the present so that the future may *be* shaped by a public acting in an enlightened partnership with the visionary artist'.[86] Behrendt's model stresses the extent to which the Romantic writer remains engaged with history even when he seems to turn away from it towards other forms such as myth, romance, epic and drama. The mythologization or plotting of history is no exercise in escapist fantasy, rather it is an act 'calculated' to 'strike the imagination', to use Whately's phrase, in the hope of influencing the way in which present history is perceived and enacted.

In this study, I am concerned with both the separate 'plottings' of Napoleon's career – the individual textual responses to specific historical moments – and with the 'plot' or history of the Romantics' developing responses to Napoleon. As the contours of Napoleon's career changed, so did the English writers' reactions to him. What the historian D. G. Wright has written of the numerous histories of Napoleon can be equally well applied to the contemporary responses:

> In the interpretation of Napoleon's career and its impact on France and Europe, a good deal depends . . . on what particular aspects and what particular chronological stages of that career are emphasised. Few can fail to admire the dynamic young Napoleon in Italy in 1796–7 and his courage in grasping power when other talented generals like Moreau and Joubert hesitated. Even fewer would attempt to defend the murder of the Duc D'Enghien or the slaughter of 2,000 disarmed French prisoners in Syria.[87]

To give a sense of the developments of the writers' responses to Napoleon and of their accumulating investments in certain representations of him, I have adopted a chronological approach. This approach, analogous to that used by French critics of Napoleonic iconograpy and historiography such as Tulard and Geyl,[88] also helps to clarify the writers' retrospective reshapings of their reactions to Napoleon.

I am concerned, on the one hand, with the private assessments of Napoleon, often carried out in letters and journals, and, on the other, with the public depiction of him. In both cases the figuring of Napoleon in language, as well as the question of what he is made to figure, are central issues. There is often a considerable overlap between the public and private responses to Napoleon. In Byron's writing of 1813–14, for example, we can trace the development of a private mode of evaluation into a public mode of representation. Often, however, the difference or disjunction between private and public responses can be revealing. While a letter or a journal entry may illustrate or explicate a public statement such as a poem, it can also call its representational strategies into question and suggest other forms of engagement that could have been adopted; alternative ways in which the writer might have responded to the challenge, threat or appeal of the complex and protean figure of Napoleon. Throughout this work, therefore, I have drawn heavily on private forms of writing such as letters, notebooks and journals, not only as a means of elucidating the public writing, but as part of an investigation into the ways in which chosen public forms and contextual pressures can often be seen to produce a simplification or glossing over of the problematic issues that were raised by Napoleon's career.

The scale of material on Napoleon in the period is vast, both in terms of the texts of the better-known writers of the Romantic period and the larger cultural contexts in which they were working. A glance through Betty Bennet's anthology, *British War Poetry in the Age of Romanticism 1793–1815*,[89] or John Ashton's *English Caricature and Satire on Napoleon I*,[90] gives some indication of the vast number of political pamphlet poems, broadsheet ballads, epics, mock-epics, satires, acrostics, songs, sonnets, lines, parodies, soliloquies, odes, plays, play-bills, dialogues, letters, epigrams, impromptus, squibs and lampoons on Napoleon that were produced in the period. Napoleon's dominant position in the caricatures and graphic satires of the period – A.M. Broadley lists an astonishing 990 English examples between 1795 and 1821[91] – effectively confirms his centrality in the political and cultural life of the Romantic era. I shall be drawing on this cultural context whenever necessary but, given the need for selectivity, I have chosen to concentrate principally on the works of Wordsworth, Coleridge, Byron and Hazlitt. Of the so-called major Romantics, these writers sustained the most intense engagement with Napoleon. To this group I have added Southey, whose involvement in Wordsworth's and Coleridge's pro- and anti-Napoleonic projects highlights the political alliance between the Lake poets. Certainly, it was as a triumvirate the Lakers appeared to Byron and Hazlitt. These two second-generation writers seized upon Napoleon as a powerful weapon in the cross-generational and intertextual debate that is such a feature of the period. Within each chapter I have focused on a particular text or group of texts and examined their representations of Napoleon within their broader historical, biographical and cultural contexts. This investigation of the polemical construction of Napoleon reveals the extent to which he was critical to the cultural politics and poetics of the Romantic period.

CHAPTER I

A 'conqueror of kings' and 'a deliverer of men': the revolutionary figure of Napoleon in the writing of Coleridge, Southey and Landor

> We are not conscious of any feeling of bitterness towards the first Consul; or, if any, only that venial prejudice, which naturally results from the having hoped proudly of an individual, and the having been miserably disappointed.
>
> S. T. Coleridge, September 1802 (*EOT* I, 319).

THE SPIRIT OF THE AGE

Given the nature of this contemporary contest over Napoleon, the importance of what was felt to be invested in it and the extreme terms in which it was conducted, it is astonishing that so little critical attention has been focused on the ways in which Napoleon was represented during the Romantic period. Byron is an exception here; his interest in Napoleon has been well served by critics such as G. Wilson Knight, Ronald Paulson, Peter Manning, Jerome McGann, Theresa Kelley and Jerome Christensen. But the fascination of the first-generation Romantics with Napoleon, particularly during the years 1798 to 1802, has been consistently underplayed in favour of a model of Romanticism that stresses the centrality of the historical events of the French Revolution to the movement but defines the crucial period of the English Romantic writers' engagement with European history as coming to an end some time in the latter half of the 1790s: a model strongly supported by works such as *The Prelude* and 'France: An Ode'. M. H. Abrams, for example, writing the 'spiritual biography' of his own generation as well as Wordsworth's under the sign of *The Prelude*[1] argues in 'English Romanticism: The Spirit of the Age' that the 'last decade of the eighteenth century included the complete cycle of the Revolution in France, from what De Quincey called its "gorgeous festival era" to the *coup d'état* of November 10, 1799, when to all but a few stubborn sympathizers it seemed betrayed from without and within, and the portent of Napoleon loomed over

Europe'.[2] He proposes that during this period the first-generation writers shifted away from an engagement with historical or political affairs 'in the very world, which is the world / Of all of us' (*The Prelude* x, 725–6) and through the imagination internalized the hopes that were prompted by the Revolution and disappointed by subsequent events. 'Hope' is 'shifted from the history of mankind to the mind of the single individual, from militant external action to an imaginative act' (p. 66).

This still-influential model of Romanticism, though originating in history, makes Napoleon a figure of little importance or interest. His rise, if mentioned at all,[3] is seen as the culmination of what Abrams has called 'the succession of disasters that began with the Reign of Terror'[4] that contributed to the first-generation writers' disillusionment with the French Revolution. Stephen Prickett, for example, in his study *England and the French Revolution* reiterates this model of the first-generation response to Napoleon:

> What turns the scale so decisively in the end and makes Burkeans of a kind out of both Wordsworth and Coleridge was not a simple linguistic or aesthetic debate but the very much more simple, and to them shocking, facts of the execution of the king and queen, the reign of terror and the inexorable rise of Napoleon, and with him a glorification of militarism worse than anything seen under the *ancien régime*.[5]

One of the factors that has encouraged this retrospective simplification of the Romantics' response to Napoleon is the involvement of the first-generation writers in the same process. This is clearly illustrated by the persistent fallacy that, at an early stage in his career, Napoleon commanded the French army which invaded Switzerland in 1798, supposedly a clear piece of evidence of his aggressive and imperialistic character. It was this invasion which 'shattered' 'Coleridge's lingering hope in the Revolution' according to Abrams,[6] and which prompted his 'Recantation' in the Miltonic 'France: An Ode'. Partly because of its climactic positioning in this poem, and partly due to Wordsworth's later statements on the subject – in his sonnet of 1806, *The Prelude, The Convention of Cintra* and the letter to James Losh of 4 December 1821 – the French invasion of Switzerland has become established as one of the culminating 'disasters' of the revolutionary course of events. Though, in fact, Napoleon took no part in this invasion, critics as influential as Ernest de Selincourt, David Erdman and Carl Woodring have followed Wordsworth and Coleridge and ascribed to him the leading role.[7] Woodring, for example, writes in *Politics in the Poetry of Coleridge* that 'the invasion of Switzerland by Bonaparte early in 1798 ended uncertainty, or at least laid down a line concerning France that the vacillating writer never quite recrossed'.[8] His comment in *Politics in English Romantic Poetry*, however, suggests the source for his belief in Napoleon's invasion. He writes that 'General Bonaparte not only drove the Austrians out of Northern Italy but subjugated Switzerland'.[9] Woodring's use of the rank of 'General' here, and his chronology of events (which goes on to include the Egyptian expedition and the *coup d'état*) make it clear that he refers to the 1798 invasion, rather than the 1802 one which Napoleon did command. His use of the verb 'subjugated', however, suggests that his principal historical source is Wordsworth's sonnet, 'Thought of a Briton on the Subjugation of Switzerland' of 1806 with its Napoleonic 'Tyrant' who drives 'Liberty' from her 'Alpine Holds' (lines 5–7). Yet, as J. C. Maxwell has shown in his concise but very informative article 'Wordsworth and the Subjugation of Switzerland',[10] in this sonnet and his other writings on the subject Wordsworth not only reconstructs his own response to historical events but conflates a number of these events, particularly the 1798 and 1802 invasions. Maxwell's examination of Wordsworth's repeated retrospective attempts to make matters clearer reveals the complexity and ambiguity of his response to the different historical events. It is, Maxwell writes, only in the years following 1802 that:

> . . . the dominant role of Napoleon as the enemy par excellence led to his being seen as also the destroyer of Swiss independence, and thus, since in fact Franco–Swiss hostilities went back to 1798, the outlines became blurred, and the highly romanticised picture given in the sonnet, though not historically true of any single period, came to include elements harking back to 1798, yet without depriving Napoleon of a position of pre-eminence he did not then hold.[11]

Maxwell's article pinpoints two fascinating processes that are characteristic of the retrospective derogation of the figure of Napoleon by both the first-generation Romantics and modern critics. Wordsworth rewrites not only his own history but that of Europe in accordance with later developments. His vision of the past, and of the rise of Napoleon, is reshaped by the continuing pressures of the Napoleonic and post-Waterloo ages, and particularly by Napoleon's assumption after 1802 of the 'dominant role as the enemy *par excellence*'. Moreover, his reformulations and replottings of Napoleon's rise to power and of the invasion of Switzerland, as well as of his own reaction to these events, have fostered the modern myth of Napoleon's Swiss invasion. The propagation of this myth has prompted critics to write Napoleon out of the plot of English

Romanticism, simplifying and dismissing him by making him an invading aggressor whose usurpation of power brought the revolution to an end in 1799.

'MORE THAN ANY DESPOT'

Yet during the period 1798–1802 Napoleon was an important 'imaginary' figure for the first-generation Romantics, particularly Coleridge and Southey, who used him to figure their political hopes, to examine the relationship of political and poetical power and to investigate new forms of leadership. Coleridge and Southey were both enthusiastic followers of Napoleon's Egyptian campaign of 1798–9, which Southey later described as the period of 'his greatness and his glory' (*SL* I, 180). The English perception of this campaign is well described by Alan J. Bewell:

> A distinctive feature of Napoleon's Expedition of 1798 was that it was not represented strictly as a military invasion, but was more generally perceived as a major cultural and scientific event: the beginning of the process whereby modern thought would unlock the mysteries of the Orient. In addition to his army, Napoleon assembled a Scientific Brigade, composed of members of France's Commission of Sciences and Arts, whose task it was, in addition to providing technical and strategic advice, to advance the cause of science in Egypt and to study and publish a full account of Egyptian history and culture . . . The Expedition placed art and politics under the banner of progress. It aimed at freeing a nation long held in bondage to the despotic government of the Ottomans, at providing Egypt with the science and government that would allow it to enter the modern world, and, at recovering, through science, the meaning of art fallen into decay and a language lost in time . . . Through this expedition, Napoleon became identified with the aims and achievements of the Revolution.[12]

In a fascinating letter of 13 May 1799 to his wife Edith, Southey represents Napoleon's Egyptian expedition as rekindling the pantisocratic hopes that had seemed extinguished in 1795. After lamenting the imprisonment of Gilbert Wakefield and Benjamin Flower, Southey declares that 'These are evil times and I believe I may write the epitaph of English liberty' (*SNL* I, 185). His condemnation of the political condition of England prompts him to turn to Napoleon's reorganized Egypt as an alternative system of government which he sees as perhaps embodying the principles of the Revolution: 'Well well Buonaparte is making a home for us in Syria, and we may perhaps enjoy freedom under the suns of the East, in a land flowing with milk and honey' (*SNL* I, 185). Here

Southey adopts the biblical idiom of the promised land from Exodus (3: 8)[13] and in so doing suggestively echoes, or even anticipates, the final lines of Coleridge's 'Kubla Khan':

> For he on honey-dew hath fed,
> And drunk the milk of Paradise. (lines 53–4)

The dating of 'Kubla Khan' is problematic, and has been put as late as October 1799 by Richard Holmes[14] – a period when Coleridge and Southey were engaged in a detailed correspondence about Napoleon. Southey's use of the idiom of Exodus suggests that it may have already gained a currency in Coleridge's immediate circle for referring to Napoleon's Egyptian campaign, just as, three years before, it had been associated with the Quantocks.[15] Southey's letter adds another suggestive piece of evidence to the argument that Coleridge had partly Napoleon, and particularly his Egyptian campaign, in mind when he wrote the poem, as David Pirie has claimed in his notes to his and William Empson's edition of the poetry.[16] Norman Rudich has argued at greater length that '"Kubla Khan" is a political poem in the sense that its basic structure contrasts the political power of the State with the creative power of the Poet' and that it is particularly 'directed against the two Tartar despots, Kubla and Napoleon'.[17] Yet Rudich's reading of the poem depends on just the type of oversimplified understanding of Coleridge's vision of Napoleon at this stage that I have been discussing. He writes that 'Napoleon's invasion of Switzerland in January 1798 marks the decisive turn from hesitations and doubts to total disillusionment, and that was the point of departure for the conservatism which shaded into the reactionary views of his later career'.[18] Certainly, if the representation of the Napoleon–Khan figure is simply a negative or pejorative one, as Rudich argues, then the final lines of the poem can be read as suggesting the visionary's potential power to build through the Imagination the Paradise of 'milk and honey' that this Napoleon–Khan figure has failed to realize through political decree. But, by basing his reading of the poem on this fallacious notion of Napoleon's role in 1798, Rudich fails to take into account Coleridge's much more ambivalent, and often positive, attitude towards Napoleon during the years in which he wrote 'Kubla Khan'. An investigation of Coleridge's and Southey's writing on Napoleon at this stage will illustrate not only how important he was for them as an 'imaginary' figure during this period, but will provide a fuller context for a reading of 'Kubla Khan' as a 'political poem', to use Rudich's phrase.

To return to 1799, on 18 October Southey enthusiastically described to Humphrey Davy his response to the recent French campaigns, including those of Napoleon in Italy and Egypt: 'Massena, Buonaparte, Switzerland, Italy, Holland, Egypt, all at once! the very spring-tide of fortune! It was a dose of gaseous oxide to me, whose powerful delight still endures.'[19] Gaseous oxide was a discovery pioneered by Davy, and Southey rapturously described its effects in a letter to his brother Tom of 12 July 1799: 'it made me laugh and tingle in every toe and finger tip. Davy has actually invented a new pleasure, for which language has no name. Oh Tom! I am going for more this evening; it makes one strong, and so happy; so gloriously happy' (*SL* II, 21). Napoleon's early career clearly induced in Southey a similar feeling of strength and glorious happiness. It seems likely that it was during this period that he considered writing a poem on Napoleon's retreat from Acre after the French army had been desolated by plague in the spring of 1799. In 1801 Southey recalled this project, while lamenting Napoleon's failure to fulfil his early promise: 'Why had the man not perished before the walls of Acre in his greatness and his glory? I *was* asked to write a poem upon that defeat, and half-tempted to do it because it went to my very heart'.[20]

In a series of letters of September and October 1799[21] Southey and Coleridge considered Napoleon's character – 'remarkably studious . . . in company reserved and silent' (*SL* II, 26) – his background and his education as a 'man of Science' (*CL* I, 294). Southey wrote that, according to his source, Napoleon 'was always the great man, always the first, always Bonaparte . . .' (*SL* II, 26). Coleridge responded excitedly, full of praise for Napoleon after his dramatic return from Egypt. As David Erdman writes, in 'Nether Stowey the fire of old Jacobin sympathies and even Gallican Sympathies kindled again, despite all the declarations of recantation and fears'.[22] Coleridge replied ecstatically to Southey on 15 October, asking 'what say you to the Resurrection and Glorification of the Saviour of the East after his tryals in the Wilderness? – I am afraid that this is a piece of Blasphemy – but it was in simple verity such an Infusion of animal Spirits into me – – Buonaparte–! Buonaparte! dear dear DEAR Buonaparte' (*CL* I, 298). Conscious here that his Messianic representation of Napoleon may appear nothing but hyperbole, Coleridge is at pains to stress the sincerity of his feelings.[23] As the rest of the letter makes clear, his adoption of Napoleon was strongly influenced by his status as an alternative and a mascot of opposition to Pitt, a contrast which Coleridge later planned to develop in a Plutarchian pairing of essays for the *Morning Post*[24] and which would be important for the whole thrust of his argument in that paper in January and February 1800.[25] His rapturous incantation of Napoleon's name, like Southey's excited list of events, strikingly illustrates the extent of his enthusiastic response to Napoleon's career. For him it was 'an Infusion of animal spirits' as for Southey it was a 'dose of gaseous oxide'.

Napoleon's *coup d'état* of November 1799, effected in conjunction with the Abbé Sieyès, was greatly disappointing to both Southey and Coleridge, who called it a 'detestable Villainy' (*CL* I, 306). Southey's friend John Rickman wrote to him and asked 'How do you and Bonaparte agree at present? I never liked the Corsican, and now he has given me new offence'.[26] Southey's violent recantation in his reply perhaps stresses the degree of hope that he had fostered for Napoleon. He writes that 'The Corsican has offended me, and even his turning out the Marmelukes will not atone for his rascally constitution . . . Buonaparte has made me Anti-Gallican' (*SL* II, 46). Even in this strident denunciation, however, there is an element of equivocation as Southey weighs Napoleon's expulsion of the despotic dynasty of Marmelukes from Egypt against his new constitution.

Yet for neither Coleridge nor Southey did their immediate reactions to the *coup* signal a full recantation from Bonaparte or a finalization of their vision of him. Coleridge wrote a series of articles for the *Morning Post* in which his representations of Napoleon are various and complex.[27] He makes him at once a heroic figure and a cowardly deserter, a 'hero of romance' and a 'fugitive and a usurper' (*EoT* I, 71, 85), and a 'popular Dictator, full of enterprise, genius and military experience' (*EoT* I, 88). His dualistic and oscillating representation of Napoleon stems partly from his ambivalence towards him at this stage, a mixture of admiration for his 'genius', 'zeal', and 'political sagacity and moderation' and detestation for his act of usurpation.[28] In his essay of 11 March 1800, a rhetorical *tour de force*, Coleridge constructs a powerful argument in favour of Napoleon's government in France which he concludes with an image which wonderfully encapsulates his ambivalence and again recalls Kubla's 'miracle of rare device': 'In his usurpation, Bonaparte stabbed his honesty in the vitals; it has perished – we admit, that it has perished – but the mausoleum, where it lies interred, is among the wonders of the world' (*EoT* I, 211). Moreover, by representing Napoleon as strong if war continues but weak if peace is established in these articles, Coleridge supports the *Morning Post*'s pro-peace editorial line.[29] He argues that if peace is made Napoleon's despotism will give way to a more democratic form of government and is prepared to believe, or at least to argue, that Napoleon is sincere in his offers of peace (*EoT* I, 76–9).

Perhaps most revealing are the two notebook comments made by Coleridge while reporting on Pitt's speech in the House of Commons on 3 February 1800. Their private nature suggests these comments are expressions of Coleridge's own opinion and involve none of the expediency or 'motive mongering' that Erdman has detected in the *Morning Post* articles.[30] Contemptuously responding to Pitt's characterization of Napoleon's government as a military despotism, Coleridge scribbled the exclamatory question: 'More that any Despot. Whats in his character of promise?' (*CNB* I, 651). The second note to the same speech suggests that for Coleridge Napoleon's value was related to his status as an alternative to the rule of the *ancien régime* monarchs: 'That a man can talk of Bourbon who has Bonaparte!' (*CNB* I, 651). These notes reveal an interest in, and an awareness of, Napoleon as a figure of potential and promise, even *after* his *coup d'état*.

Similarly, Southey refused to dwell on the damage done to Napoleon's reputation by the *coup d'état*, but stressed his multi-faceted potential in the most eulogistic terms. In February 1800, less than a month after he claimed that Napoleon had made him an anti-Gallican, he wrote:

> I do not justify his assumption of power – let the use he makes of it, do that, but in reviewing his past conduct – what I privately know of his youth – what all the world knows of his actions – the rank he holds as general – the view he entertains as a philosopher – the feelings which have made him in the career of victory the advocate of peace – I do not hesitate in pronouncing him the greatest man that events have called into action since Alexander of Macedon. (*SNL* I, 221–2[31])

Rather than dismissing Napoleon as a tyrant and seeing his rise as the culmination of the series of disasters that had begun with the execution of the king, both Coleridge and Southey looked hopefully towards him not only as a leader whose exercise of power would justify its underhand seizure but as a 'genius', a 'man of science', a 'philosopher', a 'poet' and a peacemaker. Napoleon was not one of 'the worthless Bourbons', as Southey termed them in his letter (*SNL* I, 222), or a 'plant sown and reared in a hot-house', as Coleridge described Pitt (*EoT* I, 221), but a charismatic figure, a 'man of various talent, of commanding genius, of splendid exploit' who was 'an object of superstition and enthusiasm' (*EoT* I, 208–9). Southey's admiration for Napoleon at this stage seems even to have been a matter of public knowledge or of easy inference. On 21 February 1801, he wrote to Wynn that he had been 'caricatured . . . between Fox and Norfolk – worshipping Bonaparte' (*SL* II, 134).

Given the complexity of Coleridge's and Southey's response to Napoleon during this period, Rudich's Napoleonic interpretation of 'Kubla Khan' seems over-simplistic and needs to be balanced by a more informed counter-reading. If the representation of the Khan–Napoleon figure is a positive one, as the context of this body of writing suggests it could be, in which he is seen as establishing freedom under the suns, or sunny domes, of the East, as Southey hoped Napoleon would do, then the final lines may offer an imaginative means of recreating this political miracle of rare device. This second reading of the poem is supported by the imagery of Coleridge's extraordinary notebook entry of 1802; 'A *Throne* the **Δος που στω** of Archimedes – Poet Bonaparte – Layer out of a World-garden –' (*CNB* I, 1166). This comment, while certainly ambivalent, as Erdman observes,[32] suggests that as late as May 1802 Coleridge may still have seen Napoleon as a figure of political promise and potentiality who could use his new position as Consul for Life to very real effect. Archimedes' phrase 'Give me a fulcrum [and I will move the world]' may apply to Napoleon's ambition, as Kathleen Coburn argues in her commentary on this entry in Coleridge's notebook,'[33] but it is not necessarily used to condemn it. Rather it conveys Coleridge's sense of awe at the sublimity and possibilities of the enormous power possessed by Napoleon and its potential for good or ill. After all, the comment was made less than two months after Napoleon had established the Peace of Amiens (25 March 1802) which boosted his popularity in Britain and at last fulfilled Coleridge's desire for an end to the war between France and England.

Indeed, at this stage Napoleon may well have appeared to be carrying out the mission that Coleridge tentatively envisioned for himself at this time; 'if ever I imagined myself a conqueror, it was to bring peace' (*CNB* I, 1214).[34] Coleridge, perhaps like the poet figure of 'Kubla Khan', 'turned away from these thoughts to more humane and peaceable Dreams' (*CNB* I, 1214). In Napoleon, however, both 'Poet Bonaparte' and the 'Layer out of a World-garden', he saw a powerful individual who was capable of uniting the two figures of 'Kubla Khan': the Khan, who lays out the 'gardens bright' in the first section of the poem, and the poet of the final section. Coleridge's note might suggest a belief or a hope that Bonaparte will himself prove a miracle of rare device, an embodiment of the political and poetic roles of 'Kubla Khan'.

The contrasting figures of the Khan and the poet have often been read in terms of Coleridge's later categories of the 'commanding genius', which shows itself in the world of practical affairs such as politics and warfare, and the 'absolute genius', which manifests itself in the world of the arts and the intellect, defined in *Biographia Literaria.*[35] Again Coleridge employs similar imagery. In 'tranquil times' the 'commanding genius' is formed 'to exhibit a *perfect poem* or palace or temple or *landscape-garden*' (my italics). But to use the categories of the later *Biographia Literaria* to read the earlier poem is to give 'Kubla Khan' a definitive quality that its floating juxtaposition of the two roles avoids. Rather, it seems to have been the case that the later career of Napoleon played a part in prompting Coleridge to make the important distinction between these two types of 'Genius'. If, at an early stage in Napoleon's career, Coleridge adopted him as a figure who could unite the roles of the politician – the 'Layer out of a World-Garden' – and the poet, Napoleon's later career called this figuring into question and prompted Coleridge to distinguish between political and poetic forms of genius. In his writing on Napoleon for the *Morning Post* in 1800 Coleridge makes no distinction between 'genius' and 'commanding genius', describing Napoleon as 'a popular Dictator, full of enterprise, genius, and military experience' (*EoT* I, 88), 'a man of various talent, of commanding genius, of splendid exploit' (*EoT* I, 208) and as the 'greatest genius in the world' (*EoT* I, 310). But by late 1802, when Napoleon appeared to have failed to fulfil his early promise, Coleridge began to deny him the quality of 'genius' – 'this Caesar in all things, but genius, noble birth, and fearless clemency' (*EoT* I, 399) – and to look to other figures for the quality. He describes Toussaint L'Ouverture, for example, as a 'hero as much [Napoleon's] superior in genius as in goodness' (*EoT* II, 766). By 1808, in a lecture on *Macbeth,* Coleridge first draws the distinction between action and art that characterizes his later definition of the two forms of genius:

> Hope the Master Element of Commanding Genius, meeting with an active and combining intellect of just that degree of vividness which disquiets and impels the Soul to try to realize its Images – greatly increase this creative Power and the Images become a satisfying world of themselves – i.e. we have the Poet, or original philosopher . . . (*LoL* I, 137)

Developing this definition in *Biographia* (I, 31) and Appendix C of *The Statesman's Manual,* where Napoleon is represented as a contemporary example of 'commanding genius', Coleridge completes the separation of political from poetic power, placing the 'creative, and self-sufficing power' of the 'absolute Genius' (*BL* I, 31) above the 'Restlessness and whirling Activity' of the 'commanding Genius' (*LS* 66). In this opposition, the imaginative artist is elevated above the politician or the soldier, an elevation which has been restated in numerous accounts of English Romanticism, including those of M. H. Abrams with his shift from 'militant, external action to the imaginative act'. But William Hazlitt's suggestion that the Lakers' hatred of Napoleon was prompted by their dread of him as a 'rival' and their sense of 'jealousy', quoted in the previous chapter, provides a powerful critique of this model. The implication of his satire of the Lakers is that the imaginative power of the poet is, in fact, a lesser form of the political power of the statesman. His comments suggest that behind Coleridge's distinction of 'Commanding' and 'absolute genius' may lie the frustrated hopes that either he or Napoleon would unite the roles of the poet and the politician.

'THE REPUBLICAN AND THE PARALYTIC'

Coleridge's and Southey's investment in Napoleon in the late 1790s and early 1800s and their representations of him in a series of roles as a 'genius', a 'man of science', a 'philosopher', a 'poet' and a peacemaker stress his importance to them as an 'imaginary' figure. This use of Napoleon at this time as a figure of potential who promised to revive the political hopes that had been disappointed by the earlier events of the decade can be explored most fully in the work of a poet they both admired and whom Hazlitt groups with them in his critique of their jealousy of Napoleon, Walter Savage Landor. Landor was less equivocal in his response to Napoleon than either Coleridge or Southey. He immediately claimed Napoleon as the champion of the Revolution and introduced him into the propagandist pro-French and anti-English plot of his epic *Gebir* of 1798 as 'A mortal man above all mortal praise' (VI, 193).[36] As a result *Gebir* became the first major literary work to represent Napoleon and the only contemporary English literary response to his Italian campaign of 1796–7 which announced his dramatic arrival on the international stage. *Gebir*, a work which, as Brian Wilkie has written, 'typifies an important strain of political radicalism in the 1790s',[37] provides a fascinating text for investigating this early stage in the figuring of Napoleon within the cultural context of the post-revolutionary debate in Britain.

Like many of the poems in his early volume of 1795, *Gebir* was in part the product of Landor's early political beliefs: his adherence to the French Revolution, his avowed republicanism and his hatred of monarchy. As he confessed in later years, it was written 'when our young heads were turned towards the French Revolution, and deluded by a phantom of Liberty'.[38] Born in 1775, Landor was brought up in an atmosphere of political activity. His father, having inherited a large estate, had allied himself with the Whig interest in Warwickshire in the 1790s.[39] At school, as his biographer Malcolm Elwin writes, 'news of the French Revolution in 1789 fired his imagination, and made him an ardent apostle of liberty, equality and fraternity'.[40] Whereas his father, under the influence of Burke, shifted allegiance to Pitt and the Tory party, Landor became even more vehemently a Whig, particularly under the guidance and friendship of Dr Samuel Parr, whose house was the centre of opposition activity in Warwickshire and who acted as adviser to the chief Whig politicians.[41] Elwin argues that, in addition to Parr's powerful influence, Landor's own character, his arrogance, impetuosity and antipathy to authority inspired in him a sympathetic faith in the French Revolution as a rebellion against repression.[42] Certainly, Landor's early life testifies to his characteristic combination of defiance of authority and the making of a political statement. At Rugby School he refused to use the hierarchical terms of address and was eventually removed for rebelliousness.[43] At Oxford, where he was proud to wear his hair unpowdered in the revolutionary style, he was the leader of the most vehemently Jacobin element of undergraduates who used his room as their rendezvous.[44] Southey, a contemporary of Landor's at Oxford, said later that Landor was 'notorious as a mad Jacobin', adding that 'his Jacobinism would have made me seek his acquaintaince, but for his madness'.[45] Landor's cultivation of this reputation as a political radical prompted his tutor to warn him to 'take care, or they will stone you for a republican'.[46] Perhaps most strikingly, Landor's political beliefs were characterized by a violent and iconoclastic hatred of the British monarchy. He rejoiced in sharing the date of his birthday, 30 January, with the anniversary of the execution of Charles I, and once told his mother that he wished 'the French would invade and assist us in hanging George the Third between two such thieves as the archbishops of Canterbury and York'.[47]

As Malcolm Elwin and R. H. Super have argued, Landor's *Moral Epistle, Respectfully Dedicated to Earl Stanhope*, which was published in 1795,[48] gives an indication of his political sympathies in the year before he began work on *Gebir*.[49] Stanhope, a noted radical, had opposed the war against the American colonies, delivered a congratulatory address to the National Assembly in 1789 on 'the recent glorious revolution', protested in the House of Lords against British interference in French internal affairs, and moved that the French Republic should be recognized by the British government. This last action had prompted Coleridge to address two sonnets to him in 1795 hailing him eulogistically as 'Patriot pure and just', 'the Friend of Humankind!' and the 'Champion of Freedom and her God!'[50] As Elwin notes, the *Epistle* 'laments the repressive measures introduced by Pitt's government to repel the liberal influence of the French Revolution' and 'looks forward to liberty and peace through the triumph of human brotherhood over patriotism'; themes which Landor would reiterate in *Gebir*.[51]

While he was at Oxford, Landor was accused of proposing the extravagant and threatening toast: 'May there be only two classes of people, the republican and the paralytic.'[52] This violent expression of radical sentiment, however, was more than a piece of drunken student bravado. Landor's exaltation of the republican and condemnation of any other political position characterizes the dominant plot of both his early poetry and *Gebir*, works which enact the paralysis of any force which threatens the French Republic. The last four stanzas of the short poem 'The Grape' provide a good example.[53] After describing the lyric poet Anacreon's death as a result of a grape sticking in his throat, Landor shifts his focus from the classical world to the plains of the contemporary French Republic:

> Thus far the Muse; when thro' the plains
>   Of Gallia sweeter sounds arose!
> Sounds to her liberated swains
>   How sweet! how dreadful to her foes!
>
> Her vine-clad hills the Vandal bands
>   Thro' dreary Autumn's reign had held,
> Had pluck'd with sacriligious hands
>   What unripe fruit the God would yield.
>
> But pale Disease their camp invades:
>   The Plunderer, prostrate in the dust,
> No more thro' floods of slaughter wades,
>   But sighs to see his dagger rust.
>
> – Yes, Grape! for this let all forgive
>   Anacreon's undeserved end.
> France bids the rude remainder live,
>   She makes their Tyrant, only, bend. (lines 25–40)

Here, Landor reactivates a classical sphere of reference as a means of examining contemporary political events. His depiction of the French Republic as an idyllic land inhabited by 'liberated swains', like that in

'The French Villagers', recalls the radicalization of pastoral undertaken by Coleridge and Southey in their pantisocratic schemes, and implicit in Southey's *Eclogues* and *Joan of Arc*.[54] R. H. Super effectively characterizes the imagery of Landor's first book: 'the France of the Revolution and the America of Washington were lands where the birds sang more sweetly and the palm poured more abundantly "her nectar'd balm" than in other lands, where old men and young alike led idyllic lives because tyranny had given way to justice and freedom'.[55] In 'The Grape' Landor makes his political point through allegory. Like Fox, he saw the war as a reactionary one of despotic aggression waged against social revolution.[56] In the 'Apology for Satire' he attacked directly 'the crown divine that crushes rising states' (line 114[57]). In 'The Grape' his plot implies that any Vandal-like invasion of France will end in failure: the monarchical Plunderer will be laid prostrate in the dust. Landor formulates the European situation in terms of the two categories of his defiant student toast, the republican and the paralytic.

The allegorical plot of 'The Grape', which depicts the thwarted invasion of the French Republic by the allied powers, is acted out on an epic scale in the main plot of *Gebir*. In 1796 Landor's friend Rose Aylmer suggested as a potential source for a poem a tale in Clara Reeve's *The Progress of Romance* which had been published the year before.[58] Landor probably began work on his version of the tale in the autumn of that year, when he completed most of it,[59] working on it sporadically until its publication in August 1798.[60] In Reeve's tale of the ruthless Gebir, his violent invasion of Egypt and his subsequent assassination by the Egyptian Queen Charoba, Landor would surely have recognized the basis for an epic reworking of his own political plot: the paralysis of the aggressive invading power.[61] In his version of the tale Landor softens the character of Gebir to the extent that Charoba, rather than detesting him, falls in love with him. But this softening serves only to reinforce Landor's political moral; Gebir, despite his own virtues, as a representative of the old world of conquest and monarchy is doomed. As the Nymph explains in Book VI, Gebir's death is a 'destined evil' (VI, 100), a contingent part of the passing of the old age of monarchical power:

> Gebir – 'tho generous, just, humane – inhaled
> Rank venom from these mansions [His palaces].
>
> ...
>
> With horrid chorus, Pain, Disease, Death,
> Stamp on the slippery pavement of the great,
> And ring their sounding emptiness thro' earth. (VI, 219–24)

In the final book of the poem Gebir is assassinated with a poisoned robe prepared by Dalica, the enchantress. His death re-enacts the tyrannicide anticipated in the final two stanzas of 'The Grape' and fulfils the political and apocalyptic prophecy of the 'Apology for Satire' that on the 'fated day / The prince and prelate in the dust will lay' (lines 109–10).

Moreover, as Brian Wilkie and Stuart Curran have shown in their studies of the genre of *Gebir*, Landor's ingenious invocation and subversion of the epic's form and tradition powerfully reinforces his critique of monarchy and imperialism.[62] Wilkie has classified the poem as a 'non-comic mock-epic' which takes the epic vehicle itself as one of its targets.[63] He expertly shows how Landor equates a simplified and inflexible model of the form with a notion of heroism based on violence and conquest, and by undermining the epic form itself attacks the values which it embodies. Like Wilkie, Curran sees in this procedure a parallel with Southey, writing that in 'both *Joan Of Arc* and *Gebir* Virgil is the model who is dethroned, and with him the value of an imperial mission and the warfare that sustains it'.[64] A striking example of Landor's subversion of the epic form, which also illustrates the way in which he highlights the political allegory of his poem through direct allusion to contemporary and historical figures, is Gebir's descent into the underworld in Book III. This episode is one of Landor's main additions to his source, and particularly invokes the visit to Hell in the sixth book of the *Aeneid*. However, rather than being given a vision of his glorious progeny establishing a new state as is Aeneas (VI, 752–84[65]), Gebir is confronted by his ancestors, who are allegorical portraits of British monarchs: George III (lines 185–200), William III (lines 201–10), Charles II (lines 210–15) and Charles I (lines 215–20).[66] These figures are being punished in the underworld as Tyrants, and Landor's point is that, as their living representative who has sworn to carry out their mission of conquest in Egypt (III, 241–7), Gebir must suffer the same fate. Contemporary readers were alert to the political implications of this book. De Quincey, for example, recognized the portrait of 'our worthy old George III', identified Iberia, of which Gebir is a prince, as 'spiritual England', and overall thought the poem 'too Tom-Painish' and 'up to a little treason'.[67]

In the main plot of *Gebir*, then, Landor allegorically addresses the same moment of the French Revolution as he had confronted in poems such as 'The Grape', 'The French Villagers', and the 'Apology for Satire': the moment when the new Republic was threatened with invasion by the allied powers. When his source was suggested, and when he started work on the poem, in 1796, the later stage of the Revolution in which the French armies went beyond their own borders into Germany and Italy was only just beginning. My reading of the main plot of the poem, therefore, differs from a number of influential readings which see it as a commentary on this later stage of the war. Pierre Vitoux, for example, argues that what Landor is 'transposing into the legend is the ambiguous role of the armies of the French Revolution carrying the ideals of freedom and imposing it by force on the nations around them'.[68] This stage of the Revolution, I shall argue, is treated in the pastoral sub-plot of the poem, and particularly in Book VI, as an addition to Landor's source which was probably written later than the main plot as a response to contemporary events. It is, after all, in this sixth book that Landor alludes specifically to Napoleon, a figure who, for many, embodied this later stage of the Revolution.

Like Vitoux, Stuart Curran has argued that the main plot of *Gebir* allegorizes this later stage of the war, though he is more specific and sees Landor's critique of Gebir's invasion of Egypt as a direct attack on Napoleon's own expedition to Egypt in 1798–99. He writes that 'No reader of 1798 could miss the implications of a colonial power in Egypt, where Napoleon had just landed his armies and usurped the Marmaluke government.'[69] Yet this reading of the poem is surely anachronistic, based as it is on the date of publication rather than of conception or writing. As we have seen, the plot of the invasion of Egypt was taken wholesale by Landor from his source in Clara Reeve, and it is highly unlikely that he had even heard of Napoleon at the point when he began writing the poem in 1796. Indeed, Napoleon himself would have had no idea in that year that he was destined to travel to Egypt two years later. It seems impossible, then, that such an allegorical reading of the poem can have been intended, or even grasped by the reader, in 1798 when the poem was published in August.[70] As late as November 1798, for example, Thomas Holcroft was unaware that Napoleon was in Cairo, five months after the event. Again, the direct introduction of Napoleon into the climax of the sub-plot of the poem as Tamar's progeny in Book VI makes the equation of Napoleon with Gebir made by Curran and Vitoux seem particularly misguided.

Indeed, when Landor discovered that history had mimicked art, and Napoleon had, like Gebir, invaded Egypt, he appended what purported to be an 'Extract from the French Preface' to his volume of 1800, *Poems from the Arabic and Persian.*[71] In this, under the veil of supposed translation, he extravagantly praises Napoleon's policy of encouraging the arts and sciences and writes eulogistically of France:

> No nation pursues with an equal alacrity the arts which embellish life. In the midst of a foreign, roused and resuscitated at the inextinguished beacons of a civil, war, while calamity constantly kept pace, and sometimes struggled with, glory, her general [i.e. Napoleon] meditated, and at once accomplished, the eternal deliverance of Egypt. Men of learning and men of science were the proper companions of Buonaparte . . . Conquerors like him, posterity will declare it, have never been the enemies of the human race.[72]

Like Southey and Coleridge, who were also discussing Napoleon's value as a 'Man of Science' in their correspondence of 1799, Landor viewed Napoleon's Egyptian campaign positively as an expedition undertaken on behalf of intellectual and cultural progress. Clearly he had no wish in 1800 that Napoleon should suffer a similar fate to that of Gebir and he may even have intended this paragraph to act as a specific denial of equation between the two figures in their Egyptian expeditions.

'THE HERO OF ITALY'

The dramatic rise of Napoleon did, however, present a very real ideological appeal and challenge to Landor during the period he was working on *Gebir*. With the Republic no longer threatened from without, French policy was becoming increasingly expansionist, advancing on the two fronts of Germany and Italy in 1796 and 1797. In Italy, Napoleon transformed the army and comprehensively defeated the forces of the Austrian monarchy with spectacular speed between April 1796 and April 1797.[73] The belief of many of the British Radicals and Whigs that this was a revolutionary campaign, fought to liberate the enslaved Italians from Austrian domination, rather than one of conquest fought on behalf of French ambition, seemed to be confirmed by the Treaty of Campo Formio, signed on 17 October 1797. Initiated and devised by Napoleon independently of the Directory, this treaty removed the Austrian influence from much of Northern Italy and established in their place the Cisalpine and Ligurian Republics.[74] To Landor it would have appeared that the forces of oppression were being paralysed and the spirit of Liberty was expanding beyond French borders.[75] Indeed, in the *Moral Epistle* of 1795, which had celebrated the outbreaks of the American and French Revolutions, Landor anticipated the spreading outwards from France of the Revolutionary spirit that would begin in the following year:

> Now only Liberty supremely reigns
> O'er those extended and extending plains. (lines 17–18)

1 James Gillray, *Search-Night; – or – State Watchmen, mistaking Honest-Men for Conspirators* (London, 1798).

In the 'Extract from the French Preface', Landor argues along Foxite lines that Napoleon's Italian campaign, like his Egyptian one, was the inevitable result of Allied aggression towards the French Republic. He illustrates his argument with a strikingly metaphysical image:

> But all the calamity, all the confusion, which surrounded the illustrious Buonaparte, was hurled with irresistible and destructive force on the enemies of the French Republic; which, like the mathematical compass, directed by so firm, so temperate a hand, extended the further the more heavily it was pressed.[76]

Napoleon's Italian campaign brought him to public attention in Britain shortly after Landor had begun work on *Gebir* in the autumn of 1796. A. M. Broadly writes that 'before the end of 1796 the military achievements of Napoleon Bonaparte in Italy excited almost as much interest as the invasion schemes of the Directory'.[77] During the period that Landor was working on his poem, Napoleon became an increasingly important figure in British political life; to quote David Chandler, 'in March 1796 Napoleone Buonaparte was known only to comparatively restricted circles within France, but a year later his name had become a household word throughout Europe'.[78] He was first caricatured in Britain on 12 March 1797[79] and by early 1798 had become firmly established as a mascot of opposition and radical groups in their continued support for France. On 25 January 1798, the 'Secret Committee' of England wrote to the French Directory that 'We now only wait to see the Hero of Italy and the brave veterans of the great nation. Myriads will hail their arrival with shouts of joy; they will soon finish their glorious campaign.'[80] In February a delegation of the United Irishmen on their way to France were arrested and a letter seized which invited Napoleon, 'the hero of Italy and his invincible legions', to invade.[81] Gillray satirized this adoption of Napoleon in two caricatures of 1798. In *Search-Night; – or – State-Watchmen, mistaking Honest-Men for Conspirators* (plate 1) of 20 March 1798, he depicts Pitt's and Dundas's disruption of what is presented as a subversive meeting held by Fox, Sheridan, Horne Tooke, Nicoll, Tierney and Lord Moira. In the background, bust-portraits of 'Buonapart' and 'Robertspier' hang on the wall above the motto 'Vive l'Egalité' and a *bonnet rouge*.[82] In *Shrine at St. Ann's Hill* (plate 2) of 26 May 1798, he portrays Fox praying to busts of 'Robertspeire' and 'Buonaparte' amid the standard Jacobin trappings.[83] As this pairing of icons suggests, Napoleon was often represented during this period as a representative of the French Revolution; as a Robespierre on horseback. As MacCunn points out, Lord Mornington's remark, 'Ex illo fluere et retro sublapsa referri Res

2 James Gillray, *Shrine at St Ann's Hill* (London, 1798).

Jacobin'[84] shows that he was considered to represent the crusading Republic. A number of other caricatures of the period show a portrait or bust of Napoleon labelled the 'Hero of Italy' or the 'liberator of Italy' presiding over democratic meetings at the 'Crown and Anchor' or in the background of other supposedly subversive activities. In Ansell's *A Legal Mistake or Honest Men taken for Conspirators* (plate 3) of 15 April 1798, the Attorney-General Scott attempts to break into a printer's office occupied by the radicals Tierney and John Parry. On the wall are two pictures, described in Dorothy George's *Catalogue of Political and Personal Satires* as 'one of *Buonaparte*, a swaggering soldier leaning on an impressive sabre, and one of the King, torn and suspended upside down from one corner'.[85] This description is particularly interesting in that it has a parallel with the dual nature of Landor's thought as it is revealed in *Gebir*: at once iconoclastic in its destruction of the English monarch – we remember Landor's youthful words to his mother that he wished 'that the French would invade England and assist us in hanging George the Third between two such thieves as the archbishops of Canterbury and York' – yet creating a new icon to fill the void.

In the main plot's assassination of Gebir, then, Landor had, as it were, torn up his picture of the king: both George III and monarchy as a whole. In the sub-plot, he offers in its place an image of Napoleon as the ideal political leader of the future. Bearing in mind his political sympathies, it is no surprise that Landor should have shared in the enthusiastic support for Napoleon's Italian campaign and his formation of the Cisalpine and Ligurian Republics, or that he should have incorporated a positive commentary on these events into the ambitious poem he was working on at the time. Yet this incorporation of praise for Napoleon presented Landor with a striking problem of representation. The heroic and the epic were the obvious forms that could be called upon to represent the 'hero of Italy', but, as we have seen, Landor had systematically discredited these as part of his propagandist purpose in his portrayal of Gebir in the main plot. To represent Napoleon as an epic hero would be to place him in the same condemned role. Moreover, such a standard 'heroic' or eulogistic representation of Napoleon offered an easy target for satire. As early as November 1797 the *Anti-Jacobin* had ridiculed the rhetorical paraphernalia of the 'Jacobin Poet':

> The *Jacobin* Poet would have no objection to sing battles too – but he would take a distinction. The prowess of Bonaparte indeed he might chaunt in his loftiest strains of exultation. *There* we should find nothing but trophies, and triumphs, and branches of laurel and olive, phalanxes of Republicans shouting victory,

3 Ansell, *A Legal Mistake or Honest Men taken for Conspirators* (London, 1798).

satellites of despotism biting the ground, and geniuses of liberty planting standards on mountain-tops.[86]

If Landor was to respond to the challenge of Napoleon's Italian campaign in *Gebir*, he needed to find a form of representation that would present Napoleon positively without contradicting or undermining the basic anti-heroic stance of his poem. He required a literary form which would express his hope that Napoleon would fulfil a very different role to the traditional one he had iconoclastically attacked in Prince Gebir. In the 'Extract from the French Preface' Landor memorably describes the role he still envisaged for Napoleon as late as 1800:

May the general remember, in the plentitude of his power, that many have been the masters, few the deliverers of men. Who would be an imitator when he might possibly fail, instead of an original when he surely must succeed? Who would be a Caesar that could be a Buonaparte? The republic never can suspect that the conqueror of kings will reduce himself to their level: she relies on his magnanimity and does not distrust *her own*.[87]

Landor's fascinating conception of what it is to be a 'Buonaparte' is based on, and defined in terms of, Napoleon's earlier brilliant career in Italy. In responding to the challenge of this Italian campaign in *Gebir*, Landor needed a form in which he could represent Napoleon as a 'Buonaparte', at once a 'conqueror of kings' and a 'deliverer of men'.

'A MORTAL MAN ABOVE ALL MORTAL PRAISE'

Landor found this representational form in the pastoral mode and prophetic strains of Virgil's Fourth *Eclogue*, the biblical books of Isaiah and Revelations and Milton's 'On the Morning of Christ's Nativity'. In *Gebir* he pits the epic main plot of the doomed marriage of Gebir and Charoba against the pastoral sub-plot of the happy union of Tamar the shepherd and the Nymph; a parallel which he highlights by elevating Tamar to the position of Gebir's brother.[88] (In Reeve's romance Tamar is simply one of Gebir's men.) This sub-plot is entirely new to Landor's source and is largely narrated in the epithalamic Sixth Book. This celebrates the marriage of Tamar and the Nymph, describes their flight from the dead world of Egypt to a new idyllic land, and climaxes with the Nymph's prophecy of the advent of Napoleon and her vision of a world renewed and redeemed. This sub-plot, like the main plot, works as a political allegory on both a general and a specific level, offering a prophetic vision of a new world of love and retirement based on Landor's faith in the principles of the Revolution – Freedom, Justice and Liberty. Through ingenious structural and thematic design, Landor skilfully counterpoints the advent of this redeemed world with the extinction of the old one symbolized by the death of Gebir. He underlines the relevance of these plots to the contemporary situation through a series of coded allusions. In the place of Gebir's condemned ancestors, the British monarchs, he offers Tamar's promising progeny, Napoleon Bonaparte, a 'mortal man above all mortal praise' (VI, 193).

With the lack of information about Landor's composition of *Gebir*, it is impossible to date exactly the writing of this sub-plot. It is possible that Landor had completed most of Book VI in the autumn of 1796 with the rest of the poem and simply added the prophecy about Napoleon at a later date, incorporating it into the already developed pastoral and apocalyptic plot. However, this prophecy has a central place in the design of the book which could have been written in its entirety as a response to the Italian campaign. Landor could have made additions to *Gebir* as late as the spring of 1798 when he was overseeing its printing at Ipsley Court.[89] Certainly, the sub-plot responds to the historical developments of 1796–7, and there is a strong case for arguing that much of it was written at a late stage, possibly in the early months of 1798.

The Nymph delivers her prophecy of the advent of Napoleon as she and Tamar fly from Egypt to Italy in a panoramic voyage that resembles that of Tasso's *Jerusalem Delivered* (XV, xi–xxxv).[90] As they pass over Sardinia and Corsica, the Nymph points to these two islands:

> 'Look yonder', cried the Nymph, without reply,
> 'Look yonder!' Tamar look'd, and saw two isles
> Where the waves whiten'd on the desart shore.
> Then she continued. 'That which intervenes
> Scarcely the Nymphs themselves have known from Fame:
> But mark the furthest: *there* shall once arise,
> From Tamar shall arise, 'tis Fate's decree,
> A mortal man above all mortal praise.
> Methinks already, tho' she equals Heav'n,
> Towering Trinacria to Therapne yields.' (VI, 185–95)[91]

Here Landor encodes his praise of Napoleon, perhaps as a result of his fear of prosecution or attack for sedition or treason, a dominant theme of the 'Apology for Satire' (lines 55–6, 71–2). In the opening to his *Moral Epistle* he similarly encodes his description of events unfavourable to Britain. Southey's response to Landor's 'The Phocaeans' – a poem compared to which he thought *Gebir* lucid[92] – reveals a contemporary awareness of this method of encoding subversive political sentiments within poetry. He described the poem in a letter to Rickman:

> There is more Geberish as Lamb calls it in the world. A little volume just out – with specimens of an epic 'The Phocaeans' – of which the end and aim is – how they began French Liberty. The man talks treason safely, because he uses such hard language and wraps up his meaning so that nobody will find it out. Yet there is very admirable stuff in him. You should see the book having teeth that can crack the shell – and the kernel will repay you. (*SNL* I, 292)

The shell of *Gebir* similarly needs to be cracked if we are to discover its political kernel. However, Landor's revisionary note of 1803 on the lines on the 'mortal man above all mortal praise' makes it clear that Napoleon was being referred to here. At this later stage he was redefining his loyalties and felt free to append a note identifying Napoleon as the 'mortal man' and to name Therapne as 'my Corsis' – Corsica, the island of Napoleon's birth.

Landor's praise of Napoleon is striking not only in the level of its eulogy but in its brevity. An erudite classical scholar and a competent imitator of classical poetry, as is revealed by his 'Progress of Poetry', Landor was more than capable of writing an extended panegyric on Napoleon had he wanted to.[93] After all, much of *Gebir* was originally composed in Latin, and Landor published the Latin version of the poem, *Gebirus*, in 1803. His comments on the English monarchs in Book VI show, like this brief allusion to Napoleon, that the introduction of contemporary political reference was integral to his conception of the poem. Moreover, this practice was endorsed by the conventions of the literary traditions within which he was working. The combination of prophecy and contemporary political allusion evident in the passage on Napoleon is a traditional feature of both epic and pastoral and Landor could cite both Book VI of Virgil's *Aeneid* and the fourth *Eclogue*, with its celebration of the 'first-born' of the 'Golden Age' (lines 7–89[94]) as his authorities.

But having introduced Napoleon into *Gebir* however, Landor gives us no list of his virtues or achievements, no description of his character, and no chronology of his life, any or all of which we might expect. Indeed, Napoleon is allotted fewer lines than any of the English monarchs, though he is of far greater importance. Instead, in order to present Napoleon as a figure of unrivalled excellence, Landor calls upon two of the tropes of classical panegyric. The line, 'A mortal man above all mortal praise' is a striking example of what Curtius, in his classic *European Literature and the Latin Middle Ages*, has termed the 'inexpressibility topos', whereby the orator is unable to find words which can adequately praise the person celebrated.[95] In placing Napoleon above 'all mortal praise' Landor puts him beyond the range of all the poets of the past, as well as beyond his own powers. In denying the ability to praise, Landor confirms the greatest praise of all. In the following two lines:

> Methinks already, tho' she equals Heav'n,
> Towering Trinacria to Therapne yields (VI, 194–5)

Landor employs what Curtius has called the 'outdoing topos' where the superiority and uniqueness of the person to be praised is established through comparison with the paragons of the past.[96]

Landor's adoption of this rather cryptic form of praise for Napoleon may have been a result of fear of the consequences of a more direct eulogy of Napoleon, as mentioned above. As it was, the political sentiments of the poem prompted a vicious attack from the *Anti-Jacobin Review* in February 1804 in an article on *Gebirus*, the Latin version of the poem.[97] The reviewers were apparently unaware of Landor's recantation in the second edition of the English version published the year before. His form of praise may also have been the result of the status of extended panegyric at this time, which as a form had fallen into disrepute in the eighteenth century.[98] Landor himself attacked both the form and content of panegyric in his 'Apology for Satire' (lines 10–20). Of course, any direct praise of Napoleon's achievements, virtues or career would jar with the anti-heroic sentiments and plot of the poem.

I have been arguing throughout this chapter, however, that *Gebir* is allegorical, both in general – in its destruction of an old world and its creation of a new one – and, specifically, in its portrayal of the British monarchy. Nowhere is this procedure more evident than in Book VI. In both the three lines on Napoleon, and the book as a whole, Landor uses his allegorical plot, underlined by specific political allusions, to sing the praises of Napoleon and celebrate his achievements in Italy in 1796 and 1797. He 'talks treason safely'. In invoking Napoleon as a 'mortal man' Landor implicitly figures him as a continuation of the doctrines of the French Revolution to which Landor himself was so passionately committed. In the 'Apology for Satire' he had attacked the idea of 'the crown divine' (line 114). Napoleon, by contrast, offered a powerful alternative to government based on divine right. Landor's phrase, 'a mortal man', stresses the secular and democratic nature of Napoleon's power and position, as Hazlitt would do thirty years later, championing Napoleon as a figure who opposed the *ancien régime*'s 'right divine to govern wrong'

(*HCW* VII, 81). Indeed, Landor may be further playing on this idea in the following two lines when he writes that 'Trinacria', which as I shall argue is a coded reference to the *ancien régime*, 'equals Heaven'. In the quasi-epic and romance world of *Gebir*, Napoleon is a hero unassisted by the machinery of the gods. Landor's own pointedly political use of the word 'man' is illustrated by the final invocation of his 'Ode to General Washington' when he addresses the hero of the American Revolution as 'O Man!' (line 59). Within *Gebir*, Napoleon as a 'man' is distinguished from Gebir, who is referred to throughout the poem by the titles of 'King' and 'Prince'.[99]

In the two lines that follow, moreover, Landor represents Napoleon as a 'conqueror of kings', albeit in a wrapped-up form:

> Methinks already, tho' she equals Heav'n,
> Towering Trinacria to Therapne yields. (VI, 194–5)

Indeed, in these lines Landor enacts the main political plot of *Gebir*, the supersession of the old world by the new, and specifically the replacement of the monarchs of the *ancien régime* by the figure of Napoleon, the embodiment and creator of the new world of Liberty. Landor's political and geographical allusions need some explanation here. As the *Oxford English Dictionary* reveals, 'Trinacria' is derived from the Greek for three-pointed and was the Latin term for the island of Sicily.[100] Landor's 'Towering Trinacria' that 'equals Heaven' refers, therefore, to Sicily, and particularly to its volcano Etna, described in lines 173–80. Landor uses a similarly volcanic term for Corsica, 'Therapne', a reference to another volcanic island in the Mediterranean, Thera, one of the Sporades.[101] Classical myth had it that this island had sunk, and Landor draws on this myth to image the island as rising in his poem. As mentioned, in 1803 Landor clarified this reference to Corsica; since he was redefining his loyalties he felt free to name the island more directly as 'my Corsis'. Thus the Nymph prophesies that Corsica will figuratively supersede Etna in grandeur.

This geographical imagery has a clear political dimension. 'Trinacria', with its literal meaning of three-sided, alludes to the trinity of oppressive monarchical rulers that appears in much of Landor's early poetry. To use the language of this early poetry, it is the 'triple sway' of the 'three Royal Ruffians' ('Apology for Satire', lines 143 and 149). The use of images of three to indicate reactionary monarchical powers dates back to the Triple Alliance of 1668 which had been established to prevent French expansion.[102] In these lines then, the Nymph prophesies the contemporary events of 1796 and 1797 as the monarchical powers of Europe surrender their supremacy to Napoleon, the Corsican.

Landor represents Napoleon's defeat of the *ancien régime* powers through the imagery and symbolism of the volcano, introduced in the lines on Etna (lines 173–80) and continued in the references to 'Therapne' and 'Trinacria'. In his definitive study of the symbolism of the volcano during this period, 'A Volcano's Voice in Shelley', G. M. Matthews demonstrates that it was an ambivalent and apocalyptic symbol of both destruction and creation.[103] As an image for the end of the old world and the beginning of the new, it had been been widely used to represent the French Revolution. Etna was a symbol of particular potency, having erupted in 1763 and 1796. Landor's imaging of the volcano in *Gebir* echoes images he had used for battle and war in his earlier poems. In 'The French Villagers', for example, Landor describes the battle between the army of Republican France and the 'rulers of mankind' in terms of loss of sight:

> Smoke fills the air, and dims the day:
> No more the vine of matted green
> Or thin leaved olive now are seen, (lines 49–51)

In *Gebir*, Landor describes the eruption of Etna in almost identical terms:

> Darkness with light more horrid she confounds,
> Baffles the breath, and dims the sight, of day. (VI, 175–6)

Even more strikingly, Landor's depiction of Etna's eruption, as Tamar sees it 'Hurl, from Earth's base, rocks, mountains to the skies' (line 180), is echoed by his later depiction of the Italian campaign in the 'Extract from the French Preface' in which Napoleon is described as having 'hurled with irresistible and destructive force on the enemies of the French Republic' 'all the calamity, all the confusion' which had surrounded him.[104] Again, Landor can be seen to be drawing on classical prototype in his use of the volcano as a symbol for the war between Napoleon and the *ancien régime*. As Matthews writes, the 'classic tales of the rising of the Earth's sons against Jupiter clearly record the volcanic upheavals that shaped the landscape'.[105] In his adoption of this volcanic imagery, Landor restates the theme of the early poetry which represents the new Republics of America and France as a 'rising world' and a 'rising state' ('Apology for Satire' line 114). It is an important aspect of Landor's argument in this book that the war is not portrayed as glorious but a 'necessary evil'. His use of the imagery of the volcano enables him to represent it symbolically as a violent but natural, inevitable, and irresistible process.

LANDOR'S MESSIANIC NAPOLEON

Through the Nymph's annunciation of the advent of Napoleon and of his supersession of the *ancien régime* Landor unites the two main elements of Book VI; the political prophecy of a new world and the narrative of the pastoral retirement of Tamar and the Nymph. This retirement is itself a political act; it signals a rejection of the values of monarchy and conquest and the embracing of love and liberty. Landor structures his book around the annunciation of Napoleon's birth; his plot is that of a Messianic apocalypse in which the birth of a child, in this case Napoleon, rejuvenates the earth and restores the Golden Age. In classical terms, the rebirth of ages – *nascitur ordo* – is symbolized by the birth of a boy – *nascenti pureo*. In his two prophecies, Landor reactivates both Christian and Classical myth to represent Napoleon's inauguration of this Golden Age, drawing on Virgil's Fourth *Eclogue*, Milton's 'On the Morning of Christ's Nativity' and Revelations. These prophecies foresee the ending of the old world, as symbolized by the death of Gebir (VI, 227) and the beginning of the new age of Justice, Liberty and universal brotherhood, symbolized by the triumph of Tamar's descendants (VI, 283–308). Through a nexus of allusions Landor places his own prophecy within the classical and Miltonic tradition of the Messianic apocalypse. He draws upon the common imagery, language and register of these powerful Messianic and apocalyptic works to represent mythically and on a grand, even universal, scale the effect of his hero's birth. What M. H. Abrams has written of the Romantics' imagining of the French Revolution can be applied to Landor's representation of Napoleon: he endows the promise of Napoleon with the form and impetus of one of the most compelling myths in the culture of Christian Europe.[106] If Landor represents Napoleon explicitly as 'A mortal man above all mortal praise', implicitly he represents him as the Messiah.

In narrating the journey of Tamar and the Nymph, Landor employs another motif frequently found in his early poetry, the figurative and sometimes literal flight from a land of Oppression to one of Freedom. In 'The French Villagers' the monarchical army deserts and joins the people of the French Republic in a state of 'Peace, Liberty and France / Where Pride's accused empire ends' (lines 63–4). In the *Moral Epistle* Landor invites Stanhope to 'Fly we, then, thither where their power must cease / where triumphs are prepared for liberty and peace' (lines 205–6). In *Gebir*, Tamar and the Nymph make a flight similar to that envisaged in the *Moral Epistle* and settle in an idyll (VI, 238–81) which is described in the tradition of the earthly paradise that Curtius traces back to Homer (*Iliad* XX, 8; *Odyssey* VI, 124, XVII, 205, IX, 132) and Theocritus.[107] In Virgil's fourth *Eclogue* the Utopian Golden Age is associated with the bower. In *Gebir*, Landor uses landscape to unite the pastoral plot of the narrative as the couple reach their bower with the political plot of the prophecy. He simultaneously achieves the culmination of both plots. Curran's comment on the pastoral genre that 'the momentary withdrawal from civilisation seems a symbolic act of faith in the millennial redemption whereby civilization will be absorbed within the pastoral mode'[108] suggests the way in which Landor unites the political allegory with the narrative of the sixth book. The idyll of *Gebir* is at once the setting for the couple's momentary withdrawal and a vision of the world to come after the millennial redemption brought about by Napoleon's act of liberation, when all civilization will be absorbed within the pastoral mode. The landscape is hailed by the poet as a 'Clime of unbounded liberty and love' (line 251); an embodiment of both the domestic ideal of love stressed in the narrative of Tamar and the Nymph and the political ideal of Liberty brought into the world by the French Revolution. In his depiction of the idyll Landor represents the future world prophesied in the poem, the 'extended and extending plains' of the expanding French Republic that will be inherited by Tamar's descendants. These 'Iberian hinds', like the 'shepherds' and 'liberated swains' of the early poetry, will continue the pastoral tradition embodied by their ancestors, Tamar and Napoleon. The idyll is another representation of a post-revolutionary pastoral Utopia, like those of France and America, that Landor had described in his early poetry – the world that is threatened by allied aggression in 'Apology for Satire':

> But, O ye mighty! ye whom wrongs provoke!
> Edge the keen sabre, aim the fatal stroke:
> Lest Gallia's sons in hast'ning autumn view
> Their famish'd fields the staff of life renew.
> Lest they again in lawless ease recline
> Beneath their fig, their olive, and their vine:
> Lest on the flowery banks of gentle Loire,
> New notes of gladness call the village choir. (lines 91–8)[109]

In his depiction of the retirement idyll of Tamar and the Nymph that closes the book, then, Landor represents the world to come as a continuous state of pastoral perfection in a time become timeless, following Time's abdication and entrance into the Republican revels (line 301). This world is unthreatened by outside factors, and ultimately confounds the escapism and enclosure of pastoral in a triumphant finale in which it becomes boundless. History reaches its highest point and stops.

Landor's depiction of this idyllic world may inevitably seem unrealistic, over-idealistic and too easily achieved. Indeed, Pierre Vitoux has criticized the poem on this basis:

> The doubt about the possibility of a new age for mankind is in fact at the centre of the second theme. In her more-than-human wisdom, the nymph persuades Tamar to escape with her to a pleasant retreat, and the panoramic vision of the happier future is conveyed by her to the man she has just removed from the turmoil of history in the making. The theme of her exhortation is that private happiness must be placed above the strife of politics, that *otium* is better than public life.[110]

Yet what Vitoux, like all other critics of the poem, has failed to grasp here is that the landscape where Tamar and the Nymph settle has its corollary in the real world and their happiness is a contingent part of the latest developments of contemporary European history, signalled by the reference to Napoleon. A vitally important feature of the sub-plot that has been repeatedly overlooked by critics of the poem is that Landor is specific about the geographical location of the idyll. Having flown over the Liparian islands (line 238) the couple settle on the Etruscan coast of North Italy ('Etrurian coasts' line 239). This is detailed more specifically as the Apennines (line 250). Furthermore the river that runs through the idyll (line 259) has been referred to earlier in the book:

> Behold the vast Eridanus! ere night
> We shall again behold him and rejoice. (lines 169–70)

According to Edward Tripp in his *Dictionary of Classical Mythology*, most writers, including Virgil, who set many of his *Eclogues* on its banks, thought that the Eridanus was the River Po.[111] The area in which the Nymph and Tamar settle, then, can be pinpointed as that part of Italy where the Po intersects with the Apennine mountains. Through this series of classical grid-references, Landor locates the scene of their happiness, not in a place removed from the turmoil of history in the making, as Vitoux argues, but in precisely the area of Northern Italy which had been 'liberated' by Napoleon in his campaigns of 1796–7 and where he had set up the Cisalpine and Ligurian Republics by the Treaty of Campo Formio. In his depiction of the pastoral idyll Landor is, in fact, representing the new political states that were being established even while he was working on his poem, the place where the history of a new golden age appeared to be in the making. Landor models his visionary future on these republics, which embody freedom from oppression, having been rid of the Austrians by Napoleon, and liberty, being political states established upon the principles of the French Revolution. He implies that Napoleon's Italian campaign of 1796–7 is nothing less than an apocalyptic event.

Similarly in the festivals which close the book, presumably based on the celebrations of the French Revolution designed by David, one of the images refers directly to Napoleon's political policy. The line 'yonder, Rhine / Lays his imperial sceptre at their feet' (lines 298–9) alludes to another aspect of the Treaty of Campo Formio, that the left bank of the Rhine passed from the possession of the Austrian monarchy to the French Republic.[112] It also enacts the process of democratization central to the poem. Thus the final panoramic view of the book (lines 279–88) surveys the liberated world stretching from the Pyrenees to the Rhine, as seen from the Cisalpine Republic. Indeed, the political implications of this final passage (lines 250–308) is emphasized by Landor's later excision of it, as well as of the more obvious political passages, 189–200 and 225–44 in the 1831 and 1846 editions of the poem.[113]

In *Gebir*, then, Landor's representation of Napoleon goes beyond the model of Virgil. Michael Putnam has written of the Wonder Child in the fourth *Eclogue* that the boy's role is thoroughly 'pastoral', merely the ideal of peace expanded to touch all humanity.[114] The birth and growth of the child runs parallel with the development of the Golden Age and the return to an Edenesque earthly paradise. It is the Consul Pollio who establishes the new golden age through political rule. If we decode the elaborate pastoral symbolism of *Gebir*, however, we find that it is the child himself, Napoleon, who will create the earthly paradise by overthrowing the *ancien régime* powers and establishing republics on the model of the French one. In *Gebir*, Landor represents Napoleon in the pastoral tradition of his shepherd father, Tamar. He draws on the equation of shepherd and pastor that was all but automatic by the early seventeenth century (as Curran has pointed out)[115] to represent Napoleon as the pastor who will lead his flock into the promised land, who will return them to, and restore, an Edenic earthly paradise. By appropriating the pastoral tradition of the Messianic, apocalyptic poem, Landor is able to represent Napoleon as a 'conqueror of Kings' and a 'deliverer of men'. He celebrates his achievements as a revolutionary and republican hero in a way that does not contradict the basic anti-heroism of the poem but which reactivates a powerful and compelling literary tradition to represent what Landor believed to be Napoleon's new type of heroism.

REVISIONS AND LATER VISIONS OF THE 'HERO OF ITALY'

It would be possible to be more ironical about Landor's erudite and densely packed political allegory. Despite his detailed knowledge and reconciliation of contemporary history and Classical poetic traditions, Landor's Messianic representation of Napoleon may appear naive. Yet his figuring of Napoleon as a promising embodiment of the ideals of the French Revolution offers an image of the young general that was important for all the first-generation writers of the Romantic period. Southey and Coleridge are certainly more equivocal in their expressions of hope for Napoleon, but their comments reveal that Landor's Messianic Napoleon was no isolated political fantasy. Coleridge later described Napoleon's early victories as the result of the 'enthusiasm which the spirit of freedom inspired' (*EoT* I, 395). Some time around 1799 Southey was considering writing a poem on Napoleon whom he considered a figure of 'greatness' and 'glory'.[116] His enthusiastic response to *Gebir*, which he read in 1799, reread in 1800, and reviewed favourably for the *Critical Review*, may have been as much a result of its praise of Napoleon as of its 'exquisite poetry' and its 'miraculous beauties'.[117] As we have seen, in their letters of 1799 both Coleridge and Southey saw Napoleon in a Messianic role, Coleridge describing him as 'the Saviour' (*CL* I, 298) and Southey portraying him as 'making a home for us in Syria' where 'we may perhaps enjoy freedom under the Suns of the East, in a land flowing with milk and honey' (*SNL* I, 185). Indeed, there is a certain kinship between *Gebir* and 'Kubla Khan', a poem which may have been written partly with Napoleon's Egyptian expedition in mind. 'Kubla Khan', like Book VI of *Gebir*, is a poem about a 'Layer out of a World-garden', to use Coleridge's 1802 phrase for Napoleon (*CNB* I, 1166). Landor's allegorical response to the Italian campaign and to Napoleon's reorganization of Northern Italy may even suggest this earlier historical moment as a possible context for the Khan's decree. Certainly Coleridge followed Napoleon's progress in Italy from an early stage, as a note to 'Ode to the Departing Year' of 31 December 1796 testifies (*CPW* I, 163). However, there is no further evidence to support this reading of the poem and it must remain a matter for speculation.

Yet if Landor's response to Napoleon's early campaigns has something of a paradigmatic force, then his recantation from him during the Peace of Amiens similarly dramatizes the disappointment felt by the Lakers. Landor visited Paris in August 1802 with two principal objects; to see Paris itself and to see his hero, Napoleon.[118] He was impressed by the Louvre – like Hazlitt, who was also in Paris at this time – but the visit was ultimately a disillusioning one. On 15 August, a day Landor thought would be 'the most important . . . since the commencement of the revolution',[119] he went to the Tuileries to witness the celebrations of Napoleon being made First Consul for Life. But his hero was not received with the popular support Landor expected. He described the scene in a letter:

> Buonaparte made his appearance in the centre, where his wife had sate some time in company with two other consuls. I expected that the sky would have been rent with acclamations; on the contrary he experienced such a reception as was experienced by Richard the Third. He was sensibly mortified. He bowed, but waved to & fro, and often wiped his face with his hankerchief. He retired in about ten minutes.[120]

For Landor, this was a moment of anagnorisis; dictatorship had replaced representative government. Napoleon Bonaparte, who had offered such a promising alternative to the British monarchy, was now playing the role of Shakespeare's villainous usurper, Richard III. Landor has a particular scene from this play in mind here, that in which Gloucester, seeking the support of the people, enters 'aloft, between two Bishops' (III. vii. 94–6). In his restaging of this scene at the Tuileries Landor transforms the two other consuls into these bishops and in so doing perhaps reinvokes and applies to Napoleon his youthful wish that George III would be hung 'between two such thieves as the archbishops of Canterbury and York'.[121]

Landor bitterly outlined his revised vision of the French political regime in a letter to his brother:

> Doubtless the government of Buonaparte is the best that can be contrived for Frenchmen. Monkeys must be chained, tho it may cost some grimaces. If you read attentively the last sentence of the senatus consultum, you will find that not an atom of liberty is left. This people, the most inconstant, and therefore the most contemptible in the world, seem'd to have recovered their sense when they lost their freedom. The idol is beyond their reach, but the idolatry has vanished . . . A consul of so great a genius will make the nation formidable to all the earth but England, but I hope there is no danger of anyone imitating its example. As to the cause of liberty, this cursed nation has ruined it for ever.[122]

Consequently, he republished *Gebir* in 1803 and used the extended Preface and the additional notes to reclaim and reinterpret the poem as anti-French and anti-Napoleon. To the lines on Napoleon as 'A mortal man above all mortal praise' Landor appended the note:

Bonaparte might have been so, and in the beginning of his career it was augured that he would be. But unhappily he thinks, that to produce great changes, is to perform great actions: to annihilate ancient freedom and substitute new, to give republics a monarchical government, and the provinces of monarchs a republican one; in short, to overthrow by violence all the institutions, and to tear from the heart all the social habits of men, has been the tenor of his policies to the present hour.[123]

Landor's violent recantation, like his earlier extravagant praise, exemplifies the more complex responses of the three Lake poets to the events of the time. Coleridge and Wordsworth similarly pinpointed the Peace of Amiens as the moment when they, and their country, resolved to present a united front against what they saw as the burgeoning military despotism and ambition of Napoleon. Like Landor, in their later writing on Napoleon the first-generation writers all suggest a figure who had failed to fulfil the promise of his early career. Coleridge and Southey, like Wordsworth, grieved for Buonaparte in 1802. Southey, when he felt forced to declare Napoleon a 'great rascal' and a 'fool' in December, did so to his 'utter disappointment' (*SNL* I, 299[124]). Coleridge wrote in September of having 'hoped proudly' of Napoleon, and having been 'miserably disappointed' (*EoT* I, 319). His turn against Napoleon, like his shift from arguing against the war with France to arguing for it, was a gradual process. He had long been arguing for peace which, like Southey and Wordsworth, he hoped would see the establishment of democratic government in France.[125] But as soon as the peace was negotiated he became worried by its terms. He wrote to Poole on 21 October 1801 that 'We, ie. Wordsworth and myself, regard the Peace as necessary; but the Terms as most alarming' (*CL* I, 418) and he made a marginal note, probably some time in 1801–2, that 'we made peace just at the time when war *first* became just and necessary'.[126] The 'experiment' of the peace, as Coleridge termed it (*EoT* I, 428), revealed Napoleon's 'undisguised and unqualified ambitious designs' (*EoT* I, 419) as he ordered a second invasion of Switzerland, refused to remove his army from Holland and threatened Egypt, Syria, the Greek Islands and Malta.[127] At this point Coleridge and Southey despaired of Napoleon, whose government, they now felt, had failed to justify the assumption of power as they had hoped it would do in 1800.[128]

Coleridge's vision of Napoleon was finalized during the autumn of 1802. In his Plutarchian comparison between the French Republic under Napoleon and the Roman Republic under the Caesars of September and October,[129] his attitude to Napoleon remains complex and ambivalent, though, as Erdman observes, he depicts him as changing from an Augustus to a Julius Caesar with touches of a Tiberius.[130] In October and November, however, Coleridge wrote two open letters to Charles James Fox challenging his views on Napoleon as a peacemaker.[131] These powerful pieces of invective, comparable to Burke's 'Letters on the Regicide Peace', were prompted by Fox's visit to Napoleon in Paris. They mark the end of any ambivalence in Coleridge's public representation of Napoleon, and establish the bellicose tone that characterizes his subsequent writing on him. Coleridge describes Napoleon as an 'upstart Corsican' who is driven by an 'atrocious ambition' and has established an 'iron despotism' (*EoT* I, 386, 393). Revealingly, Coleridge redraws the analogy with the Roman Empire, which only weeks before had allowed him an element of ambiguity,[132] to brand Napoleon as 'this Caesar in all things, but genius, noble birth, and fearless clemency' (*EoT* I, 399).

The heroic vision of Napoleon's first Italian campaign remains a powerful image of him throughout the Romantic period and beyond, however. Such was the power of this revolutionary myth that as early as his sonnet 'On the Extinction of the Venetian Republic' of 1802–3, Wordsworth sought to combat it by emphasizing Napoleon's destruction of the Venetian Republic in the Treaty of Campo Formio. Stendhal, Byron and Hazlitt all saw the campaign as an act of liberation. In his *Vie de Napoleon*, in which he claims Napoleon to be 'the greatest man the world has ever seen since Caesar', Stendhal describes in detail only the Italian campaigns, as Pieter Geyl has observed.[133] Stendhal writes that 'the truly poetic and noble part of Buonaparte's life comes to an end with the occupation of Venice' and that 'Here ends the heroic times of Napoleon.'[134] Byron later recalled that 'Italy required an alteration in her government' and added that 'the people were happier and more secure under Napoleon than under the Austrians'.[135] Hazlitt in his *Life of Napoleon* describes the campaign in the eulogistic and sublime terms that he elsewhere uses for the Revolution itself:

> Napoleon, during the two years of his campaigns in Italy, had filled all Europe with the renown of his arms, which gave the first stunning blow to the Coalition. Fame, after having slept a thousand years, seemed to have seized her ancient trump; and, as in the early period of Greece and Rome, freedom smiled on victory. Those who have ever felt that dawn of a brighter day, that spring-time of

hope and glow of exultation, animate their breasts, cannot easily be taught to forget it, either in the dazzling glare or the cheerless gloom that was to succeed it. But it is perhaps enough for great actions to have been and still to be remembered when they have ceased to be; and then to stir the mind in after-ages with mingled awe, admiration, and regret. (*HCW* XIII, 317)

Even Sir Walter Scott invokes this heroic vision of the first Italian campaign. In *The Field of Waterloo*, for example, he contrasts the cowardly Napoleon of his last battle with the dashing figure on 'Lodi's bridge' (stanza xiv). This conception of Napoleon as a revolutionary liberator in Italy has even become something of a literary trope. In Charlotte Brontë's novel *Shirley* (1849), for example, the Belgian industrialist Moore gives a particularly striking articulation of the pastoral representation of Napoleon which provides a useful conclusion to this chapter and anticipates the change in Napoleon's status examined in the next:

you forget the true parallel. France is Israel, and Napoleon is Moses. Europe, with her old over-gorged empires and rotten dynasties, is corrupt Egypt; gallant France is the Twelve Tribes, and her fresh and vigorous Usurper the Shepherd of Horeb . . . Oh, in Italy he was as great as any Moses! He was the right thing there; fit to head and organise measures for the regeneration of nations. It puzzles me to this day how the conqueror of Lodi should have condescended to become an emperor, a vulgar and stupid humbug . . . .[136]

CHAPTER 2

'In such strength of usurpation'[1]*: Wordsworth's Napoleonic imagination*

> My whole soul was with those who were resolved to fight it out with Bonaparte.
>
> (*MY* II, 334)

When, in 'October, 1803', William Wordsworth looked 'on the present face of things' he saw 'one Man', Napoleon Bonaparte: a single figure who dominated the age. Wordsworth's contest with the figure of Napoleon, enacted in his writing from April 1802 when he wrote his first Miltonic sonnet, 'I grieved for Buonaparte' to spring 1816 when he completed his 'Thanksgiving Ode', was crucial for him, focusing problems over his own role as well as that of the 'one Man'. In this chapter I want to develop an argument which examines the part that Napoleon plays at the very heart of Wordsworth's writing, in his conception of the 'Imagination' in Book VI of *The Prelude*. This passage, one of the key moments in the poetry, has become a battleground for critical accounts.[2]

The starting and finishing points of my argument are two moments of 'usurpation'; of, to use a dictionary definition, 'the taking possession of by force, without right, unjustly; assuming the authority, place etc. of someone or of something else; taking or borrowing, a name or a word, supplanting'.[3] Both these 'usurpations' are described in Book VI of *The Prelude* when Wordsworth recounts his journey of 1790 through the Swiss Alps. Aesthetically, both involve a frustrated desire to experience the sublime, but, while the first 'usurpation' is a disappointment, the second is part of a corresponding and compensating moment of vision, and, specifically, of 'Imagination'. What I want to suggest is that Wordsworth uses these autobiographical experiences as opportunities to reflect upon, structure, and respond to contemporary history and particularly to 'the Usurper', Napoleon Bonaparte. The first of these 'usurpations' (VI, 452–7), I shall argue, images Napoleon's own usurpation – his *coup d'état* of Brumaire 1799. In the second (VI, 525–48), when in the process of writing Wordsworth switches to the present, 1804, he responds to the historical moment by advancing a formulation of the 'Imagination' as a usurping force: as acting 'in such strength / Of usurpation' (VI, 532–3). In effect, Wordsworth usurps the usurper. The Imagination is formed both after, and in contention with, Napoleon, and Wordsworth's method of formulation is itself an act of 'usurpation'.

Moreover, by focusing on these two moments of 'usurpation' in the Alps, I will be able to distinguish my own understanding of Wordsworth's response to history and his use of it from that of other critics who have examined these passages, particularly M. H. Abrams, who uses the Simplon Pass episode to illustrate his theory of the 'Apocalypse of the Imagination',[4] and Alan Liu, who has recently provided a powerful and influential reading of the same episode with a keen awareness of its Napoleonic resonance. I have discussed Abrams' model in some detail in my previous chapter, but it will be useful to give a brief outline of Alan Liu's argument at this point. In both his essay 'Wordsworth: The History in "Imagination"',[5] and his book *Wordsworth: the Sense of History*,[6] which incorporates the earlier essay, Liu has offered a reading of Wordsworth's work as a suppression of history and of Book VI of *The Prelude* as a negation of the figure of Napoleon.[7] He argues in his essay that 'the "self" arises in a three-body problem: history, nature, self' (p. 506) and that 'Book 6's goal is to prevent the self from looking through the mask of nature, as through a lens, to underlying history' (p. 518). History is subjected to 'denial' and 'repression' (pp. 531, 539). He describes the Mont Blanc episode as a 'near-eruption' of history, the Simplon Pass one as its 'climactic veiling' (p. 528).

As will become evident from my discussion, I am greatly indebted to Liu's work, and particularly to his skilful historical elucidations, but my own approach to, and understanding of, Wordsworth's treatment of history, and of his response to the 'usurper' Napoleon, differs from his on two important counts. The first of these is that while Liu contextualizes the 'Imagination' in *The Prelude* historically, he does not examine it in the context of the rest of Wordsworth's writing on Napoleon. If this further step is made, it becomes possible to locate Wordsworth's contest with Napoleon in *The Prelude* within the context of his specific responses to and uses of him that can be traced in the sonnets.

Between 1802 and 1804 Wordsworth became obsessed with Napoleon, who had achieved a pre-eminent position in world affairs. His obsession prompted a flood of political sonnets, written in the two years before he commenced work on Book VI of *The Prelude*.[8] In these sonnets, inspired by those of Milton, Wordsworth developed much of the language and imagery, as well as the ideas, that he would use in his epic and translate on to a different plane in the 'Immortality Ode'. Whereas Liu argues that Wordsworth's 'denial' of history in Book VI looks forward to his confrontation with it in Books IX and X (p. 531), my own argument is that Wordsworth's confrontation with history in Book VI continues and develops the sonnets' direct concern with it. Does it seem reasonable to expect a poet who has spent two years writing numerous sonnets on the specific historical circumstances of his time, and his own position in them, to forget or suppress these matters when he resumes work on his autobiography? While everyone is aware that passages in Books VI, IX and X are explicitly concerned with the French Revolution, I hope to show that Wordsworth's detailed consideration of contemporary, post-1798 history, so evident in these sonnets, is not suppressed but is an integral part of his retrospective approach. Indeed, it is the intensity of Wordsworth's engagement with Napoleon, even of his identification with him, that makes his response so complex and creative. In Book VI Wordsworth not only uses autobiography as a framework for the structuring of history, but reconciles the transcendent, combative and emulative elements of his response to Napoleon detectable in the sonnets.

The second of my main differences with Liu is developed from this issue of the biographical and textual contexts of *The Prelude*. Seeing history as something that is 'denied' and 'suppressed' by Wordsworth, Liu's method is to identify the textual absences that result from this denial. As John O. Hayden has commented 'Liu is not dealing with Wordsworth's political and social views as he set them forth, but rather as he did not'; his 'major point is that contemporary social and political history continually crops up through Wordsworth's poetry unbeknownst to himself'. [9] Liu's approach is in line with the manifestos of 'new historicism',[10] a movement of which he is one of the principal theorists.[11] For example, in *The Romantic Ideology*, Jerome McGann argues that Romantic poems 'occlude and disguise their own involvement in a certain nexus of historical relations' so that history is 'evaded', 'elided', 'erased', 'displaced' and 'annihilated'.[12] Marjorie Levinson in *Wordsworth's Great Period Poems* sees history as being 'effaced', 'elided', 'displaced and 'repressed'.[13] I do not intend to take issue with this theory as a whole, which has produced some fascinating results (as in Levinson's reading of 'Tintern Abbey'). Neither do I seek to deny Wordsworth's practice of eliding, conflating and suppressing certain historical events; practices which must seem evident to any reader of Books IX and X of *The Prelude*. My argument is rather that Liu's stress on Wordsworth's denial of history in Book

VI can be countered by examining the passage in the context of his obsession with European politics and particularly with Napoleon. I hope to show that while Wordsworth's references or allusions to history in Book VI are certainly delicate and subtle, they are also conscious, considered and deliberate.[14]

This chapter is structured both historically and thematically within the framework of my argument about 'usurpation'. It will move from the first 'usurpation' of 1799 to the second of 1804 via an examination of what I have defined as the three main elements of Wordsworth's response to Napoleon – the transcendent, the combative and the emulative. All three are ultimately reconciled, I argue, in Wordsworth's conception of the 'Imagination'. Thematically, this chapter is structured by a use of the 'loss' and 'gain' structure, or more specifically the 'grief' and 'strength' exchange that is so characteristic of Wordsworth's *œuvre.* In *The Prelude* (x, 421–9) Wordsworth articulates fully this belief using the terms that I have adopted in this chapter – 'Grief' and 'Strength'. This structure has its paradigmatic statement in the 'Ode: There was a time':

> Though nothing can bring back the hour
> Of splendour in the grass, of glory in the flower;
> We will grieve not, rather find
> Strength in what remains behind . . . (lines 180–3)

Indeed, at certain moments in the chapter I shall be using the 'Ode' as a reference point: both as a means of examining Wordsworth's thought on Napoleon in terms of familiar and established patterns, and of looking, somewhat speculatively and exploratively, at what is normally seen as a non-political poem in terms of the language, imagery and structures it shares with Wordsworth's other writings on Napoleon.

'I GRIEVED FOR BUONAPARTE'

From July to October 1790 Wordsworth, in the company of his undergraduate friend Robert Jones, took a walking tour through France and Switzerland. Stephen Gill describes the motivation for their journey:

> Wordsworth and Jones crossed from Dover to Calais on 13 July at a significant moment in the history of France, the 'very eve / Of that great federal day' on which, celebrating the anniversary of the Bastille, Louis XVI pledged allegiance to the constitution at an altar erected in the Champ de Mars. But although they were caught up in the festivities of a 'whole nation . . . mad with joy', and fell in on their journey south with delegates returning home from Paris,

their route through France was determined not by a wish to be present at a turning point in European history but by an eagerness to experience for themselves what they had only read about, the sublimity of the Alps.[15]

One site where a sublime experience would seem guaranteed was Mont Blanc but, according to *The Prelude*, Wordsworth and Jones were disappointed:

> That day we first
> Beheld the summit of Mont Blanc, and grieved
> To have a soulless image on the eye
> Which had usurped upon a living thought
> That never more could be: . . . (VI, 452–6)

The materialist 'reality', as Wordsworth terms visual scenery five lines later, fails to fulfil his expectations. Wordsworth presents his experience in Lockean terms. His eye passively receives the image which is presented ready formed from without. It is a tabula rasa on which the sensation paints itself.[16] Aesthetically the summit of Mont Blanc is a disappointment. These five lines act out in miniature a similar moment of disappointment described less than one hundred lines later in the famous crossing of the Simplon Pass incident. But then the disappointment is compensated for by the realization of the 'Imagination'. Here, Wordsworth moves on to the Vale of Chamounix to be 'reconciled to realities' (VI, 461).

But Wordsworth's expression of grief at his disappointment on seeing Mont Blanc, which has no autobiographical testament in the letters or *Descriptive Sketches*, is given the weight of more than a single, easily resolved episode in an aesthetic journey. Indeed, the lines seem to suggest some form of paradigmatic experience. The cataloguing and descriptive passages immediately before and after, with their:

> . . . naked huts, wood-built, and sown like tents
> Of Indian cabins over the fresh lawns,
> And by the river side . . . (VI, 450–2)

and:

> . . . dumb cataracts and streams of ice,
> A motionless array of mighty waves,
> Five rivers broad and vast- . . . (VI, 458–60)

have a geographical specificity lacked by the lines on Mont Blanc. While indicating the mountains' lack of visual interest this may also point away from a purely geographical reading of the passage.

That something paradigmatic or symbolic is being structured within the experience at Mont Blanc is suggested by the style and structure of the passage. The tightness, regularity and formality of the passage on Mont Blanc give it a weight and an importance beyond its significance in the narrative. Furthermore, the central emotion, grief, and much of the language and tone of the passage evoke the literary tradition of elegy. We are reminded, for example, of *Lycidas*:

> But O the heavy change, now thou art gone
> Now thou art gone, and *never* must return . . . (lines 37–8, my italics)

and:

> Shall *no more be seen* (line 43, my italics)[17]

and of Lear grieving over the body of Cordelia:

> Thou'lt come *no more*,
> *Never, never, never, never, never.* (v. iii, 307–8, my italics)[18]

Wordsworth's expression of grief has all the grandeur and finality of these passages, but seems to lack their cause. At Mont Blanc Wordsworth is writing an elegy; the 'living thought' has been replaced by the dead materialist world of the 'soulless image', its life with its soul departed. But who or what is this elegy for?

There is one exception to the purity and simplicity of the diction in these lines – the word 'usurped'.[19] This word provides the clue to one of the experiences that is being structured under Mont Blanc. 'Usurped' is a word rarely used by Wordsworth. In *The Prelude* of 1805 'usurpation' is used once, later in Book vi (which I shall consider further), and 'usurped' two other times. (The first usage is seemingly unimportant (ii, 152), the second comes in the other great 'Imagination' passage, the climbing of Snowdon (xiii, 50).) In the context of Book vi, with its description of the revolutionary celebrations, 'Usurp' has a powerfully political resonance. As Paul Hamilton has commented, 'usurpations were going on all around *The Prelude*'s travellers during their trip to France and the Alps'.[20] Yet by the time Wordsworth was working on Book vi, the word had become particularly associated with Napoleon's *coup d'état* of 9–10 November 1799, or 18–19 Brumaire, Year 8, to use the revolutionary calendar. In conjunction with the Abbé Sieyès, Napoleon had overthrown the Directorate and Legislative Assemblies. In the resulting Constitution, promulgated on 24 December 1799, which Napoleon drew up, he seized control as the all-powerful First Consul.

Alan Liu, in a section of his article to which I am indebted, writes brilliantly on the contemporary meaning and implication of the word:

in the context of the years immediately preceeding 1804 [when Wordsworth wrote Book VI, probably completing it by April], *'usurper' cannot refer to anyone other than Napoleon.* After 18–19 *Brumaire*, 'usurper' was applied to Bonaparte in English parliamentary speeches, pamphlets, and newspapers with the consistency of a technical term and irrespective of party affiliation or sympathy with French republicanism. Whether he was thought merely to epitomise republicanism or to break with it, the premise was that Napoleon was a usurper. Use of the epithet peaked first in 1800 after Napoleon's offer of peace to George III, which the Government chose to perceive as an insult because Napoleon took the stance of an equal. In his splendid speech of February 3, 1800, for example, Pitt referred to Napoleon as 'a usurper' and his government as a 'usurpation'. Similarly, Sheridan spoke of Bonaparte in 1800 as 'this ferocious usurper'. Use of the epithet then peaked a second time in 1803 upon the resumption of hostilities, after the Peace of Amiens when *The Annual Register*, for example [in an edition in Wordsworth's Rydal Mount library] labelled Bonaparte 'the Corsican usurper.' Perhaps the best way to suggest the possible impact upon Wordsworth of the 'usurpation' epithet in these early years is to read Coleridge in the *Morning Post*. In 1800, Coleridge characterized Bonaparte, his regime, or various French decrees in such barbed phrases as 'This insolence in the usurper' and a 'low Harlequinade of Usurpation'. On March 11, 1800, Coleridge's rhetoric drives the point home: Napoleon's rise is a 'usurpation' he says repeatedly, and 'In his usurpation Bonaparte stabbed his honesty in the vitals.'[21]

Liu, however, gives this account of the 'usurper' in describing the Simplon Pass 'usurpation' passage, not the earlier Mont Blanc one. In his comments on the Mont Blanc passage, he hints at this context, but incorporates the episode within his model of the suppression of history:

There is some strange devil of history, I suggest, behind 'usurpation' that the poet-as-*agricola* would rather not see. The whiteness at Mont Blanc . . . is the space at which history can ghost into the present; it is not no-meaning but a panic of too much meaning. Whiteness is the page for a possible epic whose stern mood must either be recognised or thwarted. For the time being, the whiteness at Mont Blanc – protruding like a heroic bone – is simply ploughed under again.[22]

Yet Liu's contextualization of the word 'usurpation' suggests that Wordsworth himself would have been alert to its political and Napoleonic resonances. At the very least Napoleon's act of 'usurpation' provides a structure or metaphor for the working of Wordsworth's mind; Napoleon's career becomes an epistemological model. Materialist reality, the 'soulless image' usurps like Napoleon and so destroys a 'living thought'. In *The Prelude* Wordsworth presents an epic battle for power and sovereignty between the mind and the senses, led by the eye (for example XI, 170–5). He employs a political terminology, particularly of dominance and slavery, to which he adds a contemporary relevance through a reference to the career of Napoleon.

Yet the explicitness of Wordsworth's reference to Napoleon through such a vitally active epithet suggests that we may be able to locate the moment of 'usurpation' within the larger narratives of both Book VI of *The Prelude* and contemporary history. The Mont Blanc 'usurpation' follows Wordsworth's description of his experiences in France in 1790 as it celebrated the first anniversary of the fall of the Bastille:

> ... 'twas a time when Europe was rejoiced,
> France standing on the top of golden hours,
> And human nature seeming born again. (VI, 352–4)

In the previous chapter on *Gebir* I illustrated how Landor used the conventions of pastoral poetry to represent the French Revolution, drawing upon the language and ideas of poems such as Virgil's Fourth *Eclogue* and Milton's 'On The Morning of Christ's Nativity'. Wordsworth does the same here in his depiction of revolutionary France. As he journeys into Switzerland he uses its landscape and its political status as a Republic to envisage his hopes for the rebirth of the human race signalled by the French Revolution. Wordsworth's guide book for his 1790 tour, William Coxe's *Sketches of the Natural, Civil, and Political State of Switzerland*, describes Switzerland as unequalled in its prevalence of 'happiness and content . . .among the people'.[23] The Swiss symbolized Liberty for Wordsworth in 'Descriptive Sketches'[24] of 1793 and, as J. R. Watson has written, 'Switzerland was something of a symbol since it had a reputation for mountain loving freedom, and had been associated with nymphs of an Alpine Golden age in former times'.[25] It is this tradition that Wordsworth evokes in his later sonnet 'Thought of a Briton on the Subjugation of Switzerland' (October 1806 – February 1807) where his address to Liberty (line 4) echoes Milton's 'Mountain Nymph, sweet Liberty' of 'L'Allegro' (line 5).

In his depiction of the Swiss Republic in *The Prelude*, Wordsworth paints an idyllic pastoral landscape, describing its 'Sweet coverts . . . of pastoral life' (VI, 437) and its 'sanctified abodes of peaceful Man' (VI, 445). As when beholding a rainbow in the sky (see 'My heart leaps up'), the post-deluvian symbol of hope, Wordsworth's 'heart leaped up':

> . . .when first I did look down
> On that which was first seen of these deep haunts,
> A green recess, an aboriginal vale
> Quiet, and lorded over and possessed
> By naked huts, wood-built, and sown like tents
> Or Indian Cabins over the fresh lawns
> And by the river-side. (VI, 446–52)

Wordsworth's hopes for the French Revolution are modelled on, and embodied in, this Eden of the Swiss Republic – 'first', 'green', 'aboriginal', 'naked', 'fresh'. Politically man seems to have returned, like his landscape, to innocence: human nature seems born again.

Yet writing in 1804 Wordsworth superimposes on this 1790 picture of the Swiss Republic a series of other images that remind us what had happened not just in the fourteen weeks of Wordsworth's visit, but in the fourteen years of European history, during which:

> . . . become oppressors in their turn,
> Frenchmen had changed a war of self-defence
> For one of conquest, losing sight of all
> Which they had struggled for . . . (X, 791–4)

As I have illustrated in my previous chapter, it is something of a critical commonplace that the rise of Napoleon and the invasion of Switzerland by France were major causes in the loss of sympathy with the French Revolution. In 1821, Wordsworth wrote to Losh that 'after Bonaparte had violated the Independence of Switzerland, my heart turned against him. . . . Here it was that I parted, in feeling, from the Whigs, and to a certain extent united with their Adversaries.'[26] As J. C. Maxwell has pointed out in 'Wordsworth and the Subjugation of Switzerland'[27] this later comment conflates at least two incidents. The first French invasion of Switzerland was led by Menard in late 1798,[28] and Napoleon was not involved. It was this invasion which prompted Coleridge's recantation in 'France: An Ode'. Stanza IV of the ode is devoted to Switzerland and Coleridge, like Wordsworth, heightens the significance of the invasion by stressing the symbolic and pastoral nature of Switzerland: it is a 'peaceful country' (line 68) where 'peace her jealous home had built' (line 73). This 'Ode' establishes a historical and literary context for Wordsworth's treatment of the subject in Book VI, though as we shall see his reaction is not so clearly determined as Coleridge's was by this first invasion. The editorial note which prefixed the ode when it was first published in the *Morning Post* on 16 April 1798, helps to confirm the significance of Switzerland as an historical site:

> The following excellent Ode will be in unison with the feelings of every friend to Liberty and foe to Oppression; of all who, admiring the French Revolution, detest and deplore the conduct of France towards Switzerland. It is very satisfactory to find so zealous and steady an advocate for Freedom as Mr. COLERIDGE concur with us in condemning the conduct of France towards the Swiss Cantons. Indeed his concurrence is not singular; we know of no Friend to Liberty who is not of his opinion. What we most admire is the avowal of his sentiments, and public censure of the unprincipled and atrocious conduct of France. (*CPW* 243)

Napoleon, who had not been involved in the first invasion of Switzerland of 1798, led the second of 1802. According to F. J. MacCunn in *The Contemporary English View of Napoleon*,[29] this act of French aggression towards Switzerland during the Peace of Amiens, like those towards Italy, Germany and Holland, 'turned many of the Whigs against Bonaparte' in a manner similar to that later expressed by Wordsworth. Fox arraigns Bonaparte's aggression on Switzerland as scandalous in his speech of 24 May 1803 and Romilly writes on 2 November 1802 that 'there is no describing to you the effect which Bonaparte's proclamation against the Swiss has produced in this country'.[30] Newspaper poems similarly focus on Switzerland. In an 'Ode' published in *The European Magazine* (XVII) of September 1802, Bonaparte is described as:

> An enemy to all mankind,
> He left a plundered world behind,
> To execrate his name!
> Hark! how *Helvetia*, Venice, Rome,
> Lament their melancholy doom! (my italics[31])

In 'War Song' by the Revd R. Mant of May 1803 'Bonaparte Speaks':

> Me, Holland, Italy, obey:
> Her breast with many a war-wound gor'd,
> And crush'd beneath my iron sway,
> Me *Helvetia* owns her Lord. (my italics[32])

In 'Stop to a Stride' from the *Gentleman's Magazine* (LXXIII) of November 1803, Bonaparte 'strode o'er France, he threw his leg o'er *Switzerland* and Italy'.[33] A parody of Burns's 'A Man's a Man for a' that' includes the lines:

> What tho' the Swiss ha'e hunker'd down,
> An' kiss'd their looves an' a' that . . .[34]

With such a context stressing the importance for the contemporary historical vision of France's aggression towards Switzerland it would be surprising were Wordsworth to write about his experiences there *without* in some way referring to its more recent history. What is perhaps remarkable is the sophistication and skill with which he does so.

In *The Prelude,* Wordsworth uses his own journey from France to Switzerland to prefigure that of the various armies of France, and to point the contrast between 1790 and 1804. Thus his journey is 'A March . . . of military speed' (VI, 428) undertaken and described with the purpose, regularity and rhythm of a military campaign:

> Day after day, up early and down late,
> From vale to vale, from hill to hill we went,
> From Province on to Province did we pass. (VI, 431–3)

In Wordsworth's description of his journey, metaphor and simile directly hint at the destruction to come in Switzerland:

> Keen Hunters in a chase of fourteen weeks
> Eager as birds of prey. (VI, 34–5)

Here Wordsworth echoes, and may be directly alluding to, the imagery Coleridge used for his description of the French invasion of Switzerland in 'France: An Ode':

> O France
>
> . . .
>
> Are these thy boasts, Champion of human kind?
> To mix with Kings in the low lust of sway,
> Yell in the *hunt*, and share the murderous *prey*? (my italics, lines 78–92)

The Swiss pastoral landscape is 'cross[ed]' (line 437); there is even the suggestion of a military encampment – 'tents' (line 450) – in the Republic that will be subjugated – 'lorded over' (a phrase which recalls 'War Song' 'Helevetia owns her Lord') and 'possessed' (line 449) by France. The change of landscape:

> And earth did change her images and forms
> Before us . . . (VI, 429–30)

may even anticipate the change to come in the governmental form of Switzerland, from independent republic to French satellite.

Similarly, after the Mont Blanc usurpation, images of innocence – 'small birds' (line 462) and 'The maiden' (line 465) – are set beside as yet unthreatening but ominous predators – 'the eagle' (line 463) and 'the lion' (line 466).[35] At the centre of these two pairings stands 'the reaper' (line 464). Wordsworth again uses the pastoral convention of all creation living in harmony.[36] Yet in the context of the history of Switzerland, the 'eagle' and 'lion' have a threatening resonance. Both are royal and imperial emblems in heraldry, and the eagle was adopted on the standards of the Roman legions. Both denote victory and imperialism.[37] Significantly, it is these imperial animals, the eagle shortly to be officially adopted by Napoleon himself in his coronation as Emperor, that threaten the Swiss Republic. There seems a heavy irony in the lion 'Descending from the mountain to *make sport* / Among the cottages by beds of flower' (VI, 167–8, my italics).

A cross-reference with one of Wordsworth's most famous political sonnets is particularly helpful in reading this passage. His allusion to the Swiss 'Maiden' recalls his earlier sonnet 'On the Extinction of the Venetian Republic' (1802–3) in which Venice, 'the eldest child of Liberty' (line 4), the '*Maiden* City, bright and free' (my italics, line 5) is violated by the ravaging armies of Napoleon, and by Napoleon's own Treaty of Campo Formio of 1797 which declared the Republic at an end. Venice was, like Switzerland, a key historical site where a consideration of landscape seemed impossible for the Romantics without analysis of the political situation.[38] Yet its place in the contemporary consciousness meant that Wordsworth was able to invoke its contemporary historical position subtly and delicately. He makes no mention of the Treaty of Campo Formio, though in later editions an editorial note drew attention to this circumstance. Indeed, he deals with its present political position not through direct analysis, but through elegy:

> Men are we, and must grieve when even the Shade
> Of that which once was great is passed away. (lines 13–14)

Wordsworth's oblique yet powerful treatment of recent history in this sonnet, one of the first he wrote, shows him developing the techniques he would employ in his complex evocation of recent history in his description of his tour through France and Switzerland.

In the passage describing his journey from France to Switzerland Wordsworth conflates into one description his characteristic technique of double-take, of visit and revisit, vision and revision.[39] The living thought of human nature born again is usurped by more recent experience. Indeed, in the 1850 version of the poem, Wordsworth makes his description of the later French spoilations of Switzerland explicit by devoting seventy lines to the destruction of the Convent of Chartreuse, an event which occurred in May 1792, two years after Wordsworth's visit (1850, VI, 420–88). The event that Wordsworth uses to symbolize the mutation of France and which acts as a synecdoche for the failure of the French Revolution, is Napoleon's usurpation.

This is not to say that it was Napoleon's usurpation of 1799 as a single historical event that first dispelled Wordsworth's hopes for the French Revolution. When in Book x of *The Prelude* Wordsworth prepares to describe Napoleon's coronation – an event which was still to happen when he was writing in Book vi – he describes contemporary historical developments as 'the steps of our degeneracy' (x, 927). Writing in early 1804, Wordsworth seized upon the usurpation as an event which could be represented in retrospect as a clear and climactic example of these downward 'steps'. Later in the year, as we shall see, he would use Napoleon's coronation for the same purpose.

There are problems in trying to place exactly these 'steps', especially relying on *The Prelude.* As Gill writes, in 'Books x to xii, which cover the years after his return to England, dislocations of chronology, massive lacunae, recapitulations that do little to clarify obscurities, crucial vagueness of definition, all signal the effort involved in subduing biographical information to overall poetic design'.[40] One might perhaps place the first of these steps at the time of the Terror, described in x, 307–80, the guilt of which Wordsworth felt himself implicated in (x, 38–82, 373–80).[41] Yet the fall of Robespierre in July 1794 marks for Wordsworth a rebirth of his earlier hopes as he directly refers back to the 'golden hours' of 1790 described in Book vi (line 354):

> Great was my glee of spirit, great my joy
> In vengeance, and eternal justice, thus
> Made manifest. 'Come now ye golden times' . . . (x, 539–41)

With the end of the Terror 'From this time forth, in France, as is well known / Authority put on a milder face' (x, 567–68). Wordsworth himself 'The same belief . . . retained' (x, 573) though in retrospect he sees that in France 'every thing was wanting that might give / Courage to those who looked for good by light / Of rational experience' (x, 569–71). Yet at the time of the fall of Robespierre, to quote Gill again, Wordsworth's 'joy' is of 'an adherent of the French cause, able now to look with "unabated confidence" towards the future and progressive liberation of mankind'.[42]

The second major historical 'step' would be the French policy of conquest, when, 'become Oppressors in their turn, Frenchmen had changed a war of self-defence / For one of conquest' (x, 791–93). Again, this 'step' is difficult to pin to a precise historical moment. J. C. Maxwell's article

'Wordsworth and the Subjugation of Switzerland'[43] is again helpful here. Maxwell recounts the various critical opinions on the date of the advent of the French policy of conquest referred to in these lines – Mark Reed places it at 1798, F. M. Todd at 1802 (both believing that they refer to Switzerland), de Selincourt at 1794–5, Wordsworth in the letter to Losh as either 1798 or 1802, in the *Convention of Cintra* as some time before Amiens (i.e. before 1802), and Alfred Cobban as some time after 1803.[44] Maxwell reconciles the contradictory evidence in his conclusion:

> To sum up, I suspect that the course of events was something like this: 1. *The Prelude* represents with fair accuracy Wordsworth's response to the first evidences of French aggression in 1794–5. [Maxwell's previous thoughts on this response were that 'while in a way he claims to have seen it (X, 797) he also insists on his own obstinate clinging to the heart of his old position (X, 800)'[45]]. 2. The invasion of Switzerland in 1798 was not a landmark in his political development. 3. In fact, as the letter to Losh suggests, the first significant shift in his party sympathies came during the peace of Amiens in 1802–3. 4. The 1802 invasion of Switzerland, though one of the determining events, was not of overwhelming importance. 5. In the next few years the dominant role of Napoleon as the enemy *par excellence* led to his being seen also as the destroyer of Swiss independence, and thus, since in fact the Franco-Swiss hostilities went back to 1798, the outlines became blurred, and the highly romanticized picture given in the sonnet, ['Thought of a Briton on the Subjugation of Switzerland'] though not historically true of any single period, came to include elements harking back to 1798, yet without depriving Napoleon of a position of pre-eminence he did not hold then.[46]

It seems to be exactly this process that is occurring in Book VI of *The Prelude*. Wordsworth combines the invasion of Switzerland with the rise to power of Napoleon through his usurpation – conflating what he later described as the two main causes of his turn away from France in his letter of 1821 to Losh.[47] Writing *The Prelude* in 1804, Wordsworth is able to look back over past events and select the clearest historical landmark with which to indicate the end of the French Revolution, characteristically foreshortening and condensing historical events. To quote Maxwell on Wordsworth's technique, 'what Wordsworth is giving . . . is not the course of events as he saw it at the time, but as he sees it now in 1804'.[48] The 'usurpation', when the government of many was, in effect, replaced by the government of the one, would seem an obvious choice. It would have been confirmed as a significant historical 'step' for Wordsworth by the subsequent events that prompted the sonnets of 1802–4: Napoleon's elevation to Consul for Life in 1802, his government in France, his threat to invade Britain, his imperialism and his colonial policy.

4 James Gillray *Exit Liberté a la Francois! – or – Buonaparte closing the Farce of Egalité* (London, 1799).

Wordsworth's repeated reference to Napoleon as the 'Usurper' in his tract the *Convention of Cintra*[49] illustrates the potency of both the historical event and the derived term as a means of symbolizing Napoleon's rule. In Leigh Hunt's essay 'On Certain Terms Magnanimously Applied to the French Ruler' 'usurper' is the first, and by implication the most dominant, term applied to Napoleon with which Hunt takes issue.[50] Indeed, in this essay Hunt alerts us to the broader implications of the word which, he writes, refers to Bonaparte's violation of his promises to Holland and his undoing of the Independence of Switzerland, as well as to his seizure of power. Coleridge subtitled the two parts of *Zapolya*, his play of 1815 which allegorically celebrates Napoleon's defeat at Waterloo and the restoration of legitimacy, as *The Usurper's Fortune* and *The Usurper's Fate.* For him 'Usurper' could be used to represent Napoleon's whole career. Similarly, for Wordsworth in 1804 'usurpation' was a word capable of standing for the general decline of 1790–1804, and particularly 1800–4. After the uncertain course of the French Revolution in the second half of the 1790s, during which period Wordsworth's conflicting emotions were further complicated by the war and the repressive measures of Pitt's government,[51] the 'usurpation' provided a definite historical moment confirmed by subsequent events. Wordsworth's treatment of the subject in Book VI does, of course, stimulate a much more detailed probing in Books IX and X, which he wrote immediately afterwards.[52] Wordsworth's allusion to this moment of usurpation again illustrates the Romantics' habit of retrospective simplification. He chooses a particular historical event and term and makes it stand for a larger and more complex period of history.

As the public response in Britain suggests, however, even at the time, the 'usurpation' seems to have offered itself as an event that could be used to simplify the historical picture. As early as 21 November 1799, only three days after London newspapers carried full accounts of the *coup*, Gillray depicted the event as *Exit Liberté a la Francois! – or – Buonaparte closing the Farce of Egalité* (plate 4).[53] Rumour of the new French Constitution provoked a powerful reaction in England and Coleridge analysed it in great detail in a series of essays for the *Morning Post* (*EoT* I, 31–54). On 22 December 1799 Pitt wrote that it was 'a more undisguised contrivance for giving absolute power than I expected' and he saw it as the first step towards the restoration of the monarchy.[54] Fox and Sheridan in their parliamentary speeches both recognized the new Constitution as a dictatorship.[55] On 2 January 1800 the diarist Miss Berry refers to 'the man Buonaparte, absolute King of France, quietly established in the Tuileries'.[56]

There is no contemporary reaction from Wordsworth to Napoleon's usurpation, but those of Coleridge and Southey may be indicative. As I have argued in my first chapter, the usurpation did not prompt a finalization of their vision of Napoleon, but the extent of their reaction to the *coup* does suggest an event that at later stages could easily be recalled for a retrospective categorization of him. As we have seen, both Coleridge and Southey wrote positively and enthusiastically about Napoleon in their letters of 1798 and 1799, but the usurpation shook their belief in his promise. On 23 December 1799 Southey wrote despairingly to Coleridge:

> Concerning the French, I wish Buonaparte had staid in Egypt, and that Robespierre had guillotined Sieyés. These cursed complex governments are good for nothing, and will ever be in the hands of intriguers. The Jacobins were men: and one house of representatives, lodging the executive in committees, the plain and common system of government. *The cause of republicanism is over, and it is now only a struggle for dominion.* They wanted a Lycurgus after Robespierre, a man loved for his virtue, and bold, inflexible, and who should have levelled the property of France, and then would the Republic have been immortal, and the world must have been revolutionised by example. (*SNL* I, 211; my italics)

Southey's letter suggests that he, like Wordsworth, saw the period after the fall of Robespierre as a possible new beginning for the Revolution. As we have seen, like Coleridge and Landor, he had hoped Napoleon would play a role like that of Lycurgus, who founded the Spartan constitution and military system.[57] But Napoleon's usurpation seemed to betray this hope. Southey's categorical statement that 'The cause of Republicanism is over' forcefully stresses the effect of the *coup*, but also again reveals that until this moment he still believed in this cause. Coleridge replied on the 28 December:

> O for Peace and the South of France!– What a detestable Villany is not this new Constitution? . . . But the French are children. – 'Tis an infirmity to hope or fear concerning them. I wish they had a King again, if it were not only that Sieyés and Bonaparte might be hung. Guillotining is too republican a death for such Reptiles. (*CL* I, 306)

The letter gives a powerful idea of Coleridge's reaction to the *coup*. Napoleon's usurpation is seen as extinguishing Coleridge's recently revived republican hopes, and he repeats similar thoughts with varying emphases in the letters to Davy and Wedgewood on 1 January 1800. In the one to Davy he enquires about the legitimacy of tyrannicide: 'A Private Query – On our system of Death does [it] not follow, that killing a bad man mi[ght do] him a great deal of Good? And that [Bon]aparte wants a gentle dose of this kind, dagger or bullet ad libium' (*CL* I, 308). As we have seen, with finality Southey writes to Rickman on 9 January 1800: 'The Corsican has offended me . . . Buonaparte has made me Anti-Gallican' (*SL* II, 46). Of course, we have no knowledge of whether Wordsworth shared in this shocked reaction to Napoleon's usurpation, but these comments do help us to grasp the significance of the usurpation in the history of the English response, and that of Wordsworth's own circle, to the French Revolution. Certainly, looked back on from 1804, the usurpation would seem the largest historical landmark with which to symbolize the failure of the French Revolution – the final 'step' 'of our degeneracy'. One might use the formula that retrospectively Wordsworth 'grieved' to have Bonaparte, the 'soulless image', usurp upon a 'living thought that never more could be' – his hopes for the French Revolution.

The terms of Wordsworth's Miltonic sonnets of 1802–4 provide an important context for this argument. Since Napoleon's usurpation Wordsworth had been particularly concerned with him as a visual 'image', the unignorable blot on the world landscape. His sonnets on his visit to France in 1802, such as 'Festivals have I seen', frequently place the image of Napoleonic France on top of that of the revolutionary France seen during his visit of 1790. One of his most despairing sonnets, 'October, 1803', which illustrates Napoleon's place at the heart of contemporary affairs, begins:

> When, *looking on* the present face of things,
> *I see* one Man, of Men the meanest too!
> Raised up to sway the World, to do, undo . . . (my italics, lines 1–3)

It is through 'looking' and 'seeing' that Wordsworth registers Napoleon: Napoleon operates here like a 'soulless image on the eye'. His tyranny over the world is paralleled with his tyranny over the eye. In Book IX of *The Prelude*, again writing from the perspective of 1804, Wordsworth describes his friend Beaupuy as 'yet most blessed / In this, that he the fate of later times / Lived not to see, nor what we now behold / Who have as ardent hearts as he had then' (IX, 434–6). Again the narrative of the sentence progresses through the history of the French Revolution ('the fate of later times') to climax at the present moment. What Wordsworth now beholds is, of course, the reign of Napoleon Bonaparte.

This suggestion of a Napoleonic dimension in the Mont Blanc usurpation is further reinforced by the use of, and the prominence given to, the emotion of grief at this point. As used in *The Prelude*, and elsewhere, grief is an emotion with a particular political meaning (though, of course, not exclusively or dominantly so). At the end of Book x, in the last reference to France in that book, which is therefore something of a conclusion to the France books, ix and x, Wordsworth addresses Coleridge and writes:

> If for France I have grieved
> Who in the judgement of no few, hath been
> A trifler only, in her proudest day,
> Have been distressed to think of what she once
> Promised, now is, – . . . (x, 954–8)

'Grief' comes with a realization of the difference between what was 'once promised', and what 'now is': between a 'living thought' and a 'soulless image on the eye'. This passage comes only fifteen lines after the explicit introduction of Napoleon into the poem (x, 932–41). Wordsworth leaves Coleridge, and us, in no doubt that what France 'now is' is a result of the rule of Napoleon Bonaparte. In the placing of 'grieved' at the end of the line Wordsworth may even be specifically referring us back to his earlier expression of having 'grieved' in Book vi – 'That day we first / Beheld the summit of Mont Blanc, and grieved / . . .' (lines 452–3) – for these are the only two times the word is so placed in the entire poem.

This structure of grief for 'what she once / Promised, now is' may possibly hark back to Milton's *Paradise Lost*. At the end of Book xi Michael explains God's reason for the flood:

> Though late repenting him of man depraved,
> *Grieved* at his heart, when looking down he saw
> The whole earth filled with violence, and all flesh
> Corrupting each their way. (my italics, xi, 887–90)

For Wordsworth the fallen, corrupt world is that of Napoleonic, rather than revolutionary, France. Looking on, he grieves at his heart, first for France, then for Napoleon. It is this tension between Wordsworth's hopes for a renewed world and the present fallen one that E. P. Thompson sees at the heart of Wordsworth's writing:

> My argument is: the creative impulse came out of this conflict. There is a tension between a boundless aspiration – for liberty, reason, *egalité*, perfectibility – and a peculiar harsh and unregenerate reality. So long as this tension persists, the creative impulse can be felt. But once the tension slackens, the creative impulse fails also. There is nothing in disenchantment inimical to art.[58]

In Thompson's terms, Napoleon would stand as the exemplar of a 'peculiar harsh and unregenerate reality' in tension with Wordsworth's hopes for France.

It is in this sense that Wordsworth had 'grieved for Buonaparte' in his first mature sonnet of 21 May 1802,[59] which begins:

> I grieved for Buonaparte, with a vain
> And an unthinking grief . . . (lines 1–2)

This is not an expression of 'sympathetic grief', 'put paid to' when Wordsworth recognized Napoleon's 'evil propensities' as David Erdman has most recently put it.[60] Rather Wordsworth 'grieved for Buonaparte' because he failed to embody what either France or his own earlier career 'once promised'. Indeed, he now embodies the reverse. Wordsworth dismisses his grief when he realizes that Napoleon, as one trained in battle from youth, was incapable of being anything other than what he 'now is' – 'a Usurper'. Wordsworth's grief for Bonaparte anticipates his later expressions of it for Mont Blanc and for France in *The Prelude*. It even, perhaps, has some connection with his paradigmatic expression of grief in the 'Immortality Ode' which was written during these years 1802–4 – a poem which transmutes a number of terms from the political sonnets, most dazzlingly 'splendour' and 'glory', on to a different plane.

In the passage on his journey through France and Switzerland, then, Wordsworth's treats history in a much more sophisticated and consciously controlled manner than he is normally given credit for. He uses a language, a set of images and a style which alerts the reader to specific historical moments, even though these moments may be foreshortened and conflated. Within an autobiographical description Wordsworth structures and registers the events of contemporary history. He superimposes what France 'now is', an oppressor, over what she once promised – seemingly born again as a Utopian pastoral state, or political republic like that of Switzerland. The moment which Wordsworth uses to illustrate and symbolize the change from one state to another is Napoleon's usurpation.

If Napoleon's usurpation of power can be seen as one of the most significant, even climactic, of the 'steps' of contemporary European history at the time of Wordsworth's writing, then we might expect it to be further alluded to in the explicitly historical books, IX and X, of *The Prelude*. In these books, which Wordsworth probably began writing immediately after completion of Book VI in late April 1804[61] he investigates in great detail the various historical events of the period and his own response to them. Yet between Wordsworth's completion of Book VI, and that of Book X in December of the same year, there had taken place the final downward 'step' in the 'variegated journey' of contemporary history, an even more obviously symbolic crowning moment, the coronation of Napoleon as Emperor. Towards the end of Book X, in a passage that acts historically and emotionally as a conclusion to the France books, Wordsworth jumps forward from the late 1790s to describe this event which took place on 2 December 1804.[62] He thanks Coleridge, Dorothy and 'Nature's Self' (line 921) for recovering qualities in him which make it possible for him to survive the final, cataclysmic event:

Which through the steps of our degeneracy,
All degradation of this age, hath still
Upheld me, and upholds me at this day
In the catastrophe (for so they dream,
And nothing less), when, finally, to close
And rivet up the gains of France, a Pope
Is summoned in to crown an Emperor –
This last opprobrium, when we see the dog
Returning to his vomit, when the sun
That rose in splendour, was alive, and moved
In exultation among living clouds,
Hath put his function and his glory off,
And, turned into gewgaw, a machine,
Sets like an opera phantom. (X, 927–40)

Here Wordsworth makes the coronation scene serve the same function as the usurpation. It stands in *The Prelude* as a contemporary landmark for the end of the Revolution and symbol for what France 'now is', having returned to the pre-revolutionary institutional forms of church and state; papacy and empire. For Wordsworth, as for Stendhal, the coronation was 'Tyranny crowned by religion[63].' The conclusion of history in this passage – 'finally', 'close', 'rivet up', 'last' – is marked by the sense of ending as a return – the dog, drawn from Peter (2. 2. 22), returns to his vomit; a 'catastrophe' is both the final moment of a drama, and an overturning. This is surely one of the events referred to in the conclusion to the poem, when 'This Age fall back to old idolatry . . . men return to servitude as fast / As the tide ebbs' XIII, 431–3). One could perhaps say that after the glorious and blissful dawn of the new-born age of Revolution, the sun, that faded into the light of consular day, now sets on the despotic night of empire.

The coronation was not a shock to Wordsworth as it was to

Beethoven, who furiously and famously crossed out his dedication to Napoleon of the Eroica Symphony when he learned of it.[64] Rather it confirmed Wordsworth's earlier views. In one of his sonnets, '*Calais*, August, 1802', Wordsworth attacks the English tourists who were crossing the channel during the Peace of Amiens to worship the newly proclaimed First Consul for Life, also the subject of Gillray's caricature *Introduction of Citizen Volpone & his Suite, at Paris* (plate 5) of 15 November 1802, which depicts Fox's presentation to Napoleon at the Tuileries on 3 September 1802.[65] Wordsworth opens his sonnet:

> Is it a Reed that's shaken by the wind,
> Or what is it that ye go forth to see?
> Lords, Lawyers, Statesmen, Squires of low degree,
> Men known, and men unknown, Sick, Lame, and Blind,
> Post forward all, like Creatures of one kind,
> With first-fruit offerings crowd to bend the knee
> In France, before the new-born Majesty. (lines 1–7)

Here Wordsworth's mock nativity subverts the type of register Landor derived from Virgil and Milton in *Gebir*. In using the phrase 'new-born Majesty' Wordsworth comments ironically on Napoleon's position as a figure who was not born to hereditary monarchy but has been 'new-born' as a reincarnation of the *ancien régime*. The seeming innocence of 'new-born' is ironically oxymoronic when placed beside 'Majesty'. The sarcastic overtones of the phrase are highlighted by another sonnet, '*To a Friend*, Composed near Calais, on the Road leading to Ardes, August 7, 1802'. In this sonnet, addressed to Robert Jones, Wordsworth looks back to their walking tour of 1790, when they participated in the 'festivals of *new-born Liberty*' (line 4, my italics). In 'Poems Dedicated to National Independence and Liberty', '*Calais*, August, 1802' follows immediately on from 'Composed near Calais', and it is impossible to miss Wordsworth's juxtaposition of the present 'new-born Majesty' and his earlier hopes for 'new-born liberty' – a striking testament to the coherence of the sonnet sequence.

To return to the depiction of the coronation in Book x, Wordsworth points explicitly to the difference between what France 'promised' and what she 'now is' through an extraordinarily subtle punning reference back to the preceding book of *The Prelude*. In one of the most famous passages of the poem, Wordsworth and Beaupuy encounter a 'hunger-bitten girl' and Beaupuy's humanitarian response, ''Tis against that / Which we are fighting' (ix, 519–20) prompts one of Wordsworth's fullest articulations of his revolutionary hopes:

5 James Gillray, *Introduction of Citizen Volpone & his Suite, at Paris* (London, 1802).

> I with him believed
> Devoutly that a spirit was abroad
> Which could not be withstood, that poverty,
> At least like this, would in a little time
> Be found no more, that we should see the earth
> Unthwarted in her wish to recompense
> The industrious, and the lowly Child of Toil,
> All institutes forever blotted out
> That legalized exclusion, empty pomp
> Abolished, sensual state and cruel power
> Whether by the edict of the one or few –
> And finally, as sum and crown of all,
> Should see the People having a strong hand
> In making their own Laws, whence better days
> To all mankind. (IX, 520–33)

Describing the coronation, Wordsworth refers back to the climactic line here – 'And finally, as sum and crown of all, Should see,' – and rewrites it as '*finally* . . . A Pope / Is *sum*moned in to *crown* an Emperor . . . when we *see*'. The sum and crown of modern history, like the *sum*mit of Mont Blanc, is a disappointment. It brings not 'better days to all mankind' but 'the edict of one', Napoleon, symbolized and solemnized by his coronation. Wordsworth's figurative hopes for what could be achieved by the Revolution, 'the sum and crown af all', are degraded into the literal spectacle of Napoleon's coronation. The earlier linguistic formulation, like the 'living thought', is usurped by the 'soulless image' of Napoleon's coronation. The coronation itself enacts a return to what Wordsworth had hoped to see abolished by the Revolution – 'empty pomp', 'sensual state and cruel power' – and Napoleon becomes their personification.

The process of degeneration and degradation from Books IX to X is acted out in the rest of the passage. The dog returns to its vomit, as Wordsworth returns to a previously employed language and imagery. The fluid and vital natural image of the sun, a revolutionary symbol[66] that dominates much of Wordsworth's work, 'that rose in splendour, was *alive*, and moved in exultation among living clouds' (again we are reminded of the 'living thought') degenerates into a petrifying ('sets') and mechanistic imagery of theatricality and artifice ('gewgaw', 'phantom'). With this theatrical imagery, a common satirical metaphor for the coronation in Britain,[67] the 'catastrophe' – the final moment of the drama – is acted out linguistically. Wordsworth's reference to the loss of splendour and the putting off of glory is neatly glossed by the sonnet of 1802, 'Great Men have been among us', which eulogises the representatives of the English Commonwealth tradition (Sydney, Marvell, Harrington, Vane) on whose doctrine Wordsworth, like many of the French themselves and particularly the Girondins with whom he was most sympathetic, modelled his hopes for the Revolution.[68] These figures, writes Wordsworth:

> Knew how genuine *glory was put on*;
> Taught us how rightfully a nation *shone*
> *In splendor.* (lines 6–8; my italics)

Napoleon's coronation marks the final fading of Wordsworth's hopes for France achieving this 'splendor' and 'glory'.

The passage works against the essential process of coronation – the act of 'putting on' – of investiture and crowning. Wordsworth's metaphor uses the images of divestment, of 'putting off' ('hath put his function and his glory off' (line 925)). Wordsworth achieves his irony by denying Napoleon the things he implies he hopes to gain through the assumption of imperial status. Similarly, he plays on and denies the association of the sun, splendour and glory with monarchy. We think, for example of Satan's description in Book II of *Paradise Lost* of his 'imperial sovereignty, adorned / With splendour' (lines 446–7). By imaging Napoleon's coronation as a setting sun, Wordsworth simultaneously indicates his rise as synonymous with the end of the Revolution, and condemnatorily reverses the normal forms of monarchical panegyric, refusing natural authority or affinity to Napoleon.

This process of divestment in Napoleon's coronation, as with the setting sun, completes the use of one of the revolutionary metaphors of *The Prelude*, and possibly illumines the 'Immortality Ode'. In the same passage where he describes the blissful dawn of the Revolution Wordsworth writes:

> Not favoured spots alone, but the whole earth
> The beauty *wore* of promise, that which sets,
> To take an image which was felt, no doubt,
> Among the bowers of paradise itself,
> The budding rose above the rose full blown. (x, 701–5; my italics)

Again the passage uses a vocabulary that will be transformed in the coronation scene – 'sets' and 'rose' – but most importantly it uses the imagery of clothing – 'the whole earth / The beauty wore of promise' – for the dawn of the Revolution. With Napoleon's coronation this apparel is 'put off'.

In his representation of Napoleon's coronation, then, Wordsworth consummates his use of the imagery of sunrise and of clothing with which he had expressed his hopes for the French Revolution in *The Prelude*. Strikingly, in his use of these metaphors and of the ambiguous words 'glory' and 'splendor', terms of both optical and political significance, Wordsworth makes the coronation of Napoleon analogous to the 'fading' process of the 'Ode' and in so doing grants its terminology a temporary definition that the poem itself resists and avoids. Indeed, the language of the 'Ode' can be used as a means of illustrating how Wordsworth shapes the course of the Revolution and the career of Napoleon into the familiar structure of this poem. In the 'Ode':

> There was a time when meadow, grove, and stream,
> *The earth*, and every common sight,
> To me did seem
> *Apparelled* in celestial light,
> The *glory* and the freshness of a dream. (my italics, lines 1–5).

The revolutionary dawn had been a 'glorious birth' (line 16) but by 1802, following Napoleon's usurpation, there had 'passed away a *glory* from the earth' (line 19). A soulless image had usurped a living thought that never more could be:

> It is not now as it has been of yore;–
> Turn wheresoe'er I may,
> By night or day,
> The things which I have seen I now can see no more. (lines 6–9)

By 1804, when Napoleon placed the imperial crown on his head, the sun that rose in splendour set, and put his glory off, and 'nothing can bring back the hour / Of splendour in the grass, of glory in the flower' (lines 180–1).

'STRENGTH OF USURPATION'

> We will grieve not, rather find
> Strength in what remains behind . . .
> ('Ode: There was a time', lines 182–3)

In the second half of this chapter, I want to move on from 'grief', Wordsworth's grief 'for Buonaparte', to examine his search for 'Strength' with which to oppose Napoleon. I shall argue that ultimately it is in the 'Imagination', in its act of 'usurpation', that Wordsworth finds such strength.

In the two years between writing his first Miltonic sonnet, 'I grieved for Buonaparte' of April 1802,[69] and his completion of Book VI of *The Prelude* in April 1804,[70] Wordsworth became engaged in a detailed and complex investigation of the character of Napoleon, the nature of his government and his potential threat to Britain. Wordsworth carried out this investigation principally in the sonnet form,[71] and implicit throughout the sequence is his analysis of his own position as a poet, a Grasmere Volunteer and someone who had envisaged for himself an active political role. In this poetry Wordsworth responds in a number of different ways to the figure of Napoleon. While he may seek to transcend the Napoleonic figure of power and offer other forms of authority in its place, in his contest with Napoleon he uses him as a figure of his own ambition and as an *Other* against whom he can define himself. To adapt Whately's terms, more than any other writer of the time Wordsworth magnifies Napoleon to enhance the 'splendour' and 'glory' that he gains in his rhetorical conquest of him.

The transcendent impulse in Wordsworth's response to contemporary events has often been stressed by critics, be it in the form of turning within, internalization or going beyond, surpassing. Perhaps the prime model of internalization is that offered by Milton in *Paradise Lost*:

> . . . then wilt thou not be loath
> To leave this Paradise, but shalt possess
> A paradise within thee, happier far. (XII, 585–7)

Critics have often seen Wordsworth possessing a 'paradise within' as a result of, and a compensation for, the failure of the French Revolution. The model is paradigmatically put forward by M. H. Abrams who argues, following the 'Prospectus' for *The Recluse*, that Wordsworth's programme for poetry is best understood as a displacement of millenarian political expectation into an aesthetic principle that he calls the 'Apocalypse of the Imagination', a principle evolved from Christian tradition. Thus Abrams writes that:

> . . . faith in an apocalypse by revelation had been replaced by faith in an apocalypse by revolution; and this now gave way to faith in an apocalypse by imagination or cognition. In the ruling two-term frame of Romantic thought, the mind of man confronts the old heaven and earth and *possesses within* itself the power, if it will but recognize and avail itself of the power, to transform them into a new heaven and a new earth, by means of a total revolution of consciousness.[72] (my italics).

Even critics who take issue with Abrams's theory that this 'paradise within' comes with a total rejection of 'the real world which is the world of all of us' juxtapose the external and the internal worlds. E. P. Thompson writes:

> How far is it possible for men to hold on to aspirations long after there appears to be no hope of inserting them into 'the real world which is the world of all of us'? If the social context makes all insertion seem impossible – if all objective referents for these hopes are cruelly obliterated – if the attempt to live out the ideals produce their opposites – if fraternité produces fratricide, égalité produces empire, liberty produces liberticide – then aspiration can only become a transposed *interior faith*.[73] (my italics)

Wordsworth can often be seen to attempt this kind of turning inwards when confronted by Napoleon. In '*Calais*, August 15, 1802', he contrasts France as it 'now is' in 1802, celebrating Napoleon's Consulship for Life, with France as it was in 1790:

> Festivals have I seen that were not names:
> This is young Buonaparte's natal day;
> And his is henceforth an established sway,
> Consul for Life. With worship France proclaims
> Her approbation, and with pomps and games.
> Heaven grant that other cities may be gay!
> Calais is not: and I have bent my way
> To the Sea-Coast, noting that each man frames
> His business as he likes. Another time
> That was, when I was here long ago:
> The senselessness of joy was then sublime!
> Happy is he, who, caring not for Pope,
> Consul, or King, can sound himself to know
> The destiny of Man, and live in hope.

Wordsworth's concluding tercet exemplifies what Thompson has termed 'interior faith'. Faced with overwhelming evidence of the difference between what France once 'promised' and what she 'now is', Wordsworth is forced back into himself for a solution – he must 'sound' himself. Yet this act of internalization seems forced or willed, in tension with, rather than transcending, the experience of the poem. The formalized and archaic introduction of the third person singular – 'Happy is he' – may be an attempt to universalize the message of the conclusion, but it seems to contradict the experience of the 'I' in the rest of the poem – 'happy is he', but I am not. As the previous eleven lines testify, Wordsworth himself cared only too much about 'Pope, Consul and King', especially 'Consul'.

The other method of transcending Napoleon is to see beyond the 'soulless image', to 'thwart / This tyranny' of the eye, as Wordsworth terms it later in *The Prelude* (XI, 178–9). This again is an established view of the dynamics of the Wordsworthian imagination. For example, Carlos Baker writes of the Snowdon passage of *The Prelude*:

When he comes to recollect the scene's emotional impact in the tranquility of a later time, he recognizes it, not for what it was, but for what, after rumination, it had become for him: A Gestalt pattern standing for the human mind at its highest stage of development, a mind sustained

> By recognition of transcendent power
> In sense conducting to ideal form.

[Baker is using the 1850 version, XIV, 75–6]. Such minds are no longer the prisoners of sense impressions. Instead, the 'quickening impulse' provided by the sense stimuli prepare such minds all the better 'to hold fit converse with the spiritual world'.[74]

The best example of Wordsworth's attempt at this type of transcendence, when confronted with Napoleon, is the poem 'October, 1803':

> When, looking on the present face of things,
> I see one Man, of Men the meanest too!
> Raised up to sway the world, to do, undo,
> With mighty Nations for his Underlings,
> The great event with which old story rings
> Seem vain and hollow; I find nothing great;
> Nothing is left which I can venerate;
> So that almost a doubt within me springs
> Of Providence, such emptiness at length
> Seems at the heart of all things. But, great God!
> I measure back the steps which I have trod,
> And tremble, seeing, as I do, the strength
> Of such poor Instruments, with thoughts sublime
> I tremble at the sorrows of the time.

The image of Napoleon's meaningless round of creation and destruction almost undoes Wordsworth and causes a failure of the 'interior faith' – 'such emptiness at length / Seems at the heart of all things' (lines 9–10). But the final four lines suggest that it can be replaced by a new way of seeing, transforming the materialist 'seeing' of line 2 and the Napoleonic 'doing' of line 3 into a moment of not only analytic or cognitive but of transcendent vision – 'seeing as I do' (line 12). The poet now looks beyond 'the present face of things' and can see 'the strength of such poor instruments' in a moment of 'sublime' vision. The discovery of this new way of seeing comes as a result of Wordsworth's defence against the Napoleonic assault upon the eye. But again the poem's conclusion leads us to doubt its effectiveness. The standard emotion in front of the sublime, the tremble of fear, brings us back to a second tremble, now at the 'sorrows of the time' (line 14). At the end of the poem we again seem to be looking on the present face of things, uncertain of the role of 'Providence' or 'God' in the face of such violence. Wordsworth's conclusion emphasises the tension between the experiential world of the 'one Man', the 'soulless image' and the 'living thought' of sublime seeing.

The particular problem posed by Napoleon was that rather than merely representing a loss which could have been fitted into Wordsworth's characteristic pattern of loss and gain, and so a failure redeemable and recompensed with transcendent vision, he embodied the French Revolution transformed. Not only were 'hopes o'erthrown' but more than ever these were 'times of fear . . . of dereliction and dismay' (*The Prelude* II, 449, 457). From May 1803 to July 1805, the 'Army of England', as Napoleon's invasion force was termed, was encamped at Boulogne, with 2,000 vessels or landing craft capable of transporting 200,000 soldiers across the English Channel[75] and, as Wordsworth has it:

> Impatient to put out the only light
> Of liberty that yet remains on Earth! ('October 1803' lines 13–14)

Wordsworth himself was only too aware of the need to combat Napoleon poetically and physically. In his 'Lines on the Expected Invasion, 1803' he seeks to unite all political factions in the resolution:

> To have one Soul, and perish to a man,
> Or save this honoured Land from every Lord
> But British reason and the British sword. (lines 17–19)

Carl Woodring has written that in his sonnets of national defence of 1802–3 'Wordsworth's chief impulse [was] to goad all people who were in any way capable of flagging in the contest against Napoleon'.[76] It was not enough to 'sound' oneself but, as Wordsworth instructed the Men of Kent:

> Now is the time to prove your hardiment . . .
> ('To the Men of Kent' line 4)

Wordsworth himself set out to do just this. On 3 October 1803, he enrolled in the Grasmere Volunteers and donned uniform during the nationwide campaign of home defence.[77] On 9 October Dorothy wrote to Catherine Clarkson of William that 'surely there was never a more determined hater of the French nor one more willing to do his utmost to destroy them if they really do come'.[78] In another letter she apocalyptically suggests that more than the defence of Grasmere may be required: 'I have no other hope than that they will not be called out of these quiet, far-off places, except in the case of the French being successful after their landing, and in that case, what matter. We may all go together' (*EY* 403).

Wordsworth's participation in the Volunteers seems to have given an outlet for his characteristic militancy.[79] To quote Wilfred Spiegelman 'the public life, warfare, and the traditional arenas of masculine achievement are never far from his mind'.[80] In the later years of his life Wordsworth remembered that he had studied history and military strategy with great interest, that he always fancied that he had a talent for command, and he at one time thought of military life.[81] In 'Home at Grasmere' the Grasmere Volunteer-to-be wrote:

> I heard of danger met
> Or sought with courage, enterprise forlorn
> By one, soul keeper of his own intent
> Or by a resolute few, who for the sake
> Of glory fronted multitudes in arms.
> Yea, to this day I swell with like desire;
> I cannot at this moment read a tale
> Of two brave Vessels matched in deadly fight
> And fighting to the death, but I am pleased
> More than a wise Man ought to be; I wish,
> I burn, I struggle, and in soul am there. (lines 923–33)

Writing here in 1800 Wordsworth achieves 'glory' for his soul through some kind of imaginative leap. Interestingly, it is in response to the news of a naval battle that Wordsworth exercises his fantasies. On 1 August 1798 in, as we shall see, one of the most important encounters of the Napoleonic war, Nelson had destroyed Napoleon's fleet at Aboukir Bay on the mouth of the Nile, and it may be this 'deadly fight' that Wordsworth has in mind here.

Wordsworth's militancy, his need to combat Napoleon, is given a sharper edge because he tends to see Napoleon as having achieved a position and a status that he himself has failed to achieve, but to which, by nature of his character and upbringing, he believes himself to have greater right. As David Erdman has written, Bonaparte 'fulfill[ed] a role [as French Leader] which Wordsworth himself had contemplated, as he tells us in *The Prelude*'.[82] John Williams writes, the 'most important consequence of his experience in France in 1792 was not the acquisition of specific, contemporary radical political views – it was the development of a more general sense of vocation to take a practical, politically active role in affairs . . . He thus began to nurture a vision of himself as fulfilling the role of statesman.'[83] One of Wordsworth's initial and most frequent reactions to 'grief' – an emotion prompted by the failure of events to match expectations – is to offer himself, actively, as the figure who would attempt to put the world to rights. Wordsworth lodges himself in the gap between hope and disappointment. In Book x of *The Prelude* he writes of France:

> Yet did I grieve, nor only grieved, but thought
> Of opposition and of remedies:
> . . . Yet would I willingly have taken up
> A service at this time for cause so great,
> However dangerous. (x, 128–36)

In the passage that follows (x, 136–88), Wordsworth recounts his intense wishes for 'one paramount mind' who would have 'cleared a passage for just government' (x, 179, 186). His description of this role invokes his own expression of an ambition to assist the state as a 'single person' (x, 138) and suggests a contrast between what might have been had he done so and the debasing of this role by Robespierre and Napoleon.

Of course, Wordsworth's failure, and the tainting of the role of statesman by figures such as Robespierre and Napoleon, are usually seen as reinforcing Wordsworth's rejection of this role and his decision to become a 'Poet' by 1798. Gill writes that 'during the most satisfying year of his life, 1797–8, he had become convinced that he had a vocation, literally that he was called to be a major poet'.[84] In the 1803–4 work on *The Prelude*, Wordsworth shapes his material to confirm his conviction that 'the retired life of the imagination is the truely creative life, not the secular world of academic competition or of revolutionary activism'.[85] Thus in *The Prelude* Wordsworth famously disavows the world of action:

> Above all
> Did Nature bring again that wiser mood,
> More deeply reestablished in my soul,
> Which, seeing little worthy or sublime
> In what we blazon with the pompous names
> Of power and action . . . (xii, 44–9)

Yet, as John Williams has shown, matters are not this simple. Wordsworth's justification of his failure in the sphere of 'power and action' leads to a 'constant juxtaposition of active and passive principles that informs much of the later poetry'.[86] Wordsworth constantly appropriates 'pompous names' such as 'power', 'glory', 'splendour' and 'majesty' from the martial and political worlds and applies them to his own visionary or poetic one. As we have seen in 'Home at Grasmere', Wordsworth's active and heroic instincts, his desire to take on a political or martial role is being constantly suppressed, 'tamed' by Nature (lines 934–59). As Spiegelman writes, Wordsworth's 'heroic zeal does not vanish, Reason preempts and internalizes it . . . Othello's greatness, like all classical military heroes, is displaced and absorbed by the new heroic venture that Wordsworth cites in his concluding lines . . . [the result is] Wordsworth's sometimes baffling attempts to accommodate action and repose, heroic achievement and meditative calm'.[87] When he is confronted with Napoleon, Wordsworth's 'active', 'heroic' self resurfaces.

In 'I grieved for Buonaparte', Wordsworth uses Napoleon's renown as a soldier, his training in battle from youth, to disqualify him from the position of 'The Governor' (lines 1–8). Instead he offers as the exemplary education for the Governor, 'who must be wise and good' (line 6), an upbringing in the mould of his own:

> Wisdom doth live with children round her knees:
> Books, leisure, perfect freedom, and the talk
> Man holds with week-day man in the hourly walk
> Of the mind's business: these are the degrees
> By which true Sway doth mount; this is the stalk
> True Power doth grow on; and her rights are these. (lines 9–14)

Wordsworth reinforces his argument through his poetic technique. He introduces Napoleon by audaciously introducing himself, '*I* grieved for *Buonaparte*' (line 1, my italics), giving himself a position of trochaically stressed supremacy at the beginning of the sonnet. However 'Buonaparte' is stressed (it must always have four syllables) its final e (later printed as é to highlight this point) will cadence in contrast to this powerful, single-syllabled, self-asserting, opening 'I'. The effect is heightened by the caesura after seven syllables, breaking one of the standard sonnet opening line forms of six and four. Since 1798 Napoleon had signed himself Bonaparte, pronounced without the é, but here Wordsworth uses the earlier Italian form of his name. Bathetic cadence is heightened by irreverence. Wordsworth as subject is active – 'I grieved' – Napoleon, the paradigmatic man of action, as object is passive – 'for Buonaparte'.

In the rest of the quatrain:

> . . . the vital blood
> Of that Man's mind what can it be? What food
> Fed his first hopes? what knowledge could he gain? (lines 2–4)

Wordsworth appears to forget himself and concentrate on Napoleon. Yet this very stress on the third person singular – 'his', 'he' – and the definition of Napoleon through absence remind the reader that there is another presence in the poem – 'I'. Wordsworth knows only too well what the vital blood of *his own* mind is, what food had fed his first hopes and what knowledge *he himself* had gained. These are perennial Wordsworthian questions, the ones behind *The Prelude* and 'Tintern Abbey', the idiom of which he is adopting:

> But oft, in lonely rooms, and mid the din
> Of towns and cities, I have owed to them,
> In hours of weariness, sensations sweet,
> *Felt in the blood, and felt along the heart,*
> *And passing even into purer mind*
> With tranquil restoration. (my italics, lines 26–31)

and

> . . . but with pleasing thoughts
> That in this moment there is life and *food*
> For future years. And so I dare to *hope* . . . (my italics, lines 64–6)

Similarly, in the *Essay on Morals* Wordsworth writes of the need for things to 'melt into our affections, to incorporate itself with the blood and juices of our minds'.[88] Napoleon is the absence of those very qualities of thought and experience that make Wordsworth 'I'. In this sonnet, to consider Bonaparte is to consider what he is not: to consider what he is not, is to consider what 'I' am.

As the sonnet progresses from 'I' and 'he' to 'we' again both Bonaparte and 'I' seem to have been left behind. Yet throughout the description of the prototype 'Governor' the reader is aware that the two initial figures in the poem are being measured against the list of credentials, and, as Napoleon does not fit the pattern, 'I' becomes the only available candidate. The process of applying a Wordsworthian language to Napoleon is now reversed. The language of Napoleonic command – 'true Sway' (line 13), 'True Power' (line 14) – is applied, and redefined by the process of application, to the Wordsworthian lifestyle and combined with the familiar language of organic growth. Confronted with Napoleon, Wordsworth appropriates the Napoleonic realm of 'true Sway' and 'True Power' to his own life. By the criteria of 'I grieved', *The*

Prelude, a propaedeutic work, becomes a curriculum vitae for the 'Governor who must be wise and good' (line 6). It is an interesting exercise to put this sonnet next to 'I am not one' which gives a similar view of Wordsworth's life. In 'I grieved', Wordsworth's confrontation with Napoleon forces him to shape and justify his early life not as creating a 'Poet', as it does in that poem, but as preparation for the role of 'Governor'.

One poem in which Wordsworth strikingly images his desire to achieve a position and a status that can be described as Napoleonic is 'It is no Spirit'. This lyric can even be seen as an allegorical consideration of Napoleon's rise and of Wordsworth's own response to it. Wordsworth wrote this poem in November or December 1802,[89] after a summer of poetic contemplations of Napoleon's elevation to the pre-eminent position – 'his is henceforth an established sway / Consul for life' ('Festivals have I seen' lines 2–3). In it Wordsworth contemplates the evening star:

> It is no Spirit who from Heaven hath flown,
> And is descending on his embassy;
> Nor Traveller gone from Earth the Heavens to Espy!
> 'Tis Hesperus – there he stands with glittering crown,
> First admonition that the sun is down!
> For yet it is broad day-light: clouds pass by;
> A few are near him still – and now the sky,
> He hath it to himself – 'tis all his own.
> O most ambitious Star! an inquest wrought
> Within me when I recognised thy light;
> A moment I was startled at the sight:
> And, while I gazed, there came to me a thought
> That I might step beyond my natural race
> As thou seem'st now to do; might one day trace
> Some ground not mine; and, strong her strength above,
> My Soul, an Apparition in the place,
> Tread there, with steps that no one shall reprove.

As with Mont Blanc, Wordsworth may well be using a natural phenomenon to formulate his reaction to Napoleon's rise. As in the coronation scene of *The Prelude*, the rise of the Napoleonic evening star occurs against the background of the setting of the revolutionary sun – 'first admonition that the sun is down' (line 5). Napoleon's emergence from the First Consul of a triumvirate – 'A few are near him still' (line 7) – to pre-eminence as Consul for life in an effective dictatorship – 'He hath it to himself – 'tis all his own' (lines 8–9) – is allegorized in the rise of the Evening Star. The timing of the poem, after a summer of 'inquest' into

Napoleon, the apostrophe to the 'most ambitious Star', and the reprehensible nature of its rise, the reproved steps (secured, of course, by a usurpation), all point inexorably to Napoleon.

Alluding to *Macbeth*, the main revolutionary text of *The Prelude*, Wordsworth plays Banquo to Napoleon's Macbeth:

> Thou hast it now: King, Cawdor, Glamis, all . . . (III. i. 1)

As for Banquo, the recognition of Napoleon's rise to power prompts Wordsworth to consider his own ambitions. He is stimulated to simulate Napoleon's rise. As in 'Home at Grasmere' Wordsworth wishes to place his soul, here feminized, into the place of power, but, as in 'I grieved', he presents himself as a more suitable candidate for the position, who can do so blamelessly – 'with steps that no one shall reprove' (line 17). Wordsworth seeks to emulate and gain the place of Napoleon: to usurp the usurper.

The complexity of Wordsworth's responses to Napoleon in the poetry of 1802–4 needs to be borne in mind when considering the second 'usurpation' of Book VI of *The Prelude*. The Simplon Pass incident, which Hartman has called 'perhaps the most significant in *The Prelude*',[90] takes the same form of hope and disappointment as the Mont Blanc one, and again I shall use Stephen Gill's description:

> On that day, he and Jones set off with others from Brig to cross the Alps at the Simplon Pass. They ate at midday at the Old Stockalper Spittal, but lingered at the main table longer than the main party, which set off again without them. When they did continue, Wordsworth and Jones thought to catch up with the group as they followed a track which led, as they expected, still higher, but they did not do so. Questioning a peasant they learned that they had mistaken their way. Back they must go to where they had branched off up the mountain track and thence downwards, following the current of the stream. Jones and Wordsworth were still keyed up for an ultimate experience of the sublime, but what the peasant was trying to tell them, through the barriers of language and their reluctance to believe, was that they had, in fact, already crossed the Alps.[91]

As with the summit of Mont Blanc, the hope for some crowning experience of the sublime is disappointingly frustrated. In the 1850 version, Wordsworth uses a familiar formulation of 'hope' and 'grief':

> Loth to believe what we so grieved to hear,
> For still we had hopes that pointed to the clouds . . . (1850: VI, 586–7)

But now, recalled at the time of writing in 1804, the moment of grief produces a new strength, when the 'Imagination' comes athwart Wordsworth in 'such strength of usurpation':

Imagination! – lifting up itself
Before the eye and progress of my song
Like an unfathered vapour, here that power,
In all the might of its endowments, came
Athwart me, I was lost as in a cloud,
Halted without a struggle to break through,
And now, recovering, to my soul I say
'I recognise thy glory'. In such strength
Of usurpation, in such visitings
Of awful promise, when the light of sense
Goes out in flashes that have shewn to us
The invisible world, doth greatness make abode,
There harbours whether we be young or old.
Our destiny, our nature, and our home,
Is with infinitude – and only there;
With hope it is, hope that can never die,
Effort, and expectation, and desire,
And something evermore about to be.
The mind beneath such banners militant
Thinks not of spoils or trophies, nor of aught
That may attest its prowess, blest in thoughts
That are their own perfection and reward –
Strong in itself, and in the access of joy
Which hides it like the overflowing Nile. (VI, 525–48)

The 'Imagination', in its 'strength of usurpation', echoes and responds to the usurpation imaged in the Mont Blanc passage seventy lines before, which, as I've been arguing, can be seen as structured upon Napoleon's usurpation of 1799 and symbolically his rule as a whole. The disappointment experienced crossing the Alps follows the same structure as that encountered at Mont Blanc. It too, as Abrams points out, reflects the failure of Wordsworth's 'unbounded and so impossible hopes in the French Revolution'.[92] But now Wordsworth finds in the Imagination a power that compensates for this failure of reality. He does so by appropriating the very act that he used to symbolize the end of the Revolution. He usurps the usurpation, at once seizing it as a structure, and supplanting materialist reality, 'the soulless image', and possibly Napoleon, with the 'Imagination'. In doing so Wordsworth transforms usurpation from a negative into a positive act. The past tense of 'had usurped' switches to the present tense 'usurpation'. Whereas Napoleon's usurpation had been an act of destructive finality – 'upon a living thought that *never more could be*' – Wordsworth's imaginative usurpation is one of eternal creation – 'something *evermore about to be*'. Thus

Wordsworth no longer grieves to have a soulless image on the eye that had usurped a living thought, but corrects his grief and finds strength in the 'Imagination', 'in such strength of usurpation'.

Wordsworth's imaginative act of usurpation raises his soul to Napoleonic heights. In 'Home at Grasmere' he had swelled with desire to achieve 'glory' and did so through an imaginative leap:

> I wish
> I burn, I struggle, and in soul am there. (lines 932–3)

In 'It is no Spirit', he looked on the Napoleon-Hesperus figure, and, having 'recognised his light' wished to assume a similar place of pre-eminence for his soul (lines 10, 11–16). Now, under the influence of the 'Imagination', Wordsworth turns to his Soul and says 'I recognise thy glory' (line 532). The faded glory of the French Revolution, that will be finally 'put off' by Napoleon at his coronation, is transferred to Wordsworth's soul. Wordsworth puts his own soul in the place of the 'soulless image' and fills the emptiness at the heart of all things.

There is a similar process of usurpation throughout the passage in terms of vocabulary: Wordsworth plunders the Napoleonic, combative, and militant as a means of reinforcing his formulation of the 'Imagination' – 'power', 'might', 'strength', 'greatness', 'banners militant', 'prowess', 'strong'. But as desired in 'It is no Spirit' Wordsworth's powerfulness is achieved without reproof. As Liu has pointed out,[93] unlike Napoleon, notorious for his 'spoilations' of invaded countries, the 'Imagination' 'thinks not of spoils or trophies' (line 545). It needs no Star of the Legion of Honour to 'attest its prowess' (line 543). Similarly, Greatness makes its abode in the 'Imagination', not in the palace of Malmaison where Napoleon held court, and it is in the 'Imagination' that it 'harbours', not at Boulogne waiting to invade England with two thousand ships.

After two years poetic engagement with the French Consul in the sonnets, then, Wordsworth's formulation and legitimization of the 'Imagination' can perhaps be said to involve the process of Napoleonization. The Imagination acts like a purified and idealized Napoleon. Wordsworth achieves an 'ennobling interchange' with Napoleon (*The Prelude*, XII, 376), distilling what might be termed 'The excellence, pure spirit, and best power . . . of the object seen' (XII, 377–8), the 'one Man', the 'soulless image on the eye', Napoleon. The Napoleonic usurpation becomes a model for the working of the 'Imagination'. Hartman has described the 'Imagination' in this passage as 'consciousness of self raised to apocalyptic pitch'[94] and one could perhaps rephrase this as 'consciousness of self raised to Napoleonic pitch'. In his 'Essay, supplementary to the Preface' of 1815, Wordsworth describes the poet, the original genius, as being 'in the condition of Hannibal among the Alps'.[95] Napoleon was 'the present-day Hannibal' (*EoT* II, 138) to quote Coleridge, and as is illustrated by the inscriptions at the base of David's *Napoleon crossing the Alps*. The Alps were the sights of his greatest triumphs in the campaigns of 1796–7 and 1800. In 1804, describing his own experience among the Alps, Wordsworth makes them the scene of one of the greatest triumphs of his 'Imagination'. It could perhaps be said that he images himself as the 'present-day Hannibal' and crowns himself as the Napoleon of the 'Imagination'.

While providing an outlet for Wordsworth's Napoleonic instinct, what Gill has termed the 'imperious, self-willed Wordsworth who wanted to be recognised as an intellectual power',[96] the Imagination seeks to transcend the Napoleonic and the immediate. It goes beyond 'the things that pass away' to a 'shew / Of objects that endure' (XII, 35–6). Indeed, the lines:

> Our destiny, our nature, and our home,
> Is with infinitude, and only there,
> With hope it is, hope that can never die . . . (lines 540–2)

reiterate Wordsworth's earlier attempt at transcendence when faced with Napoleon in '*Calais*, August, 1802':

> Happy is he who . . .
> . . . can sound himself
> To know the *destiny* of Man, and live in *hope*. (my italics, lines 11–14)

The possibility of transcendence is no longer wished on to a third person. Through the Imagination it is now available to all – '*our* destiny, *our* nature, and *our* home'. The 'Imagination' enables one to see beyond 'the soulless image' of 'one Man raised up to sway the world' and shows us instead 'the invisible world'. As in Book XIII of *The Prelude*, where Wordsworth gives the other main description of the 'Imagination', 'reality', the 'real sea', is 'Usurped upon as far as sight could reach' (XIII, 49–51). It is as a result of being, amongst other things, to quote again from Book XIII, 'in opposition set against an enemy' (XIII, 30–1) that Wordsworth discovers the strength of the Imagination. Rather than outmanoeuvering the Napoleonic assault on the eye, the 'Imagination' confronts it and commandeers its vocabulary. Only once this has been done, the usurper usurped, can the 'Imagination' truly transcend.

Yet, while the 'Imagination' involves itself linguistically and thematically with Napoleon, in its transcendence it may seem to ignore the immediate 'destiny of man', whether or not Napoleon would invade 'our homes', and seems to fail to vindicate Wordsworth's combative nature and efforts. Wordsworth was, we remember, described by Dorothy as a determined hater of the French who was 'willing to do his utmost to destroy them'.[97] It is possible that the mind's enlistment beneath 'banners militant' parallels Wordsworth's own enlistment in the Grasmere Volunteers. If so, the general militancy of the passage may be not only metaphorical but an allusion to the contemporary situation of a country set 'to prove its hardiment', stoically determined to resist Napoleon with 'hope that can never die / Effort, and expectation, and desire' (line 54). This is supported by Alan Liu's suggestion that the militant diction of the passage culminates with a reference to the Battle of the Nile, when Nelson destroyed the French fleet at Aboukir Bay. This, he argues, was the main symbol of hope during the period of the threatened invasion, ' a moral victory, the prophecy of defeat even in the years of greatest French conquest'.[98] If this is the case, then Liu's suggestion can perhaps be developed to explore Wordsworth's reconciliation of his combative, transcendent and emulative responses to Napoleon. To use the language of 'October, 1803' the Nile was 'a great event' (line 5) that did not seem 'vain and hollow' (line 6). The reference to it at the conclusion of the 'Imagination' passage may be taken to allude to faith in the armed struggle against Napoleon and a belief in his eventual defeat. As Colin Pedley has revealed, Wordsworth's sonnet '*Anticipation*, October, 1803', which looks forward to the defeat of Napoleon's invasion force, does so by alluding to a popular poem which celebrates the Battle of the Nile. Its opening, 'Shout for a mighty victory is won' echoes the first line of Bowles's 'Song of the Battle of the Nile' of 1799 – 'Shout! for the Lord hath triumphed gloriously'.[99] In this sonnet, as in the 'Imagination' passage, Wordsworth draws on the symbolic status of the battle of the Nile as an anticipation of the victory over Napoleon. The power of the reference is again seen in *The Convention of Cintra* when Wordsworth draws on the implicit militancy of the image to portray the combined regular and irregular armies of Spain: 'A military spirit should be there, and a military action, not confined like an ordinary river in one channel, but spreading like the Nile over the whole face of the land' (*CoC* 234). The specific reference to the Nile in the 'Imagination' passage of 1804 makes a similar demand for a 'military spirit' and a commitment to resist Napoleon through 'military action'.

The 'Imagination' passage of Book VI of *The Prelude*, one of the paradigmatic passages of English Romanticism, can be seen as the culmination of the two-year period during which Wordsworth had been constantly engaged with Napoleon. It is the site of Wordsworth's contest with him, and in it Wordsworth's 'Imagination', 'the main essential power' (XIII, 289), 'the moving soul / Of our long labour (XIII, 171–2)', takes on Napoleon in both the combative and the appropriative sense. Wordsworth absorbs him within the structures of the imagination. He internalizes Napoleon in *The Prelude*, as he does the epic and the heroic. Wordsworth's 'Imagination' can be seen as Napoleonic, acting 'in such strength of usurpation', as Wordsworth appropriates his power and status. Wordsworth might be said to offer himself as the Napoleon of the 'Imagination'. Yet the 'Imagination' fights against Napoleon. It is not, as Abrams calls it, a state of 'spiritual quietism' and 'wise passiveness'.[100] Neither is it, as Jonathan Bate has criticized Liu for arguing, a power that is privileged at the expense of the suppression of history.[101] Rather, the 'Imagination' is a militant, active and political force that both evolves out of and is directly engaged in Wordsworth's contest with Napoleon. Even while seeking to transcend – to see beyond the 'One Man', beyond the 'soulless image on the eye' to the 'invisible world' – the 'Imagination' continues to operate in 'the very world which is the world / Of all of us' (X, 725–6), fighting the 'tyranny' both of the eye and of Napoleon. Significantly, as we shall see, over the next decade Wordsworth repeatedly addresses himself to Napoleon's place in the 'Imagination'. Indeed, it is not until Napoleon's final defeat at Waterloo that Wordsworth's 'Imagination' was 'satisfied' ('Thanksgiving Ode', lines 163–7). Thus it was with some feeling of justification that he could look back in 1816 and write that 'My whole soul was with those who were resolved to fight it out with Bonaparte' (*MY* II, 334).

CHAPTER 3

'Historiographer[s] to the King of Hell':[1] *The Lake poets' Peninsular campaign*

> We combated for victory in the empire of reason, for strong-holds in the imagination.
>
> Wordsworth, *The Convention of Cintra* (*CoC* 261)

Wordsworth's tract on the Convention of Cintra of 1809 marks the beginning of a remarkable resurgence of the Lakers' writing on Napoleon and signals a new stage in the methods and purposes of their representation of him. If their engagement with Napoleon in the years 1798–1804 was characterized by their complex use of him as an 'imaginary' figure – at once a figure of their own desires, an *Other* and, in Wordsworth's case, a figure of the imagination – in their various writings of 1809 and after they were more concerned with establishing that Napoleon's power was imaginary – located within the 'imagination' itself. They continue to use Napoleon as an 'imaginary' figure, representing him fantastically in their writing on the Peninsular war as a monstrous *Other* who threatens the destruction of 'everything which gives life its value – of virtue, of reason, of repose in God, or in truth' (*CoC* 241). The production of this Napoleonic *Other* enables the Lakers to redefine their own political allegiances. But increasingly in this body of writing their concern is with finding figurative forms which will help them drive him out of the public 'imagination'.

In his tract, Wordsworth locates the decisive battles of the war against Napoleon as being fought not in Spain or Portugal, but in the 'imagination'. He argues that Napoleon's real power lies in his tyrannical hold over the 'imaginations of men' (*CoC* 249), not in his domination of Europe. The most important effect of Wellington's initial victories at Rolica and Vimiero was not the promise of the deliverance of Portugal or the humiliation and weakening of the French, but the fact that 'there was an anticipation of a shock to his [Napoleon's] power, where that power is strongest, in the imaginations of men, which are sure to fall under the bondage of long-continued success' (*CoC* 249). In *The Prelude*,

Wordsworth sought through an act of appropriation to assimilate Napoleon within the 'Imagination', reconciling both his combative and emulative responses towards him. In *The Convention of Cintra* he strives to drive him out of it. He sees the strength and value of the forces that have resisted Napoleon not in their actual territorial success, but in the inroads they have made into his mythical power. It is this essentially imaginative nature of the war in the Peninsula that the British generals who ratified the Convention have failed to grasp. As Wordsworth declares, 'Lisbon and Portugal, as city and soil, were chiefly prized by us as a *language*; but our Generals mistook the counters of the game for the stakes played for' (*CoC* 261–2).

Coleridge, similarly, establishes the imagination as the vital arena of the war in his 'Letters on the Spaniards' – a series which he wrote for *The Courier* in December 1809 and January 1810 and which, he commented, he 'should be proud to consider . . . as an Appendix' to Wordsworth's Pamphlet (*EoT* II, 77). In the sixth of these 'Letters', he pronounces that the 'main strength of Bonaparte, Sir, is in the imaginations of men which are dazzled and blinded by the splendid robes and gaudy trappings, which have been purchased by guilt for its own disguise' (*EoT* II, 75). By representing Napoleon's power as imaginary, located within the 'imagination' itself, both Wordsworth and Coleridge create an arena for their own rhetorical conquests of him and mark out the 'imagination' itself as political. Their attempts to drive Napoleon from the 'imagination' involve an elevation of themselves and their roles above those of the politician or the soldier. By adopting the roles of biblical and political prophets, it is they who are able to take up where the British generals have left off; combating Napoleon with *language* and repeatedly emphasising that the 'game' that is being played is essentially imaginative and that military and diplomatic events are only counters in it.

Yet this new stage in the Lakers' representation of Napoleon is fraught with contradiction. While both writers acknowledge Napoleon's place in the imagination, one that he himself had fostered throughout his career, their attempts to drive him out of it force them to adopt strategies of demonizing and Satanizing that paradoxically acknowledge and refigure Napoleon's imaginary power. Hazlitt's comment on John Stoddard's use of passages from *Paradise Lost* to describe Napoleon's fall is equally applicable to the Lakers' writing on him in 1809 and after. By representing Napoleon as Satanic, they were acknowledging that he had 'realized a conception of himself in the mind of his enemies on a par with the most stupendous creations of the imagination' (*HCW* XVII, 22).

Coleridge himself was aware of this problem and addressed it in his post-Waterloo writing.

In this chapter I am concerned with the shift to this new stage in the Lakers' representation of Napoleon, a shift which needs to be seen within the context of the changed cultural perception of Napoleon during the Peninsular war. I am particularly concerned with the figurative forms with which the Lakers sought to enact their conquest of Napoleon in the 'Imagination'. I shall be focusing on Wordsworth's and Coleridge's adoption of the Satanic analogy in these years and with Coleridge's later rethinking of it, but I shall also be considering Southey's *The Curse of Kehama*, in which he adopts similar rhetorical strategies.

SATANIZING NAPOLEON: WORDSWORTH'S TRACT

The Convention of Cintra, ratified on 30 August 1808, created a crisis for the Lake poets' representation of the war against Napoleon just when the meaning of the war had appeared to be becoming clear.[2] In May 1808, the rising of the Spanish people against Napoleon's army of invasion had made possible a new and attractively simple formulation of international affairs. These spontaneous shows of resistance to Napoleon's imperialism had enabled the Lakers to reinterpret the war as a battle conducted on behalf of liberty and freedom and against tyranny and oppression. Moreover, the British government's military support of the Spanish and Portuguese enabled the three writers to realign themselves with their countrymen, their government and 'Liberty', and so to close, at last, the schism that had been opened by the outbreak of the war in 1793. As Coleridge famously declared in 1809, joyfully adopting the English republican idiom of Wordsworth's sonnets of 1802 and 1803:

> it was the noble efforts of Spanish Patriotism, that first restored us, without distinction of party, to our characteristic enthusiasm for *liberty*; and, presenting in its genuine form, incapable of being confounded with its French counterfeit, enabled us once more to utter the names of our Hampdens, Sidneys, and Russells, without hazard of alarming the quiet subject, or offending the zealous loyalist. (*EoT* II, 38)

But the Convention of Cintra suddenly and dramatically called into question the war's new-found meaning. By allowing the French Marshal Junot to evacuate his defeated army from Portugal in British ships, complete with stolen booty, the British generals who signed the Convention seemed to betray the cause of 'Liberty', now synonymous with the cause of the people of the Peninsula. The Convention reopened the schism between the Lakers' natural sympathy for Liberty and official British policy.

Wordsworth's tract on the Convention of Cintra, which emerged out of the Lakers' frustrated attempts to organize a meeting on the subject, signals a change in his engagement with contemporary history from the type seen in *The Prelude* and the sonnets of 1802–3. His major strategy in his epic response to the Convention is enacted in miniature by Southey in a letter of 15 October 1808 to Senhouse. In this Southey argues that Sir Hugh Dalrymple, one of the British signatories of the treaty, has:

> abandoned our vantage ground, betrayed the cause of Spain and Portugal, and disclaimed, as far as his authority extends, the feelings which the Spaniards are inculcating, and in which lie their strength and their salvation, by degrading into a common and petty war between soldier and soldier, that which is the struggle of a nation against a foreign usurper, a business of natural life and death, a war of virtue against vice, light against darkness, the good principle against the evil one. (*SL* III, 176)

Southey's passionate outcry at the news of the Convention came after a six-month period during which he had come to take an increasingly polarized view of the war against Napoleon, as his letters reveal. By the late summer of 1808 he had accumulated a significant investment in the Spanish as a people who showed a 'true love of liberty, and a true spirit of patriotism' and who would begin the 'deliverance of Europe' (*SL* III, 155–6, 157). He had moved from 'hardly [daring to] indulge a hope' on their behalf to confidently asserting a 'firm conviction' that they 'will eventually destroy [Napoleon]' (*SL* III, 148, 158). The Convention of Cintra was obviously a staggering and rather embarrassing blow to these hopes. It called into question the supposed purpose and meaning of the war and so degraded it into 'a common and petty war between soldier and soldier'. Southey's response, typified by this letter, is to upgrade the 'common and petty war' into a 'holy war', as Coleridge later termed it (*EoT* II, 178). He compensates for the disappointments of historical actuality by transforming the war into a series of apocalyptic oppositions of black and white, elevating it beyond a matter of politics or diplomacy into the realm of morality and religion and so mythologizing it as a Christian and libertarian crusade. By the assertion of this convenient, providential and biblically endorsed plot, Southey regains the vantage ground that he feared had been lost by the ratification of the Convention.

Wordsworth effects a similar transformation, elevation and

mythologization of the war throughout *The Convention of Cintra*. Like Southey he fights to gain the moral high ground, claiming that 'the Spanish and Portuguese Nations stand upon the loftiest ground of principle and passion' and demanding that Britain should not 'negligently or timidly descend from those heights of magnanimity to which as a nation we were raised, when they first represented to us their wars and entreated our assistance' (*CoC* 248). Wordsworth strives to elevate the readers' understanding of the war (*CoC* 237). It is not, he claims, an 'ordinary war' (*CoC* 225) but a 'subject which requires the highest mode of thinking and feeling of which human nature is capable' (*CoC* 291). This is not to say that Wordsworth neglects the details or actualities of the Peninsular War, which he spent much time researching and verifying.[3] But when he does 'descend to particulars' as he terms such a move (*CoC* 300), he does so to support an argument that he is conducting on a higher plain.

Wordsworth's move to the moral high ground marks a retreat from both the probing examinations of his own response to historical events of the type seen in Books IX and X of *The Prelude* and from the ambivalent and reflexive goadings of the Miltonic sonnets of 1802–4.[4] Of course, Wordsworth's political and moral thinking in the tract is complicated by his indictment of the British generals who, by ratifying the Convention, have failed to play their allotted roles as agents of good in the apocalyptic series of events enacted in the Peninsula.[5] While Wordsworth claims to speak on behalf of the British 'people' in the tract, he is nonetheless writing from a position of opposition to government policy that he considered dangerous (*CoC* 223[6]). But, like Southey, rather than allowing the policy of the British generals to shatter his new-found belief in the war, Wordsworth compensates for the inadequacy of history with a defensive exercise of the imagination, remorselessly asserting a simple apocalyptic plot as the basis of his prophecy.

Certainly, the historical events in the Peninsula were a major factor in Wordsworth's simplified vision of the war. He shared his enthusiasm for the Spanish cause not only with Southey and Coleridge, but with most of his countrymen. Radical and mainstream opinion in Britain reacted indignantly to Napoleon's diplomatic trickery and his expansionist policy in Spain. British politicians who normally inclined toward Napoleon, such as Whitbread, Holland and Sheridan, saw him as a political aggressor for the first time and interpreted the war against Spain as one fought against a people rather than against princes. As Southey melodramatically commented, Napoleon's intervention in

6 James Gillray, *The Plumb-pudding in danger* (London, 1805).

Spain 'was the first incident in which Buonaparte unequivocally displayed himself in his true character of pure devil'.[7] But while Southey makes Napoleon's policy the origin of this new vision of him, his hyperbolical and categorical tone suggest that the events in the Peninsula were something of a pretext for a radical redefinition of loyalties, enacted through the diabolical figuring of Napoleon.

For Wordsworth, the events in Spain offered an opportunity to clarify his own political position after a complex period of equivocation over the status of the wars fought against France in Europe. In the years before the Spanish rising, and particularly after the effective end of the invasion threat to Britain in 1805, Wordsworth had found himself with no contemporary political cause with which he could unite against Napoleon. He argues in the tract that while there had been for some years a spirit of unity amongst the British in their determination to resist Napoleonic aggression, it was not until the Spanish rising that any real enthusiasm was felt for the struggle. Before 1808, he argues, 'the effort [to resist French ambition], if it had the determination, wanted the cheerfulness of duty. Our condition savoured too much of a grinding constraint – too much of the vassalage of necessity; – it had too much of fear, and therefore of selfishness, not to be contemplated in the main with rueful emotion. We desponded though we did not despair' (*CoC* 227).

During this period of 'despondency' from 1805 to 1808, Napoleon had spectacularly defeated Austria and Russia at Austerlitz in December 1805 and Prussia at Jena in October 1806 in campaigns that, it was often argued by the Whigs, had been forced upon him by Allied aggression.[8] He had become, in Southey's phrase, 'master of the Continent' (*SL* II, 357), gaining a position of supremacy in Europe graphically illustrated by Gillray in his caricatures of 1805 and 1806. In *The Plumb-pudding in danger* (plate 6) of 26 February 1805, for example, Gillray depicts Napoleon cutting with his sabre that portion of the globe made up of the European nations of France, Holland, Spain, Switzerland and Italy, while Pitt carves for himself the Atlantic ocean, including the West Indies.[9] In *Tiddy-Doll, the great French-Gingerbread-Baker* (plate 7) of 23 January 1806, Gillray satirizes Napoleon's imperial and dynastic reconstruction of Europe in the period after Austerlitz, depicting his destruction of the rulers of the old regime and his creation of new 'kinglings.'[10]

In a letter of 1808, Southey gave a revealingly ambivalent explanation of Napoleon's military success in the years before the Spanish rising,

7 James Gillray, *Tiddy-Doll, the great French-Gingerbread-Baker, drawing out a new Batch of Kings* (London, 1806).

arguing that 'the truth of the present history is, that a great military despotism, in its youth and full vigour – like that of France – will and must beat down corrupt establishments and worn-out governments' (*SL* III, 155–6). Wordsworth too showed little sympathy for the vanquished *ancien régime* powers on these occasions. In the sonnet 'November, 1806' he described the Prussian defeat as 'Another mighty Empire overthrown' (line 2). Even at this late date he clearly felt no enthusiasm for the cause of 'Empires'. In *The Convention of Cintra* he stresses that the difference between Napoleon's wars of 1805–7 and that against the Spanish is that the Spanish are 'a PEOPLE, and not a mere army or set of armies' (*CoC* 236–7). As late as March 1811, in his published letter to C. W. Pasley, Wordsworth represents the series of French victories in the years 1805–7 as the triumph of one sort of tyranny over another, implying that Napoleon, though a tyrant, was no worse than the tyrannies he shattered and replaced (*MY* I, 480–1).

Indeed, it is Wordsworth's ambivalent response to the wars in Europe during these years that reveal the extent of his use of the events in Spain to redefine his loyalties. His Byronic or Hazlittean representation of Napoleon's role in the letter to Pasley as a destroyer of the 'detestable governments with which the nations have been afflicted' (*MY* I, 480–1) was one that he could have applied to Napoleon's intervention in Spain. He was dramatically confronted by such a positive appreciation of Napoleon's role as late as March 1809, in an encounter which he did his best to make comic in his description of it in a letter to Thomas De Quincey:

> Mr Crump, my landlord, called here this morning; he did not stay much above two hours, as soon as he had heard the dismal tale of the chimneys and the cellars, he began to crow; and over what, think you? The inert, the lazy, the helpless, the worthless Spaniards, clapping his wings at the same time in honour of Buonaparte – this was the truth, though perhaps he was not aware how his wings were employed. Mr. Crump introduced the subject and his words were 'Well, Mr. W., is there no good to come out of this? What do you say to rooting out the Friars – abolishing the Inquisition – sweeping away the feudal tenures' in short, though he did not mean to defend Buonaparte, 'Oh no, on no account! yet certainly he would be a great Benefactor to the Spaniards'. (*MY* I, 306)

Crump represents Napoleon's army in Spain as the bringers of the liberal ideas of the French Revolution who would establish enlightened government in the place of the twin tyrannies of *ancien régime* monarchy and the Inquisition.[11] If his vision of events idealizes the French role, it nonetheless points to elements in the Spanish cause that Wordsworth

8 James Gillray, *Spanish-Patriots attacking the French-Banditti. Loyal Britons lending a lift* (London, 1808).

would not automatically have sympathised with. These elements are graphically illustrated by James Gillray in his caricature of 1808, *Spanish Patriots attacking the French-Banditti* (plate 8) of 15 August 1808[12] in which he represents the Spanish not as the embodiment of liberty, but as representatives of the *ancien régime* alliance of monarchy and papacy. Gillray depicts the Spanish force as consisting of nuns, monks and noblemen fighting under a banner which proclaims 'Vive le Roi FERDINAND VII'.

Crump's and Gillray's representations of the Spanish cause might suggest a potential conflict of allegiances for Wordsworth. In 1804, he had directed his invective at the twin tyrannies of papacy and monarchy in his attack on Napoleon's coronation, representing it in *The Prelude* as 'a Pope / . . . summoned in to crown an Emperor' (x, 932–3). As the editors of the Norton *Prelude* comment, stressing the two-pronged nature of Wordsworth's criticism in these lines, to Wordsworth's 'indignation the French people had not only returned to monarchy . . . but had called upon the church to ratify their backsliding'.[13] Now, with the Spanish rising, the tyrant was at last resisted, but he was resisted by forces who fought under the same detested banners of monarchy and papacy. Such a potential conflict immediately recalls Wordsworth's complex and ambivalent response to the commencement of the war between France and England in 1793, as explored in *The Prelude*. In Book x of this poem, written only four years before the Convention was signed, Wordsworth had continued to wrestle with the meaning of the events of 1793 and after, describing 'the ravage of this most unnatural strife / In my own heart' (lines 250–1) and the 'conflict of sensations without a name' that had resulted (line 265).

In *The Convention of Cintra*, however, Wordsworth retreats from any comparable struggle with the meaning of history; he steadfastly ignores any other possible interpretation of the events in the Peninsula. R. J. White has criticized the tract on this basis, observing that 'Wordsworth could not bring himself to apply his principle of nationality to the French people . . . The idea that the French might have beaten, and for long continue to beat, their enemies by reason of a burning faith in a superior social system brought to birth under the banner of Liberty, Equality and Fraternity, seems to have eluded him'.[14] White's use of 'eluded' is probably unfair to Wordsworth, as Manning has suggested.[15] The tract must be seen, at least in part, as a piece of propaganda which skilfully negotiates the problems of boosting British morale while indicting the British generals. But the pressure of the war had taken its toll on Wordsworth. The tract exhibits a fascinating combination of persuasion and self-persuasion as Wordsworth exhorts his readership to ascribe a clear cause and a noble purpose to the war. It is possible that by 1808 he had, to adapt *The Prelude* (X, 900), yielded up historical questions in despair, and needed a simplified and coherent understanding of the war against France. Fifteen exhausting years of self-examination and enquiry into the historical and political meaning of the war, conducted in a national culture that was increasingly bellicose and chauvinistic, had had their apogee in Books IX and X of *The Prelude*, books which are characterized by their elisions, conflations, repressions, lacunae, dislocations of chronology and obscurity and which reveal the effort involved in subduing historical as well as biographical material to poetic design.[16] By 1808 Wordsworth was 'wearied out with contrarieties' (X, 900), desperate to find a cause with which he could ally himself against Napoleon, and this cause offered itself in the form of the people of the Peninsula. As a result he retreated from the kind of historical engagement he describes in *The Prelude*; a work in which he had focused on the problematic and unresolvable conflict of his sensations and loyalties. By contrast, in *The Convention of Cintra* he maps a very clear path of his reactions to the historical development, clarifies his own sympathies and loyalties and makes high-minded sense of the war to answer his own doubts about it as well as those of his readers. The Spanish cause was by no means as perfect a political cause as Wordsworth makes it appear in *The Convention of Cintra*, but it served his own purposes perfectly.

Wordsworth's simplification of his own response to the war in the tract is illustrated once again by his attempt to retrospectively reshape and clarify an earlier obscure period and in the process to establish his own political credentials and authority as a writer. In the long third paragraph of the tract, Wordsworth locates the crucial period of the shift in both his own sympathies and those of the 'body of the people' from France to Britain rather vaguely between 1798 and 1802 – years which he had elided in Book X of *The Prelude* and treated with complexity and subtlety in Book VI. He writes:

> This just and necessary war, as we have been accustomed to hear it styled from the beginning of the contest in the year 1793, had some time before the Treaty of Amiens, viz. after the subjugation of Switzerland, and not till then, begun to be regarded by the body of the people, as indeed just and necessary. (*CoC* 226)

The characteristic mixture of confidence and chronological vagueness here suggests a ruthless omission of any ambivalence that may have been felt either by Wordsworth or the 'body of the people' at the time. As we have seen, it was during these years that Wordsworth's close friends, Southey and Coleridge, had enthused about Napoleon's expedition to Egypt in 1798–9, had reconciled themselves to his usurpation in 1800, and had remained ambivalent and equivocal about him until the disillusioning events of 1802 – events that came after the signing of the Treaty of Amiens. As late as 12 May 1802, Southey had written to his brother that war seemed inevitable, 'and yet God knows what it is all about'.[17] Indeed, in October 1801, Coleridge reported that Wordsworth, like himself, felt peace with France was 'necessary' (*CL* I, 418). But Wordsworth evades the now dangerous complexity of this period and refuses to engage with Napoleon's early promise, simplifying his complex reaction to this earlier period in the light of more recent developments.

Wordsworth goes on to argue that those who 'had most eagerly opposed the war in its commencement and who regret that this nation had ever borne a part in it' (*CoC* 226) – a group in which he clearly includes himself – were consistent in their support of the war with France at this later stage. This was because, he continues, 'they only combated the same enemy opposed to them under a different shape; and that enemy was the spirit of selfish tyranny and lawless ambition' (*CoC* 226). Rather than examining the events of the years 1798 to 1802 in detail, Wordsworth retreats behind abstractions, branding the French as the new example of 'selfish tyranny and lawless ambition' (*CoC* 226). He continues to use this tactic throughout the paragraph, asserting that this 'spirit' 'became undeniably embodied in the French government' (*CoC* 226) but without arguing in detail how, or why or when. Fifty lines into the paragraph, Wordsworth is able to state that 'in opposition to French tyranny growing daily more insatiable and implacable, [the people of England] ranged themselves zealously under their Government' (*CoC* 227). By the end of this vital paragraph, Wordsworth has succeeded not only in representing France and Napoleon as an embodiment of 'tyranny' but in vindicating his own political history and in justifying his opposition to the nation he had initially sided with in the war.

Wordsworth exploits these political oppositions throughout the tract, representing the war as the modern enactment of an archetypal plot – 'the present effort of liberty against oppression' (*CoC* 237) – and investing it with an epic and heroic grandeur (*CoC* 228–30). In representing the Peninsular War as a battle of 'liberty' against invading 'tyranny', Wordsworth redeploys the terms of his earlier sonnet sequence, and particularly 'Thought of a Briton on the Subjugation of Switzerland' of 1806. But in describing the reaction to the Spanish rising he cites St Paul's revelatory moment from the First Epistle to the Corinthians (15: 51–4) – 'this corruptible put on incorruption, and this mortal put on immortality' – translating the war against Napoleon into a mythic apocalypse. In *The Convention of Cintra* Wordsworth does not internalize apocalypse, as Abrams argues he does in *The Prelude*, but projects it on to the public sphere, as during the millenial phase of responses to the French Revolution. Wordsworth represents the war as a divinely ordered and teleologically structured battle between contraries; a struggle of good against evil, virtue against vice, darkness against the 'noblest services of light' (*CoC* 301). He no longer figures Napoleon in the human terms of the sonnets as 'young Buonaparte' ('*Calais*, August 15, 1802' line 2), or as the political aggressor in Spain, but as the incarnation of moral evil, the 'evil-doer' (*CoC* 247), who commits 'the worst deeds of darkness' (*CoC* 301) and who 'aims at the extinction of . . . every thing which gives life its value – of virtue, of reason, of repose in God, or in truth' (*CoC* 241). By representing Napoleon and the war in this way Wordsworth is able to fall back on the Christian assumption that 'good . . . is stronger than evil' (*CoC* 334).

Within this polarized vision of the war, in which Napoleon operates in binary opposition to all that is valuable, Wordsworth represents him particularly in terms of Milton's Satan. *The Convention of Cintra* is a curiously literary work, both in style and in the numerous quotations and allusions Wordsworth employs. Passages from Virgil, Dante, Sidney, Petrarch and Plutarch, as well as the biblical books of Paul, Acts, Matthew and Daniel[18] are deployed throughout the text; 'disposed as it were in a tesselated pavement' (*CoC* 230), to use Wordsworth's image. Like Wordsworth's repeated references to the heroes of the English Civil War (*CoC* 288, 336), these quotations place the Peninsular War firmly in the tradition of an archetypal struggle for liberty, and place the tract itself in a tradition of libertarian writing. Wordsworth uses 'the records of past ages' as 'sanction and authority' for both his own argument and the war as a whole (*CoC* 304, 228).

The most important of these libertarian models for Wordsworth in the tract is Milton whom he saw as a republican writer and political inspirer of England. We know from Wordsworth's letters that he was seeking Milton's prose works in July 1808 (*MY* I, 257) and the tract reveals their obvious stylistic influence.[19] Southey, for example, imputed 'Wordsworth's want of perspicuity' in the tract to 'two causes, – his admiration of Milton's prose, and his habit of dictating instead of writing' (*SL* III, 246). Yet Milton's real importance for Wordsworth lay in his achievement as a poet, and particularly as the writer of *Paradise Lost*, the inspirational national epic for all the Romantic poets. In 1803–4 Wordsworth had adopted the sonnet form of Milton, as well as his tones and ethos, to unite the English at a time of national crisis. From 1808 to 1809 he turned again to the model and authority of Milton for the same purpose, but he did so now on an epic scale. The events of the Peninsular War offered Wordsworth a modern equivalent to 'some old / Romantic tale by Milton left unsung' which he had considered as a subject fit for his epic ambition in the opening book of *The Prelude* (I, 179–80). Moreover, while Milton provides Wordsworth with a vital source of strength in a time of crisis, the crisis also enables Wordsworth to claim for himself the role of Milton, achieving an ambition identified by Hazlitt, who wrote of Wordsworth that 'Milton is his great idol, and he sometimes dares to compare himself with him' (*HCW* XI, 92).

Throughout the tract, as in the well-known sonnet 'London, 1802', Wordsworth associates Milton with the glorious republican past of England during the Commonwealth. His writing embodies for Wordsworth the values that he believes should be symbolized by England as the home of liberty (*CoC* 280). It is this glorious past and inheritance that has been shamed by the generals who ratified the Convention. In a particularly striking passage, as Wordsworth laments their betrayal of this heritage, he himself inherits the voice and role of Milton:

> O sorrow! O misery for England, the land of liberty and courage and peace; the land trustworthy and long approved; the home of lofty example and benign precept; the central orb to which, as to a fountain, the nations of the earth 'ought to repair, and in their golden urn draw light;' – O sorrow and shame for our country; for the grass which grows upon her fields and the dust which is in her graves;– for her good men who now look upon her days;– and her long train of deliverers and defenders, her Alfreds, her Sidneys, and her Miltons; whose voice yet speaketh for our own reproach; and whose actions survive in memory to confound us, or to redeem! (*CoC* 288)

Just as the 'nations of the earth' repair to England as the land of liberty, so Wordsworth repairs to the language as well as the 'lofty example and benign precept' of Milton, quoting *Paradise Lost* VII, 365.[20] The parallel is highlighted by Wordsworth's imaging of England as 'the central orb' which echoes the lines in *The Excursion* in which he autobiographically describes the early reading of the Wanderer:

Among the hills
He gazed upon that mighty orb of song,
The divine Milton. (I, 248–50)

While appropriating the authority of Milton, Wordsworth claims for himself a position as the latest in the 'line of deliverers and defenders' whom he had also so often evoked in the sonnets of 1802–3. Milton was not living at this hour, but Wordsworth was and could assume his voice to speak a reproach to his own age. Indeed, in the tract we can see Wordsworth assuming the Miltonic role that he had described in a sonnet of around 1806:

Amid the dark control of lawless sway
Ambition's rivalry, fanatick hate,
And various ills that shook the unsettled State,
The dauntless Bard pursued his studious way,
Not more his lofty genius to display
Than raise and dignify our mortal state,
And sing the blessings which the Just await . . .[21]

By assuming the Bardic role and prophetic voice of Milton in the tract, Wordsworth is able to bear what he describes in a somewhat Bloomean phrase as 'the burthen of the past' (*CoC* 281) – an inheritance both literary and political – which would otherwise have been 'insupportable'. By appropriating and internalizing Milton, Wordsworth transforms the memory of the past into something redemptive rather than confounding.

Wordsworth's use of the Miltonic voice, and his recourse to Milton's 'mighty orb of song', are at their most powerful and suggestive in his representation of Napoleon, who perhaps inevitably is associated throughout *The Convention of Cintra* with Milton's Satan.[22] Wordsworth draws from the Miltonic fountain a nexus of quotations with which he establishes a Satanic iconography for Napoleon, forcefully characterizing him as a personification of evil whose ultimate defeat by the forces of good is reassuringly predetermined. When Wordsworth first names Napoleon in the tract, after some 480 lines, he immediately establishes this analogy, writing that 'courage and enthusiasm have equally characterized the best and worst beings, a Satan equally with an ABDIEL – a BONAPARTE equally with a LEONIDAS' (*CoC* 236). Until this point in the text, Wordsworth's sources for analogy have been historical. The allusion to Leonidas, for example, recalls and develops the comparison of the Spanish cause with 'the opposition of the Greek Republic to the Persian Invader at Thermopylae and Marathon' (*CoC* 229). Yet with the introduction of 'BONAPARTE' into the text, Wordsworth dramatically shifts registers, introducing him not as a historical figure, but as a mythical character endowed with considerable biblical and literary status and meaning.

Wordsworth explains his recourse to 'writers of fiction' rather than 'historians' in his representations of Napoleon three paragraphs later. Having described Napoleon's 'bloody mindedness', his 'scoffs and insults' and his 'heinous contempt of the most awful truths', he writes that 'Merciless ferocity is an evil familiar to our thoughts; but these combinations of malevolence historians have not yet been called upon to record; and writers of fiction, if they have ever ventured to create passions resembling them, have confined, out of reverence for the acknowledged constitution of human nature, those passions to reprobate Spirits' (*CoC* 241). While Wordsworth represents the Spanish and British armies as heroic in historical terms, then, he argues that for analogy with Napoleon he must go beyond the records of historians to the 'fictions' describing the 'reprobate Spirits'; the definitive version of which is, of course, *Paradise Lost*. In making this point, Wordsworth not only dehumanizes and dehistoricizes Napoleon, he demonizes and Satanizes him. The analogy with Satan gives a powerful literary form to the representation of Napoleon that reinforces Wordsworth's conceptual polarization of the war as a Christian crusade myth. Yet Wordsworth's recourse to the Satanic analogy demonstrates the rather paradoxical strength of Napoleon's hold over Wordsworth's imagination and the 'imaginations of men'. Such was Napoleon's status and power that Wordsworth was forced to adopt the ultimate demonizing tactic, yet in so doing he consistently represents him in terms of one of the dominant and most compelling mythic types of Christian Europe and the British literary tradition.

Having explicitly established the analogy between Napoleon and Satan, Wordsworth is able to draw on it throughout the tract, as, for example, when he describes Napoleon as the 'adversary of all good' who performs 'the worst deeds of darkness' (*CoC* 301). At other points in the tract Wordsworth alludes to specific passages in *Paradise Lost* and invokes the full force of their context.[23] He compares Napoleon with Milton's Satan as commanders of their respective armies:

> I have yet to speak of the influence of such concessions upon the French ruler and his army. With what Satanic pride must he have contemplated the devotion of his servants and adherents to their law, the steadiness and zeal of their perverse loyalty, and the faithfulness with which they stand by him and each other!

How must his heart have distended with false glory, while he contrasted the qualities of his subjects with the insensibility and slackness of his British enemies! (*CoC* 272)

Wordsworth's use of the adjective 'Satanic' reintroduces the analogy and primes the reader for the direct quotation from Book I of *Paradise Lost* – 'And now his heart / Distends with pride, and hardening in his strength / Glories' (I, 571–3). Wordsworth rewrites the quotation to drive home his point. Whereas Milton's presentation of Satan in Book I is notoriously ambivalent, awaiting his degradation later in the poem, Wordsworth refuses this ambivalence in his representation of the Satanic Napoleon. Napoleon's 'glory' – a key word in *The Convention of Cintra* as elsewhere in Wordsworth's work – is defined as 'false'. Wordsworth makes explicit what he believes is implicit in Milton's text, and in so doing not only develops the Napoleon-Satan analogy but provides his own mini-critique of the character of Satan. It is indicative of the change of the nature of Wordsworth's engagement with Napoleon that he is now simply dismissive of Napoleon's claims to 'glory'; a term which he treated in a much more complex way in his poetry of 1802–4.

In Wordsworth's most detailed and important analysis of Napoleon, he again introduces the analogy through his use of one of Milton's terms for Satan – 'Chief' (*Paradise Lost* I, 128, 566; II, 527) – and highlights it by describing Napoleon as the 'Enemy of mankind' (*Paradise Lost* IX, 494). In this passage Wordsworth develops his argument that Napoleon's character is one of the two inherent features of the French domination of Europe and claims for its permanence. He writes of Napoleon:

For the second – namely the personal character of the Chief; I shall at present content myself with noting (to prevent misconception) that this basis is not laid in any superiority of talent in him, but in his utter rejection of the restraints of morality – in wickedness which acknowledges no limit but the extent of its own power. Let anyone reflect a moment; and he will feel that a new world of forces is opened to a Being who has made this desperate leap. It is a tremendous principle to be adopted, and steadily adhered to, by a man in the station which Buonaparte occupies; and he has taken the full benefit of it. (*CoC* 312)

Wordsworth had developed these ideas on Napoleon's 'utter rejection of the restraints of morality' in conjunction with Coleridge.[24] In a letter to George Beaumont of 14 December 1808, Coleridge anticipates both the language and ideas of this passage (*CL* III, 731) and in both the sixth issue of *The Friend* and the seventh of the 'Letters on the Spaniards' he reiterates this conception of Napoleon's power and, by quoting Satan's notorious avowal 'evil be thou my good' from Book IV of *Paradise Lost* (IV, 110), makes explicit the Satanic model that underpins Wordsworth's 'principle' (*EoT* II, 83).

Both Coleridge and Wordsworth paradoxically use the Satanic analogy to stress Napoleon's ordinariness: he has a mind 'of an ordinary constitution', he is without any 'superiority of talents', and his dominion has not been achieved as a result of any 'endowments of intellect which are rarely bestowed, or . . . [an] uncommon accumulation of knowledge'. The analogy enables them to explain away Napoleon's position of power without giving him any of the credit for it, and so to undermine his hold over the European imagination of the time. As Wordsworth goes on to argue, he has achieved his 'station' and gained dominion through 'circumstances over which he has no influence' (*CoC* 313), and has only been able to maintain them 'by the utter rejection of the restraints of morality – in wickedness which acknowledges no limit but the extent of its own power'. In this way Wordsworth and Coleridge are able to resist and debunk the heroic myth of Napoleon as an 'extraordinary man' or a 'genius' that was being advanced at this time by Whitbread and Sir George Ponsonby in the House of Commons.

Wordsworth's analogizing of Napoleon and Satan does more than provide him with a pattern of literary allusions; it implies a notion of plot. Just as Wordsworth's polarization of the war suggests the inevitable apocalyptic outcome in which good will triumph over evil, so the analogy with Satan brings with it a powerful inherent prophecy of Napoleon's ultimate defeat in his war against the 'Almighty' – a term used by both Milton and Wordsworth. Wordsworth's combination of practical political analysis and mythic transformation of Napoleon through Miltonic allusion is best seen in the closing pages of the tract. While Wordsworth continues to exhort Christian virtue as necessary to oppose the evil basis of Napoleon's power, he also recalls his earlier argument that because the basis of Napoleon's power is evil, it is necessarily 'weak, perilous and self-destructive'. This is a further cause for optimism:

> I have announced the feelings of those who hope; yet one word more to those who despond. And first; *he* stands upon a hideous precipice (and it will be the same with all who may succeed to him and his iron sceptre) – he who has outlawed himself from society by proclaiming, with word and act, that he acknowledges no mastery but power. This truth must be evident to all who had breath – from the dawn of childhood, till the last gleam of twilight is lost in the darkness of dotage. (*CoC* 341)

Wordsworth supports this argument with pragmatic considerations and an analysis of the specific political circumstances of Napoleon's rule. Because Napoleon is an outlaw he is vulnerable to any opposition. There is nothing '*inherent* or *permanent*' in Napoleon's power (*CoC* 313). He is fighting a war that he cannot win morally or physically. His enemies are inspired by their fight for good, his own generals are likely to desert to the 'righteous cause'. His multi-national army will crumble and his troops desert. The myth of his invincibility has been shattered and 'two signal overthrows in pitched battle would . . . go far to destroy' 'his power' (*CoC* 313). Wordsworth demands that Britain 'redeem' herself by taking a more active role in the war (*CoC* 314). Furthermore, Napoleon's power is weakened by the demands for freedom from French imperialism in Germany, Switzerland, Florence, Venice, Genoa, Rome, Poland, Hungary and, of course, Spain, which Wordsworth describes in an eloquent passage comparable to Paine's vision of impending revolution in the *Rights of Man* (*CoC* 341). It is the force of liberty that will deliver Europe from French dominion; as Wordsworth argues, 'Upon liberty, and upon liberty alone, can there be permanent dependence' (*CoC* 341). This, of course, provides the subject-matter of Part II of the *Sonnets dedicated to National Independence and Liberty*.[25]

Wordsworth, then, argues in detail to explain why he believes Napoleon's power is 'weak, perilous and self-destructive'. But the image which he chooses to illustrate Napoleon's perilous position – 'he stands upon a hideous precipice' – reveals the subtle way in which Wordsworth uses Milton to mythologize Napoleon. Obviously, the image suggests the precariousness of Napoleon's position and his imminent fall. Yet the real force of the phrase derives from its nexus of allusions to important passages of *Paradise Lost*. Wordsworth roots the analogy of Napoleon and Satan in a literary and mythic narrative which acts as a prophecy of his inevitable downfall. He draws the image of the precipice from Satan's account of the defeat and fall of his troops in Book I:

> . . . the sulphorous hail
> Shot after us in storm, o'erblown hath laid
> The fiery surge, that from the precipice
> Of heaven received us falling . . . (I, 171–4)

Wordsworth's annotations to Richard Payne Knight's *An Analytical Inquiry into the Principles of Taste* (1806) which he made between March and April 1808 – only eight months before he commenced work on the tract – help to establish the Miltonic resonances of the rest of the phrase.

Wordsworth identified as a familiar and favourite passage in *Paradise Lost* that which describes Satan's fall. He wrote that '*Him* the Almighty hurled headlong &c. sees one of the most wonderful sentences ever formed by the mind of man'.[26] This 'wonderful sentence' in full reads:

Him the almighty power
Hurled headlong flaming from the ethereal sky
With hideous ruin and combustion down
To bottomless perdition, there to dwell
In adamantine flames and penal fire,
Who durst defy the omnipotent to arms. (I, 44–9)

It seems likely that Wordsworth has drawn the adjective 'hideous' from this 'wonderful sentence' when in *The Convention* he describes the 'precipice' Napoleon stands on. In doing so he conflates two of the main descriptions of Satan's fall which, when applied to Napoleon, are rich in resonance and implication.[27]

Wordsworth also commented upon Knight's analysis of the lines from *Paradise Lost* which begin:

He above the rest,
In shape and gesture proudly eminent,
Stood like a tower . . . (I, 589–91)[28]

This passage was particularly well known because Burke had chosen it as an instance of the sublime in his *Philosophical Enquiry*. When Wordsworth writes 'He stands upon a hideous precipice' there may be an implicit allusion to Satan – 'He . . . stood'. Indeed, in *Paradise Lost* this passage appears only twenty lines after that which Wordsworth has already quoted directly in describing Napoleon's 'Satanic Pride' and the way 'his heart [must] have distended with false glory'. The context of the passage in *Paradise Lost* is Satan's review of his troops, the moment at which his power seems greatest, and is certainly at its most impressive:

. . . and now
Advanced in view, they stand, a horrid front
Of dreadful length and dazzling arms, in guise
Of warriors old with ordered spear and shield,
Awaiting what command their mighty chief
Had to impose: he through the armed files
Darts his experienced eye, and soon traverse
The whole battalion views, their order due,
Their visages and stature as of gods,
Their number last he sums. And now his heart
Distends with pride, and hardening with strength

Glories: for never since created man,
Met such embodied force . . . (I, 562–74)

Wordsworth's allusion to Satan standing like a tower summons the broader analogy with Napoleon that had already been established by his direct quotation of these lines. It implies that Napoleon's position in 1809 is analogous to Satan in Book I, feeling at the height of his powers and revelling in the might of his force. Yet the brilliance of Wordsworth's use of this analogy lies in his exploitation of the reader's knowledge that Satan at this moment is already defeated, flung down from the precipice. In his use of the precipice image, Satan echoes Michael's warning to him in Book VI, where the verb 'precipitate', derived from the same Latin root 'praeceps', is used:

Hence then, and evil go with thee along
Thy offspring, to the place of evil, hell,
Thou and thy wicked crew; there mingle broils,
Ere this avenging sword begin thy doom,
Or some more sudden vengeance winged from God
Precipitate thee with augmented pain. (VI, 275–80)

In appropriating the image of the precipice in the tract, Wordsworth assumes the role of the Archangel Michael, prophesying that Napoleon, like Satan, will at any moment be precipitated by sudden vengeance with augmented pain.

If such a reading of the line from the tract seems forced, it is supported by Wordsworth's use of precisely this synthetic technique in his sonnet 'Look now on that Adventurer' which represents the apotheosis and epitome of his appropriation of Milton's Satan for the contemporary figure of Napoleon. Wordsworth probably wrote this sonnet around 30 March 1809, at about the same time he was putting the finishing touches to the tract.[29] Without specific dates for either the poem or the prose passage it is impossible to come to a conclusion about the relationship between the two. The sonnet may have been the initial form in which Wordsworth experimented with the analogy to Satan and the method of allusion to *Paradise Lost*, which he then condensed and employed in the tract, or it may be a more detailed and developed examination of the analogy of the characters and careers of Napoleon and Satan. Whichever, the sonnet confirms the value of *Paradise Lost* as a narrative source and a linguistic fountain from which Wordsworth could draw in his representation of Napoleon. As the poem is little known, I shall quote it in full:

Look now on that Adventurer who hath paid
His vows to fortune; who, in cruel slight
Of virtuous hope, of liberty, and right,
Hath followed wheresoe'er a way was made
By the blind Goddess; – ruthless, undismayed;
And so hath gained at length a prosperous Height,
Round which the Elements of worldly might
Beneath his haughty feet, like clouds, are laid.
O joyless power that stands by lawless force!
Curses are his dire portion, scorn, and hate,
Internal darkness and unquiet breath;
And, if old judgements keep their sacred course,
Him from that Height shall Heaven precipitate
By violent and ignominious death.[30]

In its opening line the poem presents itself as an updating of the 1803 sonnet 'When looking on the present face of things', and like that poem it is concerned with 'one man . . . raised up', Napoleon Bonaparte. However, whereas in 1803 Wordsworth's focus had moved from 'one Man' (line 2) to his own 'thoughts sublime' (line 13), it now remains resolutely fixed upon the 'Adventurer'. In the context of the tract Wordsworth's representation of Napoleon's career is a familiar one. His power is not derived from any special talents but from the following of fortune and the refusal to let anything – 'virtuous hope', 'liberty' or 'right' – stop his pursuit and maintainance of it. Wordsworth again exploits one of the great premises of the Christian tradition that if 'old judgements keep their sacred course' Napoleon will be thrown down by heaven.

What is most striking about the sonnet, however, is its Miltonic tone, diction, syntax and grammar. It is as if Wordsworth has compiled the final seven lines out of *Paradise Lost.* Not only is the sonnet's diction unmistakably Miltonic, but Wordsworth represents Napoleon in the terms that Milton had chosen for Satan. Satan's walk is described as 'haughty': he 'went haughty on' (IV, 858), 'Satan with vast and haughty strides advanced' (VI, 109). Napoleon, likewise, stands on 'haughty feet'. The qualities which are Napoleon's 'dire portion' in the sonnet are similarly derived from Satan. Satan both feels himself 'cursed' by God in his opening speech in Book IV (line 71) and is cursed by God in Book X (line 174). He feels 'scorn', breathes 'scorn', is 'filled with scorn' and three times speaks in scorn, but his scorn is repeatedly met with scorn (I, 619; II, 697; IV, 827, 834, 902; V, 904; IV, 834; V, 906). Perhaps the one characteristic and word which defines Satan in *Paradise Lost* is 'hate'. He feels 'steadfast hate' and swears 'immortal hate' (I, 57, 107). When he first sees Adam and Eve he stands 'Stupidly good, of enmity disarmed' but soon 'Fierce hate he recollects' (IX, 465–71) and it is 'hate' which he then announces as his motivation (IX, 473–6). Napoleon's 'portion' then is a state of mind which is like that of Satan's after his fall, an inner torment that is symbolized by Hell:

> Such place Eternal Justice had prepared
> For those rebellious, here their prison ordained,
> In utter darkness, and their *portion* set
> As far removed from God and light of heaven
> As from the centre thrice to the utmost pole. (I, 70; my italics)

Wordsworth's use of the adjective 'dire' again recalls the fall of the rebel angels – a 'dire event', a 'dire calamity' and a 'dire change' (I, 134, 189, 624, 625).

Even while in power, at the 'prosperous Height', Napoleon's 'dire portion' is to be subject, like Satan after his fall, to an inner hell; to feel curses, scorn and hate, internal darkness and unquiet breath. Napoleon is his own hell. Napoleon's power is one that 'stands' by lawless force, again perhaps suggesting the moment when Satan stood, feeling pride at the strength of his army. Yet, as the parallel with Satan emphasizes, Napoleon's height is one from which he must fall. In Book I of *Paradise Lost* height is associated not with achievement, but with distance fallen: 'From what height fallen' (I, 92) and 'fallen such a pernicious height' (I, 282). In his sonnet, Wordsworth again utilizes the Miltonic precipice / precipitate image and verb that he had used in the tract:

> Him from that Height shall Heaven precipitate
> By violent and ignominious death.

What is more, in this sonnet he places it within a sentence that is modelled on Milton's 'most wonderful sentence'. In his comment on this sentence in his annotations to Knight, Wordsworth continues 'the instances of imagined and impassioned inversion in Milton are innumerable.[31] In his chosen example the imaginative and impassioned inversion is an object – subject – verb one – '*Him* the Almighty Power / Hurled headlong'. It is exactly this form of inversion that Wordsworth himself adopts for hurling Napoleon down. He starts with a similar stress on the third-person pronoun, 'Him' and uses the object – subject – verb inversion form: 'Him . . . shall Heaven precipitate'. Like Milton, Wordsworth uses a phrasal verb; he models 'from that height' on 'from the ethereal sky'. In Milton's 'with hideous ruin and combustion' we can also perhaps find a model for Wordsworth's 'violent and ignominious death'. 'Ignominious' is yet another word used by Milton to describe the fallen angels after their defeat (VI, 395, VI, 207).

In this sonnet, then, Wordsworth conflates the same two passages of *Paradise Lost* describing the fall of Satan that he had used in the tract as a means of prophesying the downfall of Napoleon. His reversion to the sonnet form in his representation of Napoleon as Milton's Satan serves to emphasize the poetic inspiration behind his writing in *The Convention of Cintra*. Wordsworth had, of course, first used the form for 'I grieved for Buonaparte' after Dorothy had read Milton's sonnets to him, and now in 1809 he returned to it to give full poetic expression to the Miltonic urge that is so evident in the tract. In both the sonnet 'Look now on that Adventurer' and *The Convention of Cintra*, 'our own Milton' provided Wordsworth with a prophetic role and an inspirational voice. By adopting Milton as his prime model and authority, and by repairing to his 'mighty orb of song' as to a fountain from which he can draw his language, Wordsworth invests his optimistic mythologizing of the war with a specifically literary dimension as well as a particularly English one. Wordsworth transforms Milton into his most powerful weapon in his epic prose offensive that seeks to drive Napoleon from his 'strong-holds in the imaginations' and so hasten his fall from the 'hideous precipice'.

AN 'EASTERN *ALTER EGO*':[32] *THE CURSE OF KEHAMA*

For all its Miltonic intonations and grandeur, however, the *Convention of Cintra* failed to make the public impact Wordsworth had hoped for. Dorothy noted in August 1809 that 'nobody buys' the pamphlet (*MY* I, 370) and 178 remaining copies were sold for waste paper in 1811.[33] If Wordsworth found a 'fit audience' for his Miltonic epic, it was certainly 'few'.[34] Yet he continued to conduct his anti-Napoleonic campaign in the sonnet form, writing twenty-nine sonnets between late 1808 and March 1811.[35] Coleridge, who had assisted Wordsworth in the writing of his tract, and Southey, who had eagerly looked forward to its publication, both took up the pen against Napoleon, perhaps as a result of the failure of the tract which they had hoped would speak for all three of them. In the rest of this chapter I want to concentrate on the continuing anti-Napoleonic campaigns of these other two writers.

Wordsworth's and Coleridge's prophetic and propagandist use of Milton's Satan as a demonizing mythic type has much in common with another powerful literary incarnation of Napoleon of these years,

Southey's Oriental tyrant Kehama. Stuart Curran has drawn attention to the similarity of Satan and Kehama, writing that in *The Curse of Kehama* the 'heroic quest is inverted with something like the scrupulous logic Milton gives to Satan, but Kehama is truly a paper tiger. His evil is total, but it is not interesting.'[36] But Curran's curt dismissal of *The Curse of Kehama* misses the poem's historical meaning; had he identified the target of Southey's paper bullets, he might have found Southey's object in presenting a totally evil figure more interesting. Southey was involved with Coleridge and Wordsworth in the attempts to organize a public protest against the Convention and he had promised to write on it if Wordsworth failed to do so. In its final version *The Curse of Kehama*, which was published in 1810, is a work which emerges out of this context of writing on Spain. In it Southey dresses up his patriotic, pro-Spanish and anti-Napoleonic propaganda as an Oriental epic-romance.

The poem narrates the career of Kehama, an evil Hindu magician whom Marilyn Butler has described as 'an Eastern *alter ego* of Napoleon'.[37] Kehama has achieved dominion on earth through a series of vows and Southey explains the nature of these vows, in the 'Preface' to the poem:

> In the religion of the Hindoos, which of all false religions is the most monstrous in its fables, and the most fatal in its effects, there is one remarkable peculiarity. Prayers, penances, and sacrifices are supposed to possess an inherent and actual value, in no degree depending on the disposition or the motive of the person who performs them. They are drafts upon Heaven, for which the Gods cannot refuse payment. The worst men, bent upon the worst designs, have in this manner obtained power which has made them formidable to the Supreme Deities themselves, and rendered an *Avatar*, or Incarnation of Veshnoo the Preserver, necessary. This belief is the foundation of the following Poem.

Southey's use of this Hindu idea of 'Prayers, penances and sacrifices' here to explain the source of Kehama's power recalls Coleridge's and Wordsworth's appropriation of the Satanic avowal 'evil be thou my good' to explain Napoleon's power, and echoes Wordsworth's description of him in his sonnet as an 'Adventurer who hath paid / His vows to fortune'. Like them, he immediately marks his protagonist as 'evil' and denies him the credit for achieving his positions of power. Southey's term the 'worst men' also echoes Wordsworth's definition of Napoleon and Satan as 'the worst beings'. The poem traces Kehama's attempt to extend his evil empire to heaven and focuses on his persecution of an old man, Ladurlad, and his daughter, Kaiyal. Of course, just at the moment when Kehama appears to be about to triumph and realize his dream of universal dominion he is violently punished for his evil actions and overthrown.

Southey himself made explicit the comparison between Napoleon and Kehama in a letter of 1811, writing that 'if Canning would but compare Bonaparte to Kehama in the House of Commons, I might get half as much by my next poem' (*SL* III, 303). While Southey obviously seeks the publicity that such a notice would bring, his comment also reveals a fascinating desire on his part to have his poem read and interpreted allegorically in the light of contemporary events. It also suggests that there was a demand for exactly the type of poetry that could be read in this way, which would boost the sales of Southey's next poem. In my earlier chapter on Landor, I illustrated how Southey's response to *Gebir* and *The Phocaeans* revealed his alertness to potential political readings of a literary text. His comments on his own writing during the period while he was working on *The Curse of Kehama* stress that he similarly thought about his own writing as a means of intervening in contemporary affairs. In 1808, for example, he wrote of his translation of the *Chronicles of the Cid* that 'it is not a text for entering directly upon the Spanish affairs, though a fine one for *touching* upon them' (*SL* III, 186). His plans for another poem reveal the way in which he saw his own texts as a means of boosting British morale over the events in Spain. He wrote that he was 'planning something of great importance, a poem upon Pelayo, the first restorer of Spain: it has long been one of my chosen subjects; and those late events which have warmed every heart that has right British blood circulating through it, have revived and strengthened old resolutions' (*SL* III, 178).[38] Such comments could well be applied to *The Curse of Kehama.* In this poem Southey produced a text with which he and the reader could enter directly upon the present Spanish affairs and which would warm every heart that has right British blood circulating through it.

Moreover, in a fascinating letter of 1812, which has implications for all Southey's long poetry, he discusses his use of myth as a means of presenting Christian allegory:

> My next mythological poem, should I ever write another, would be founded upon the system of Zoroaster. I should represent the chief personages as persecuted by evil powers, and make every calamity they brought upon him the means of evolving some virtue which would otherwise never have been called into action. In the hope that the fables of false religion may be made subservient to the true, by exalting and strengthening Christian feelings. (*SL* III, 352)

This comment has a direct bearing on Southey's allegorical procedure in *The Curse of Kehama.* In this poem he adopts a 'fable' from the Hindu religion which, as he announces in the Preface to the poem, 'of all false religions is the most monstrous in its fables'. This 'false fable' he then applies to the Spanish situation and converts both into a narrative derived from his own Christian myth, with the hope of 'exalting and strengthening Christian feelings'.

Kenneth Curry, though denying that *The Curse of Kehama* can be read allegorically, sees certain parallels in the careers of Kehama and Napoleon, two ambitious, cruel and seemingly invincible tyrants. The poem's 'lesson', he argues, is an encouraging one because 'faith, fortitude and righteousness will triumph, and the poem makes clear that power in the universe will ultimately see that justice is done'.[39] Curry's reading of the poem clearly aligns it with Wordsworth's mythical plotting of the war in *The Convention of Cintra*, and shows how its narrative force rests upon the same reassuring Christian assumptions. Indeed, contrary to Curry's surprising claim that the poem will not bear an allegorical reading, the whole poem can be read as a political and religious allegory based on Southey's formulation of the Peninsular War into a mythical Christian narrative of history akin to that presented in *The Convention of Cintra*. In *The Curse of Kehama* Southey personifies the Christian virtues which he saw as resisting Napoleon in Spain and which he hoped would bring about his eventual defeat in Kaiyal and Ladurlad. For example, Ladurlad defies Kehama by falling back on his thinly disguised Christian faith:

> . . . for though all other things
> Were subject to the starry influencings,
> And bow'd submissive to thy tyranny,
> The virtuous heart and resolute mind are free.
> Thus in their wisdom did the Gods decree
> When they created man. Let come what will,
> This is our rock of strength; in every
> Sorrow, oppression, pain and agony,
> The spirit of the good is unsubdued,
> And, suffer as they may, they triumph still. (XVIII, 10, 129–38)[40]

The history of Southey's composition of *The Curse of Kehama* helps recover the poem's historical force. He began writing the poem in May 1801 but seems to have quickly left off its composition. It seems to have been in 1806 that he picked it up again, as he wrote in a letter of 17 June: 'I have been inserting occasional rhymes in Kehama, and in this way altered and amended about six hundred lines. When what is already written shall be got through in this manner, I shall think the poem in the way of completion: indeed, it will most likely supply my ways and means for next winter, instead of reviewing' (*SL* III, 44). Later in the same letter he described the process of his writing of *Kehama* as 'revising and re-revising over and over again' (*SL* III, 44). It is surely not coincidental that Southey started rewriting and revising *The Curse of Kehama* during the period when he was horrified to see Napoleon realizing a seemingly unchallengeable dominance in world affairs. In a letter of 1 January 1806 Southey had written that the 'extraordinary success of Bonaparte, or, rather, the wretched misconduct of Austria, has left the Continent completely under the control of France' (*SL* III, 11). Napoleon's victory at Austerlitz had fully justified Southey's fears that he would become 'the master of the Continent' (*SL* II, 357). In the early months of 1806, Southey may well have seen parallels between Napoleon and the eponymous fictional tyrant of his uncompleted poem of 1801, who is described in the final version of the poem as the 'King of the world', 'the Tyrant of the World', and the 'Master of Mankind' (I, 5, 77; XII, 1, 12; I, 5, 81). Certainly, Southey's description of Kehama's ascent to power seems to re-envision the triumphant progress of Napoleon during these years:

> He went on
> Conquering in irresistible career,
> Till his triumphant car had measured o'er
> The insufficient earth, and all the Kings
> Of men received his yoke; then had he won
> His will, to ride upon their necks elate
> And crown his conquests with the sacrifice
> That should, to men and gods, proclaim him Lord
> And Sovereign Master of the vassal world,
> Sole Rajah, the Omnipotent below. (VII, 11, 269–78)

Furthermore, in 1808, when Southey had again left off composition of the poem, mainly for financial reasons, he met Walter Savage Landor, whom he knew and respected principally as 'the author of Gebir' (*SL* III, 138). Landor's allegorical and pro-Napoleonic epic was, as we have seen, greatly admired by Southey when it was first published, though both writers had by now revised their judgements of Napoleon. Southey was keen to describe his own present literary projects to Landor, as he recounts in a letter:

> I told him of the series of mythological poems which I had planned, – mentioned some of the leading incidents on which they were to have been formed, and also told him for what reasons they were laid aside; – in plain English, that I could not afford to write them. Landor's reply was 'Go on with them, and I will pay for printing them . . .'. (*SL* III, 137–8)

Southey refused this offer of financial help from Landor, but took heart from his encouragement and returned to the writing of *Kehama*, sending completed sections of it to him (*SL* III, 196–7). Southey's report of the meeting is very generalized, but it would seem likely that *The Curse of Kehama* was one of the 'mythological poems' they discussed, particularly as it was this poem that Southey then returned to and completed.

As we have seen, Landor had undergone a complete reversal in his attitude to Napoleon in 1802, and he in fact went to Spain to fight against Napoleon later in 1808, much to Southey's delight (*SL* III, 162). It is possible that hearing Southey's description of *The Curse of Kehama* he grasped the anti-Napoleonic thrust of its narrative. Alternatively, Southey may have made this explicit in his description of the 'leading incidents' on which the poem was founded. By encouraging Southey's anti-Napoleonic offensive in *The Curse of Kehama* and by offering to fund the printing of the poem, Landor may have been making amends for his own earlier praise of Napoleon. *The Curse of Kehama* offered itself as a powerful antidote or corrective to *Gebir*'s panegyric of 'a mortal man above all mortal praise' (VI, 193). Indeed, in its narrative and its anti-imperialist message, *The Curse of Kehama* re-enacts the main plot of *Gebir*, but it does so with Napoleon in the role of villain and as the target of its critical invective.[41] Just as Gebir is killed with the poisoned cloak when he is about to marry Charoba (*Gebir* VII, 159–81), so Kehama is punished at the moment he had hoped would see the apotheosis of his power. This punishment is dramatized through his drinking from the Amreeta cup, the symbol of 'Retribution':

> The deed is done,
> The dreadful liquor works the will of Fate.
> Immortal he would be,
> Immortal he is made, but through his veins
> Torture at once and immortality,
> A stream of poison doth the Amreeta run,
> And while within the burning anguish flows,
> His outward body glows
> Like molten ore, beneath the avenging Eye,
> Doom'd thus to live and burn eternally. (XXIV, 18, 222–31)

Like Wordsworth and Coleridge, then, Southey transforms the war against Napoleon into a Christian mythical narrative of good against evil, based on the reassuring assumption that good will eventually triumph. Yet, whereas they deploy Milton's Satan as the mythical type through which they could represent Napoleon's role in this predetermined narrative, Southey uses the figure of the Oriental tyrant and dresses the narrative up as an Oriental epic-romance. Both incarnations effectively demonize and mythologize Napoleon, shifting the reader's conception of him away from historical actuality and representing him as an archetypal embodiment of evil. Thus while J. R. de J. Jackson's criticism of *The Curse of Kehama* that the 'characters . . . are too good, or bad, to be true'[42] may have validity as a literary judgement, it also serves to emphasize the essential propagandist strategy of the poem which confers a literary form on Southey's polarized vision of the war as 'a business of natural life and death, a war of virtue against vice, light against darkness, the good principle against the evil one' (*SL* III, 175).

'A SORT OF FABULOUS MONSTER':[43] COLERIDGE'S NAPOLEON

The paradoxes and dangers of the Lakers' representation of their own fight against Napoleon as a battle for and in the 'imaginations of men' is most fully explored by Coleridge. Coleridge had been aware of Napoleon's ability to capture the imagination since the Egyptian campaign. In 1800 he described him as an 'object of superstition and enthusiasm' (*EoT* I, 208) and in a notebook comment of late 1801 he had commented on Napoleon's potential iconic status: 'Courage – That courage which the Soldier derives from B – B being God – His General' (*CNB* I, 1082). Yet Coleridge had always been aware of the potential dangers of Napoleon's imaginative appeal, the 'brilliance' and 'splendour' of which 'dazzled and blinded' the observer, preventing any real judgement of his political qualities.[44] Unlike Washington, whom Coleridge described as possessing a 'solid greatness . . . without any obtrusive appeal to the imagination' (*EoT* I, 229), Napoleon's appeal to the imagination was so 'obtrusive' that he was able to use it as a 'disguise'. This imagery of 'disguise' is constantly employed by Coleridge in his writing on Napoleon and can be traced back to the essays of 1800 for the *Morning Post* in which he had described Napoleon's new French constitution as a 'rhetorical domino' (*EoT* I, 9) and a 'miserable masquerade domino, to throw around the nakedness of despotism' (*EoT* I, 52). Coleridge's description of Bonaparte dazzling and blinding the 'imaginations of men' with 'splendid robes and gaudy trappings' is directed particularly at Napoleon's assumption of imperial status. Elsewhere, however, he is more general in his stress on the 'palliative' – cloaking or disguising – effect of Napoleon's appeal to the imagination. In 1811 he succinctly encapsulated the source of both Napoleon's fascination and his danger when he wrote that he possessed 'those daring and dazzling qualities that too often make a tyrant pass for a hero' (*EoT* II, 150).

In his essays of 1800 for the *Morning Post* Coleridge had defined Napoleon's imaginative appeal as principally a consequence of his military success. In an article of 3 January, for example, he described Napoleon as 'the man, who has achieved by his exploits the splendour of a hero in romance' (*EoT* I, 71). The use of a literary sphere of reference here is interesting; in his later writing Coleridge will make a crucial distinction between 'poetic' and 'historic' figures in the acceptability of their imaginative appeal. In his writing on Napoleon during the Peninsular War, Coleridge redefined Napoleon's imaginative appeal as a result of his status as an object of 'Power', of which his military success is a tangible form. In a later lecture on Shakespeare of 1818, Coleridge wrote that Shakespeare 'had read Nature too heedfully not to know, that Courage, Intellect, and strength of Character were the most impressive Forms of Power; and that to Power in itself; without any reference to any moral end, an inevitable Admiration and Complacency appertains, whether it be displayed in the conquests of a Napoleon or a Tamerlaine, or in the foam and thunder of a Cataract' (*LoL* II, 328). Lecturing here in 1818, more than two years after Napoleon's fall, Coleridge was freer to comment on Napoleon's 'Power' 'without any reference to moral end' because the propagandist objective of his writing on Napoleon was no longer imperative. Yet before 1815 Coleridge had written with the precise aim of countering this separation of the admiration for Napoleon as an object of power from the moral imperative to condemn him as wicked. He had definitively stated this in the sixth of the 'Letters on the Spaniards', in a passage which immediately precedes his definition of Napoleon's main strength as being in the 'imaginations of men':

> The error, which of all others most besets the public mind, and which yet of all others is the most degrading in its nature, the most tremendous in its consequences, is an inward prostration of the soul before enormous POWER, and a readiness to palliate and forget all iniquities to which prosperity has wedded itself; as if man were only a puppet without free will, and without the conscience which is the offspring of their union, a puppet played off by some unknown power! as if success were the broad seal of the divine approbation, and tyranny itself the Almighty's inauguration of a Tyrant. (*EoT* II, 75)

Coleridge's whole object in his writing on Napoleon is to repudiate this 'error' and to urge his readers to use their 'conscience'. The rhetorical question which follows the 'imaginations of men' passage makes clear Coleridge's aim:

Is it to be borne by good men without an attempt on their part to stem or counteract the delusion, that the power or prosperity, which derive their very being from the excess of wickedness, should secure for that wickedness an immunity from our hatred and execration? (*EoT* II, 75)

Coleridge aims in his writing on Napoleon, then, to weaken his hold over the 'imaginations of men' and to promote 'hatred and execration' of him. His writing is self-confessedly bellicose and propagandist. He described it in 1811 to his editor Stuart as prompted by 'the necessity of ever re-fuelling the moral feelings of the People as to the monstrosity of the Giant-fiend, that menaces them' (*CL* III, 828). As this comment suggests, Coleridge's boosting of British morale and demonization of Napoleon was prompted by the need to combat an increasing spirit of public war-weariness. After the initial period of enthusiasm for the Spanish cause, public support for the war had flagged, particularly after Napoleon's victory at Wagram, his capture of Vienna and Britain's apparent failure to gain a significant victory in the Peninsula. Following the battle of Talavera in July 1809, Wellington had withdrawn from Spain into Portugal. In November the Spanish army of La Mancha had been destroyed at Thames and Ocana, ending all regular Spanish resistance to France. From mid-September 1809 Whig criticism of the war intensified, and as a result of the failure of the Walcheren expedition and consequent intrigues, Canning, Castlereagh and Portland resigned.[45] By December 1809, as Coleridge wrote in the second of the 'Letters on the Spaniards', there had been a 'depression of our hopes, and the alienation of our friendly feelings from the Spanish cause' (*EoT* II, 44). As Christie has pointed out, it was not until July 1812 when Wellesley beat Marmont in the first decisive Allied victory in open battle that British criticism of the war against France was stilled.[46]

Coleridge's overall method of 're-fuelling the moral feelings of the People as to the monstrosity of the Giant-fiend, that menaces them' is much the same as Wordsworth's. He too aligns the war against Napoleon with the same Christian libertarian crusade myth, transforming it into 'this holy war of man against the enemy of human nature' (*EoT* II, 178). Having mythologized the war in this way, Coleridge claims that it not only justifies, but demands, the mobilization of his full rhetorical powers:

is this not an unexampled, an extraordinary war, which cannot be adequately supported but by extraordinary means? Is it not a war in which we are all alike interested, not only as patriots . . . but likewise as Christians and even as men? Are not the lively convictions and strong moral feelings of the community at large, an essential and most important part and condition of those extraordinary means? And how can these convictions and feelings be impressed, but by proclaiming aloud and in the strongest language, though no language can be adequately strong, the baseness, the injustice, the perfidy, and the remorseless cruelty of the enemy, against whom we are to fight for everything that makes life worth living for. (*EoT* II, 193)

As this comment indicates, Coleridge's principal strategy in his fight to ensure the continued prosecution of the war is the remorseless dehumanization and demonization of Napoleon. As Coleridge vows, 'whilst life and language last . . . we shall always apply to this man and his crimes every epithet of deepest reproach and keenest execration' (*EoT* II, 199). He invokes the Bible as authority for his anti-Napoleonic crusade:

There is a book, Sir, which we have not yet learnt to treat with contempt, that abounds with examples of words and phrases that seem on fire with anger, and indignant reprobation, and these used by inspired wisdom itself to scare the vicious as with thunder, and to kindle the hearts of good men like the blast of a trumpet calling them to battle against the giants that war against Heaven. For assuredly against Heaven doth that man wage war, whose whole career is in defiance of all the principles which alone give meaning to our erect form, and entitle us to look towards Heaven as to our natural and destined country. (*EoT* II, 75–6)

Once again, biblical authority is exploited to transform the war against Napoleon into an enactment of the Apocalypse.

In his representations of Napoleon during the war, Coleridge strives to turn Napoleon into an object of fear and hatred. He stresses the 'menace' of the 'Giant-fiend' and repeatedly lists the 'long and black catalogue of his crimes' because 'with his crimes we confirm his infamy; with his infamy we perpetuate our resistance' (*EoT* II, 194, 195, 193[47]). The dual character of Coleridge's representation of Napoleon is uncannily captured by Victor Hugo in his depiction of the French Restoration's satirical representation of him in *Les Misérables.* Hugo writes that 'Buonaparte had become a sort of fabulous monster, and to make him comprehensible to the simple minds of the people he had been depicted in every kind of terrifying guise, from the awe-inspiring and grandiose to the ugly and grotesque, as a Tiberius and as a buffoon. In referring to Buonaparte one might gnash one's teeth or explode with laughter, provided always that the basis was hatred.'[48] Coleridge similarly makes a 'sort of fabulous monster' out of Napoleon. His incarnations of him are essentially twofold, and have some correspondence with the categories of the sublime and the grotesque which Paulson examines in Goya's giants looming over the Spanish countryside and Gillray's caricatures of 'little Boney'.[49]

In sublime mode, Coleridge represents Napoleon as an enormous monstrous figure; a 'Giant-fiend'[50] and a 'Horrible Monster',[51] whose epic feats of destruction are performed on an awe-inspiring and terrifying scale: 'He has dyed every country with blood, he has sacrificed millions to his ambition . . .' (*EoT* II, 198). Coleridge's writing in this vein is perhaps at its most powerful when Napoleon is not only dehumanized but is transformed into an abstract yet devastating force. In the following passage, for example, Coleridge builds from specific, albeit rather fantasized, historical events to a representation of Napoleon in terms of an Old Testament plague:

> The death of Buonaparte would be the greatest blessing, which by any event could at present befall mankind, since his life has been the most grievous curse to humanity in our time. Setting aside the assassinations, poisoning &c. he has procured, his whole history has been, and is even at this day, one dismal tale of blood, rapine and devastation. Without pretext for war, without the shew even of a quarrel, he has inundated whole nations with fire and sword, massacring the loyal to their king by thousands in the streets of the capital, because they were loyal; . . . Can we contemplate the widows and orphans he has made, the towns he has ruined, the nations he has rendered wretched, he still stretching further his arm of pestilence and death, chiefly anxious to thrust it into the bowels of our own country, without viewing with horror and indignation, those who would throw up any fence, under any circumstances, for the protection of the person or character of so great a monster? (*EoT* II, 200)

Paulson's understanding of Goya's giants in terms of the Burkean sublime can be applied to Coleridge's representation of Napoleon in these passages. Paulson argues that the 'giant is linked in size and sublimity to Burke's associations of it in his *Philosophical Enquiry* with "tyranny, cruelty, injustice, and everything horrid and abominable. We paint the giant ravaging the countryside, plundering the innocent traveller, and afterwards gorged with half living flesh".'[52] Coleridge draws on this eighteenth-century tradition of the sublime giant to present Napoleon in a truly 'terrifying guise', to use Hugo's term.

In the grotesque mode, Coleridge represents Napoleon reductively as a low-life figure who is often involved in a world of petty crime. Napoleon becomes an 'outlaw' (*EoT* II, 201), an 'adventurer' (*EoT* II, 368, 347), a 'footpad' (F II, 332), a 'base, unmanly and . . . cowardly ruffian' (*EoT* II, 194) and, perhaps most famously, an 'upstart Corsican' (*EoT* I, 399). This type of representation doesn't make Napoleon any less threatening ; the reader was, after all, more likely to have experience of encountering a footpad than a giant. Rather it aims to demystify Napoleon, stripping him of any charismatic grandeur or heroism. Coleridge was seeking to combat the vision of Napoleon as a 'Great Man' put forward by figures like Ponsonby, who claimed in 1810 that Napoleon was 'the greatest man that has ever appeared on the face of the earth'.[53] To resist this glorification of Napoleon, a prime example of what Coleridge saw as the palliative effect of his appeal to the imagination, Coleridge calls upon the well-established humanist tradition of attacks on 'greatness' exemplified in the eighteenth century by the various representations of the 'Great Man' Horace Walpole as an outlaw, a footpad and a ruffian.

Coleridge's most frequently used weapon in his war of words against the French Emperor is his insistent stress on Napoleon's 'wickedness'. Coleridge frequently returns to the Satanic model as a way of representing this as the basis of his power and as a source for a powerful demonizing idiom.[54] For example, he opens his article of December 1812 on 'Bonaparte and the Emperor Julian' with allusions to *Paradise Lost*:

> There is nothing new under the sun – even the fortunes of Buonaparte, the eccentricities of that comet, 'which, from its horrid hair, shakes pestilence and war,' and 'with the fear of change, perplexes Monarchs,' are not unexampled. [*Paradise Lost* II, 710–11, I, 588–9] (*EoT* II, 349)

The analogy Coleridge goes on to explore is that with the Emperor Julian, but in quoting from *Paradise Lost* he again implies the analogy with Satan. In another powerful passage Coleridge presents Napoleon as going beyond even the model of Satan, and so damns Napoleon even more than Milton damns Satan. Commenting on Napoleon's twenty-ninth Bulletin of the Grand Army on the retreat from Moscow, which was translated in London newspapers on 24 December 1812, Coleridge writes:

> Never, surely, was anything so horrible – so unnatural – as this. Our great Bard, even when his sublime imagination was struggling to embody consummate wickedness in the person of *Satan*, never in his bitterest conception, hit upon sentiments so diabolical as these. When the rebel champion of Pandemonium has experienced a defeat, even the stern genius of Milton was relaxed, and he represents the great author of human woe, relenting for the moment, and shedding such tears as Angels might, over the fruitless fidelity, the unavailing courage, and fallen fortunes, of his unhappy followers [*Paradise Lost* I, 620]. Satan's taunts are directed only against his Conqueror – it was reserved for the '*mild and merciful*' Napoleon, to exhibit an original trait of infernal ingratitude, such as poetry could never feign, nor the mind of Milton conceive! (*EoT* II, 357)

This passage succeeds in its propagandist use of Satan as a means of embodying Napoleon's 'consummate wickedness'. Yet it also suggests that Coleridge felt that the analogy between the two figures was limiting and reductive. The problem of the analogy was not that it reduced Napoleon to a personification of evil who was uninteresting in historical terms; this reduction was an essential part of Coleridge's determination to 'fight the same good fight', as the newspaper *The Journal* described his anti-Napoleonic campaign.[55] Rather, the problem was that the analogy threatened to restrict Coleridge's interpretation and appreciation of Milton's Satan, a figure who captured his imagination like that of so many other writers in the period. This passage indicates a relish of the 'sublime imagination' and 'stern genius' of Milton, 'our great Bard', and an interest in the figure of Satan as a 'poetic' conception that goes beyond the requirements of their invocation for propagandist purposes.

Yet, just as Napoleon had become Satanic in Wordsworth's and Coleridge's writing during the Peninsular War, so Satan had become Napoleonic. One could not be thought of without bringing to mind the other, as Hazlitt commented in his essay 'On Means and Ends' (*HCW* XVII, 22). In a lecture of April 1814, for example, Coleridge followed his description of the character of Satan 'with a full analytical character of the late "French Emperor"' (*LoL* II, 13). Obviously the figure of Satan gave Coleridge a wonderful opportunity to celebrate the fall of Napoleon at the time of his first abdication, yet the seemingly smooth transition from Satan to Napoleon suggests their close association during this period. Moreover, this was an association that was widely exploited during the months that led up to Napoleon's abdication. John Stoddard, for example, constantly referred to Napoleon in Satanic terms such as 'the Rebel Chief' and the 'Arch Rebel' in his editorials for *The Times*. Edward Stirling, in his 'Vetus' articles of December 1813 and January 1814 for the same newspaper frequently quoted passages of *Paradise Lost* on the fall of Satan and applied them to Napoleon.[56] Southey, in a piece of sublime propaganda of 1814, 'Ode Written During the Negotiations with Buonaparte', joined forces with Wordsworth and Coleridge in the projection of a Satanic iconography for Napoleon, declaring that 'Evil was his Good' (line 50).

Coleridge continued to draw the analogy between Napoleon and Satan in the years after Waterloo. However, he now made a crucial distinction between the different criteria that he believed were necessary when judging a 'historical' figure, such as Napoleon, and a 'poetic' character, such as Satan. He strove to liberate Satan from the tainting analogy with Napoleon, so that he could again be appreciated as a model of poetic sublimity in line with eighteenth-century readings of him. In a lecture on literature (which presents some problems of dating[57]) Coleridge makes this distinction between the 'political' Napoleon and the 'poetic' Satan:

> The character of Satan is pride and sensual indulgence, finding in self the sole motive of action. It is the character so often seen *in little* on the political stage. It exhibits all the restlessness, temerity, and cunning which have marked the mighty hunters of mankind from Nimrod to Napoleon. The common fascination of men is, that these great men, as they are called, must act from some great motive. Milton has carefully marked in his Satan the intense selfishness, the alcohol of egotism, which would rather reign in hell than serve in heaven. To place this lust of self in opposition to denial of self or duty, and to show what exertions it would make, and what pains endure to accomplish its end, is Milton's particular object in the character of Satan. But around this character he has thrown a singularity of daring, a grandeur of sufferance, and a ruined splendour which constitute the very height of poetic sublimity. (*LoL* II, 427)

As ever, Coleridge is alert to the dangerous appeal to the imagination of these 'great men', an appeal stressed by his use of the word 'fascination' with its literal meaning of 'bewitchment' or 'enchantment'. Coleridge uses his analysis of Satan to demystify these 'great men'. Yet in the final sentence he radically changes register. He moves from a condemnation of these character traits to an appreciation of Satan as a literary character. The image of a cloak suggested by 'thrown' recalls Coleridge's use of the imagery of disguise for Napoleon, such as the 'miserable masquerade domino, to *throw* around the nakedness of despotism' (*EoT* I, 52, my italics). Napoleon's appeal to the imagination was 'palliative', we remember; it acted as a 'disguise'. When he had used this imagery for Napoleon, Coleridge had implied that his own role as a writer was to disrobe Napoleon and to reveal the nakedness of his power base. However, Coleridge is positive in his appraisal of Satan's imaginative appeal, which constitutes the 'very height of poetic sublimity'. It is his stress on 'poetic' here that is crucial; it is this which distinguishes Satan from a figure such as Napoleon and which sanctions Coleridge's appreciation of him. Coleridge refuses to extend his aesthetic judgement to Napoleon. The cloak of 'sublimity' can be thrown round 'poetic' characters, but it must be stripped from historical ones like Napoleon, who perform on the 'political stage'.

Coleridge's need to distinguish between the sublime appeal to the imagination of the poetic Satan and the historical Napoleon reveals the paradox of the Lakers' figurative battle to drive Napoleon from the 'imagination'. Their demonization of him was prompted by personal and propagandist needs, the result not only of the historical events in the Peninsular War but of the rhetorical demands of their anti-Napoleonic campaigns; a series of literary and often Miltonic interventions in national and international politics. In representing Napoleon as Satan and in transforming the war into an apocalyptic plot, the Lakers had gone as far as they could go in their writing on the subject until history enacted their prophetic and political fantasies at Waterloo. Yet, their turn to Milton's Satan – the ultimate literary representation of evil – as a means of embodying Napoleon's 'consummate wickedness' emphasizes the French Emperor's dominant position both on the Continent and in the 'imaginations of men'. Such was his sway over these regions that this ultimate representational form was necessary as a means of combating him. This form paradoxically testified to Napoleon's imaginative power; a paradox which Hazlitt would exploit in his heterodox championing of both Satan and Napoleon after Waterloo.

CHAPTER 4

Staging history: Byron and Napoleon, 1813–1814

I blame the manner of [Napoleon's] death: he showed he possessed much of his Italian character in consenting to live. There he lost himself in his dramatic character, in my estimation. He was master of his own destiny; of that, at least, his enemies could not deprive him. He should have gone off stage like a hero: it was expected of him.

Medwin's Conversations of Lord Byron[1]

. . . there are two distinct tempers of mind in which we judge of things – the worldly, theatrical and pantomimical; and the unearthly, spiritual and etherial – in the former Buonaparte, Lord Byron and this Charmian hold the first place in our Minds; . . .

John Keats, letter of 14–31 October 1818[2]

'REALMS OF RHYME'

In one of the most remarkable acts of self-representation in *Don Juan*, even in the whole of Romantic poetry, Byron dramatizes himself through analogy with Napoleon Bonaparte, for him the supreme embodiment of the 'talents of *action* – of war – or the Senate', to which he aspired (*BLJ* III, 179). In canto XI of his epic, written in 1823, Byron retrospectively considers his own career as a poet:

> Even I – albeit I'm sure I did not know it,
> Nor sought of foolscap subjects to be king, –
> Was reckoned, a considerable time,
> The grand Napoleon of the realms of rhyme. (XI, 55, 5–8)

Byron's irony – itself partly a product of a post-Waterloo world view which questions the viability of the heroic mode – enables him to unite himself as a writer of 'rhyme' with Napoleon, the 'man of action'. Despite being a prolific poet, Byron was notoriously dismissive of the role[3] and by playing Napoleon was able to negotiate between two vocations which he normally saw as diametrically opposed. Moreover, this was a highly public gesture. Byron represents himself as playing his Napoleonic role in the public imagination as well as his own – 'I . . . was reckoned'.

Yet the effectiveness of Byron's pantomimical presentation of himself as the 'grand Napoleon of the realms of rhyme' comes from the way he maintains the tension between the tongue-in-cheek grandeur of his heroic claim for himself and the evident disparity between the two figures. In terms of the poetry–action dialectic in Byron's work, typified by his remark 'Who would write, who had anything better to do ?' (*BLJ* III, 220), the two phrases – 'the grand Napoleon' and 'the realms of rhyme' – are oxymoronic. Indeed, Byron had originally written line 6 as 'Nor wished of such frail realms to be the King',[4] highlighting the inferior status of the poetic domain. Byron's grand claim subsides into the bathos of the mockingly alliterative 'realms of rhyme' which again elevates him to a position of dominion yet enacts the contrast between the political world of 'realms' and the poetic one of 'rhyme'. Indeed, this disparity has the further effect of calling into question Napoleon's own status, about which Byron had always been equivocal. As he later commented of a comparison made in the English papers between himself and Bonaparte: 'Poor Napoleon. He little dreamed to what "vile comparisons" the turn of the Wheel would reduce him' (*BLJ* IX, 74). The result is that Byron's representation of himself in terms of Napoleon is at once heroic and mock-heroic, or, to use a Napoleonic formulation that Byron used for himself, simultaneously sublime and ridiculous.[5]

Yet this public moment of identification was to some extent the culmination of Byron's lifelong engagement with the figure of Napoleon. His ongoing struggle to grasp and formulate Napoleon's political and imaginative meaning played an important part in his own continuous process of self-assessment and self-representation. Napoleon dominated Byron's imagination like no other contemporary political figure, both satisfying and frustrating his characteristic craving for the heroic, famously expressed in the opening of *Don Juan* – 'I want a hero' (I, 1). Yet this craving was held in check by Byron's sense of living in an age in which the heroic mode had itself become questionable, an age in which no 'hero' had proved to be the 'true one' (*Don Juan* I, 1). Napoleon's character and career played an important part in this scepticism. He was certainly a less exemplary figure than George Washington, as Byron wrote in *The Age of Bronze*, 'A single step into the right had made /

This man the Washington of Worlds betrayed' (lines 233–4). But Napoleon's flawed greatness made him all the more exciting and Byronic.

Byron not only uses Napoleon as a figure for heroic or mock-heroic self-projection in his work. He consciously dramatizes Napoleon's career in an attempt to make him publicly perform a role on a world stage that is at once historical and literary, peopled with classical rulers and Shakespearean tragic heroes. Keats's description of both Byron and Napoleon as of the 'worldly, theatrical and pantomimical' temper captures the element of performance that is familiar in the Byronic pose; what McGann has termed the 'grand, even theatrical way in which Byron conceives and represents himself'.[6] But it also serves to introduce Byron's transformation of history into drama. This dramatization is no shallow gesture, but an attempt to register the impact and shape of Napoleon's career and his status as a 'hero' within the widest possible frame of reference. To use Stephen Behrendt's model that I discuss in my introduction, Byron strives to transform Napoleon into 'myth'[7] while remaining attentive to the historical developments of his career.

The texts I am concerned with in this chapter – the letters and the journal of 1813–14 and the 'Ode to Napoleon Buonaparte' – powerfully display Byron's complex response to Napoleon on the one hand, and his dramatization of both himself as part spectator / part protagonist and Napoleon as 'hero' on the other. During the period in which they were written, which climaxed with Napoleon's first abdication in April 1814, Byron was engaged in an evaluation of his own role in a society from which he felt increasingly alienated. In the context of his prolonged self-examination, part of a larger analysis of the politics of heroism and action, he repeatedly turned to Napoleon, whose apparent exit from the world stage enacted several of the key issues. Yet while Napoleon's exit was of great personal significance, Byron was keenly aware of its political impact, realizing that the final act of the drama would determine the public perception of the whole period since 1789. His dramatization and plotting of Napoleon's career in the privacy of his letters and journal reveal the importance he laid on Napoleon's enactment of a heroic role in determining the public's final response to the whole revolutionary period. This concern ultimately led him to the public statement of the 'Ode to Napoleon Buonaparte', a work in which he seeks to confer a mythic status on Napoleon with the aim of transforming his meaning in the public's political imagination.

THE 'ANAKIM OF ANARCHY'

Byron's journal entry of 17 November 1813 provides a useful starting-point for examining the complexities of his response to Napoleon's career. Byron had begun his journal only three days before and its fluidity and freedom – 'every page should confute, refute, and utterly abjure its predecessor' (*BLJ* III, 233) – made it the perfect form for engaging with the antithetical figure of Napoleon, who had been occupying an increasingly important place in his thought and his letters since 1812.[8] Byron opened his journal with a disillusioned record of personal failure and, as Leslie Marchand notes in his biography, neither his hectic social life nor the success of his writing could suppress his feelings that his powers were being wasted at this time.[9] His entry of 17 November begins with a reference to Napoleon's retreat from Leipzig, where he had been defeated in the so-called 'Battle of Nations' the previous month:

> What strange tidings from the Anakim of anarchy – Buonaparte! (*BLJ* III, 210)

The Anak were a tribe of Old Testament giants[10] and, in the political idiom of the day, 'anarchy' was the result of 'excess of liberty', the dialectical opposite of 'tyranny'.[11] Byron represents Napoleon as a monstrous form, a giant, who continues the liberating 'excess' of the French Revolution. Such a conception of Napoleon suggests that Byron's view of him was at least partly favourable, particularly if placed in the Whig tradition which saw the friends of freedom as driven to 'excess' by anti-revolutionary pressure.[12]

Indeed, Byron's admiration for Napoleon needs to be located within the context of the party system that dominated British politics. As Malcolm Kelsall has argued, Byron's political allegiance was to the Whigs, particularly during the period before Waterloo.[13] Byron had joined a Whig club at Cambridge in 1807, where his friend Matthews was known as the 'citoyen'.[14] While resident in England, he was a member of the social and political circles of the Whigs, who, as Whately comments, adopted Napoleon as an embodiment of liberty and opposition to monarchical power.[15] In 1812 he joined both the Union Club and the London Hampden Club and became a member of the Holland House circle, the glamorous centre of opposition support.[16] Many in these circles, led by Whitbread in the Commons after Fox's death in 1806 and by Holland in the Lords, admired Napoleon. In 1802 Fox had notoriously stated that since 'there is to be no political liberty in the world, I really believe that Buonaparte is the fittest to be master'.[17] Lord

Holland praised Napoleon as 'the greatest statesman and ablest general of ancient or modern times'.[18] Ponsonby, the leader of the Opposition in the Commons, eulogized him in 1810 as 'the greatest man that has ever appeared on the face of the earth', claiming that he was an 'extraordinary' man 'unparalleled in the history of the world, both as a military man, and a general statesman'.[19] The Whigs saw Napoleon as a reformer of French institutions, as the designer of a civil code which embodied the fundamental principles of the Revolution, as a political symbol who represented the last hope of an otherwise lost cause and as a 'genius' and a 'great man'.[20]

Byron shared his associates' admiration for Napoleon. His friends from Cambridge, Hobhouse and Scrope Davies, were passionate Napoleonists. Hobhouse, in particular, fuelled Byron's interest, telling him 'ten thousand anecdotes . . . of this extraordinary man; all in favour of his intellect and courage, but against his *bonhomie*' (*BLJ* III, 243–4). Like Hobhouse and Scrope Davies, Byron adopted Napoleon as a figure of opposition to *ancien régime* monarchy. He wrote to Moore in January 1814 that he hoped Napoleon would 'rally and rout your legitimate sovereigns, having a mortal hate to all royal entails' (*BLJ* IV, 19). He would certainly have agreed with Moore, who wrote to him that 'We owe great gratitude to this thunderstorm of a fellow for clearing the air of all the old legitimate fogs that have settled upon us, and I trust his task is not over yet.'[21] Like many European liberals such as Stendhal, whom he met in 1816, and Lord Holland, to whom he turned for political advice in 1812,[22] Byron saw Napoleon's regime as a more enlightened alternative to that of the *ancien régime*, commenting that 'Italy required an alteration in her government. The people were happier and more secure under Napoleon than under the Austrians'.[23] Indeed, in July 1813 he expressed a pragmatic desire to see Napoleon play the liberator in another country particularly close to his imagination, tentatively prophesying that the 'Greeks will, sooner or later, rise against them [the Turks], but if they do not make haste, I hope Bonaparte will come and drive the useless rascals away'.[24] Byron's admiration for what he termed Napoleon's 'talent' (*BLJ* IV, 101) was heightened by his increasing contempt for the impotent figures who dominated the political scene in England, which he satirized in a letter to Lady Melbourne of September 1813:

> Tis said – *Indifference* marks the present time
> Then hear the reason – though 'tis told in rhyme –
> A King who *can't* – a Prince of Wales who *don't* –
> Patriots who *shan't* – Ministers who *won't* –

What matters who are *in* or *out* of place
The *Mad* – the *Bad* – the *Useless* – or the *Base*? (*BLJ* III, 117)

Like many Whigs, Byron feared that Napoleon's defeat would lead to the restoration of the *ancien régime* rather than to the establishment of the French Republic he desired. As he commented in November 1813: 'here we are, retrograding to the dull, stupid old system, – balance of Europe – poising straws upon king's noses, instead of wringing them off' (*BLJ* III, 218). For Byron, then, as for many of his circle, much was invested in Napoleon as a figure of his political hopes and beliefs.

Yet as the obvious ambivalence of the phrase 'Anakim of anarchy' suggests, Byron's response to Napoleon was complex. He was equally aware of the tyranny of Napoleon's imperialism, on which he focused in his account of the Spanish war in canto I of *Childe Harold's Pilgrimage* (1812). Initially, he represents Napoleon as 'the Scourger of the world', fulfilling the classical mission *debellare superbos*:[25]

. . . but he whose nod
Has tumbled feebler despots from their sway,
A moment pauseth ere he lifts the rod;
A little moment deigneth to delay:
Soon will his legions sweep through these their way;
The West must own the Scourger of the world. (I, 52, 1–6)

Byron implies Napoleon's supremacy over the other European rulers – 'feebler despots' – while not denying his despotism (or theirs). However, in the following lines, he reinterprets Napoleon's career in the context of the people, the 'Sons of Spain':

Ah! Spain! how sad will be thy reckoning-day,
When soars Gaul's Vulture, with his wings unfurl'd,
And thou shalt view thy sons in crowds to Hades hurl'd.

And must they fall? the young, the proud, the brave,
To swell one bloated Chief's unwholesome reign. (I, 52–3)

The phrase 'the Anakim of anarchy', then, encapsulates Byron's political ambivalence towards 'the iconoclast who became an icon', to quote Frederick Raphael.[26] This ambivalence is brilliantly enacted in a moment in the journal of 6 March 1814. With a characteristically Bonapartist gesture, Byron had sent his 'fine print' of Napoleon to be framed and was evidently pleased with the result, writing that 'It is framed; and the Emperor becomes his robes as if he had been hatched in them' (*BLJ* III, 248). Here Byron fuses his judgement on the framing of the picture with a wry comment on Gérard's representation of Napoleon in his coronation robes, the portrait from which the print was engraved. He expresses pleasure at the suitability of the frame to the 'print', using as a metaphor the imagery of the engraving. Yet he also implies that Napoleon, though not a monarch by birth, is fully suited to his imperial status, perhaps even more so than any of the contemporary monarchs who had been born to the role. In thus framing Napoleon, Byron makes him represent a meritocratic ideal which can nonetheless gain imperial status with all its associated splendour.

'HIS DRAMATIC CHARACTER'

The complex interplay of Byron's responses to Napoleon is maintained throughout the rest of the journal entry of 17 November 1813:

> Ever since I defended my bust of him at Harrow against the rascally time-servers, when war broke out in 1803, he has been a 'Héros de Roman' of mine – on the continent; I don't want him here. But I don't like those same flights – leaving of armies, &c. &c. I am sure when I fought for his bust at school, I did not think he would run away from himself. But I should not wonder if he banged them yet. To be beat by men would be something; but by three stupid, legitimate-old-dynasty boobies of regular-bred sovereigns – O-hone-a-rie! – O-hone-a-rie! (*BLJ* III, 210)

The passage twists and turns as Byron investigates not only the Napoleonic career but the tension between his own investment in certain historical and literary versions of it and the events on the Continent. In recalling his early support (of which there is no contemporary record), he first thinks of Napoleon in historical and possibly classical terms as a 'bust' and then transforms him into a literary figure, a 'Héros de Roman'. Yet Byron immediately questions this literary and historic ennobling of Napoleon, undercutting the florid 'Héros de Roman' with the matter-of-fact 'on the continent, I don't want him here'. He pricks the heroic bubble that he has just blown, playing off his investment in his hero against the disappointment of present events – 'I don't like those same flights.'

Byron's investment in Napoleon was partly a result of his enactment of the heroic career of the great man. Napoleon seemed to have a place in world history and a mission to fulfil similar to that which, as McGann has suggested, Byron believed himself fated to accomplish.[27] Malcolm Kelsall traces this belief in the career of the great man to Byron's Whiggish education, arguing that 'the classic training of the patrician "caste" (to use Byron's word) was the record of the lives of the great men. What constituted true greatness, an honourable name and fame, was subject to debate, but history was made by the way that great men and women shaped the destiny of nations and empires'.[28] But Napoleon's present actions called into question both his own fitness for this role – as Byron commented in August 1813 'by all accounts the Emperor is rather more frail than becomes a hero' (*BLJ* III, 86) – and the viability of the role itself. As Byron wrote later in November:

> *Vide* Napoleon's last twelvemonth. It has completely upset my system of fatalism. I thought, if crushed, he would have fallen, when '*fractus illabitur orbis*,' and not have been pared away to gradual insignificance; – that all this was not a mere jeu of the gods, but a prelude to greater changes and mightier events. (*BLJ* III, 218)

With his retreat from Moscow and his defeat at Leipzig, Napoleon had been 'crushed', but he had failed to exit in an apocalyptic blaze of glory or to enact the tragic plot implied by Byron's system of fatalism. Instead, the seeming anticlimax of his exit from the world stage – 'pared away to gradual insignificance' – reinforces Byron's own renunciation of an active role – '. . . all I can do now is to make life an amusement, and look on, while others play' (*BLJ* III, 217–18). Napoleon had, at least, been a progressive force, symbolic of the forward movement of the French Revolution. His failure embodied the failure of the Whiggish belief in the gradual progress of liberty led by patrician figures.

Indeed, to return to the 'Anakim of anarchy' entry, Napoleon's failure to enact the grand role that Byron has scripted for him prompts Byron to acknowledge the difference between his 'imaginary' Napoleon, the 'Héros de Roman', and the Napoleon who deserted his army. As he comments, 'I did not think he would run away from himself.' Byron often conceives Napoleon's 'imaginary' self in dramatic terms. As he later commented, in failing to go 'off stage like a hero' Napoleon 'lost himself in his dramatic character'.[29] Byron scripted this 'dramatic character' for Napoleon in his letters and journal throughout the winter of 1813–14, but it was a role that Napoleon repeatedly acted badly or forgot to play at all. For example, Byron wrote to Lady Melbourne on 12 January 1814:

> By the bye – don't you pity poor Napoleon – and are these your heroes? – Commend me to the Romans – or Macbeth – or Richard 3d. – this man's spirit seems broken – it is but a bastard devil at last – and a sad whining example to your future Conquerors – it will work a moral revolution – he must *feel* doubtless – if he did not there would be little merit in insensibility – but why shew it to the

world – a thorough mind would either rise from the rebound or at least go out 'with harness on its back'. (*BLJ* IV, 27)

Clearly, the 'dramatic character' that Byron expected Napoleon to play on the European stage was a tragic Shakespearean one. The 'Romans', Brutus and Cassius, had committed suicide; Macbeth and Richard III had both died in battle. But through the winter of 1813–14 Napoleon failed to achieve this status as a tragic hero; he did not go out with 'harness' on his 'back', as Macbeth did. Byron's response reflects his awareness of Napoleon's impact on the public's political imagination. Had he cut a tragic and heroic figure, Napoleon would have provided a model for future generations and joined the ranks of the great figures of the past, becoming part of the *dramatis personae* of history. But Napoleon has shown his feelings to 'the world' – he has failed to play his part.

A striking feature of all these passages from Byron's letters and journal is Byron's own place in them. Implicit throughout the section quoted from the 'Anakim of anarchy' entry, which balances eight first-person pronouns with seven third-person pronouns, is a comparison between Byron's role and that of his hero. Byron parallels his own defence of Napoleon's bust against the 'rascally time-servers' with Napoleon's opposition against the 'three legitimate-old-dynasty boobies' and he contrasts his own schoolboy fighting with Napoleon's 'leaving of armies'. Byron's identification with Napoleon certainly involved an element of heroic self-projection, particularly during periods of boredom and frustration. Throughout the winter of 1813–14, Byron drew a series of parallels between himself and his hero, comparing his own snowbound situation at Newstead with the retreat from Moscow. But, as this passage indicates, it is also a political act in which Byron unites himself and Napoleon against the forces of reaction, be they the 'rascally time-servers' or the 'regular-bred sovereigns'.

Yet Byron's interest in Napoleon was not simply a matter of the vicarious satisfaction of his own active impulses after his own planned career in the Lords had ended in frustration. (He wrote to Augusta in March 1813 that he had 'no intention to "strut another hour" on that stage' (*BLJ* III, 32).) The uncertainty of Napoleon acting out the heroic drama on a world stage provides an excuse for Byron's own inaction – if Napoleon has failed all must fail. Yet it leaves a void in the world which Byron imagines fulfilling by incorporating himself within a pantheon of republican heroes from classical and modern history: 'To be the first man – not the Dictator – nor the Sylla, but the Washington or the Aristides – the leader in talent and truth – is next to the Divinity! Franklin, Penn, and, next to these, either Brutus or Cassius – even Mirabeau – or St. Just' (*BLJ* III, 218). Yet once again Byron swings from this expression of political ambition to a renunciation of it in which he achieves a dramatic self-consciousness while representing himself as occupying a place in the public imagination: 'I shall never be anything, or rather always be nothing. The most I can hope is, that some will say, "He might, perhaps, if he would"' (*BLJ* III, 218).

Byron's crisis over Napoleon, then, prompted a crisis of personal identity. Jerome Christensen, analysing a later passage from the journal of 9 April 1814, identifies a recurrent pattern in Byron's writing on Napoleon, commenting that 'in his journal entry Lord Byron mourns that he is not and can never be Napoleon Bonaparte – a Byronic trope, but now turned with an ironic finality: Byron can never be Napoleon because Napoleon cannot be himself'.[30] Christensen's analysis can be equally well applied to the 'Anakim of anarchy' passage, with Byron's avowal that Napoleon has 'run away from himself'. But the sentence that follows in that journal entry should not be overlooked – 'But I should not wonder if he banged them yet' (*BLJ* III, 210). Even while Byron laments Napoleon's failure to enact the tragic plot – 'to be beat by men would be something' – he still begins to reinvest in Napoleon as an antagonist and an alternative to the *ancien régime*. Such a process of reinvestment, of refusing to give up Napoleon, recurs throughout Byron's writing during this period and it is frequently facilitated by Byron's use of drama.

Byron's turn to drama as a way of reinvesting in and transforming history can be seen most clearly in the journal entry of 9 April 1814 to which Christensen alludes. This entry responds to the climax in this crisis over Napoleon when Byron discovered, probably from an announcement in the *Gazette Extraordinary*, that Napoleon had abdicated.[31] This was the supreme moment of anagnorisis. It confirmed Napoleon's failure to enact the role that Byron had scripted for him in the belief that it would have made such an impact on the popular imagination and called into question the validity of a role which Byron envisaged for himself. Byron had invested his faith in the Revolution in Napoleon, but now it was as if the Revolution had never happened. Napoleon's fall took away a powerful source and symbol of hope and opposition and appeared to vindicate the 'cant' of the Tories who now could delight in the anticlimax of Napoleon's career. Byron's fear that Napoleon's lame exit would discredit him totally is borne out by a letter from the Duke of Cumberland to the Prince Regent:

Hallelujah! thank God you have succeeded now in all your endeavours, and you in England has gained the day, for she alone never did recognise that wretch, and I think the baseness he has shown at the end prove him to be baser than any man that ever has existed. France must feel itself humbled at having submitted so long to the despotism of such a man; had he fallen gloriously in battle, had he rushed when he saw he could do nothing to the cannon's mouth, one might have said he was great in the end, but to submit tamely and ask for his treasure proves a soul as mean in his misfortune as it was cruel in prosperity.[32]

In his journal entry of 9 April, Byron draws on his mental storehouse of historical examples to make a series of parallels between figures who had resigned and Napoleon who falls short when measured against the decreasing standard of 'finest' to 'but so so':

I mark this day!

Napoleon Buonaparte has abdicated the throne of the world. 'Excellent well.' Methinks Sylla did better; for he revenged and resigned in the height of his sway, red with the slaughter of his foes – the finest instance of glorious contempt of the rascals upon record. Dioclesian did well too – Amurath not amiss, had he become aught except a dervise – Charles the Fifth but so so – but Napoleon, worst of all. What! wait till they were in his capital, and then talk of his readiness to give up what is already gone!! (*BLJ* III, 256)

Byron appropriates literary quotations – from *Venice Preserved* (IV. ii) and *Antony and Cleopatra* (III. ii) – as a way of attempting to make sense of confusing contemporary events, continuing: '"What whinging monk art thou – what holy cheat?" 'Sdeath! – Dionysius at Corinth was yet a king to this. The "Isle of Elba" to retire to! – Well – if it had been Caprea, I should have marvelled less. "I see men's minds are but a parcel of their fortunes"' (*BLJ* III, 256). But Napoleon's failure to enact any of the possible roles prompts a breakdown in Byron's prose – 'I am utterly bewildered and confounded' (*BLJ* III, 256).

Byron's bewilderment may result as much from his ways of assessing events as from the events themselves. As he continues, he uses several methods to try to understand and come to terms with events, employing a multitude of familiar patterns of experience which may, however, be inadequate as a means of appreciating the complexities of Napoleon's character and situation:

I don't know – but I think I, even I (an insect compared with this creature), have set my life on casts not a millionth part of this man's. But, after all, a crown may not be worth dying for. Yet to outlive *Lodi* for this!!! Oh that Juvenal or Johnson could rise from the dead! 'Expende – quot libras in duce summo invenies?' I knew they were light in the balance of mortality; but I thought their living dust weighed more *carats*. Alas this imperial diamond hath a flaw in it, and is now hardly fit to stick in a glazier's pencil: – the pen of the historian won't rate it worth a ducat. (*BLJ* III, 256–7)

Byron tentatively introduces himself into the already chaotic arena of assessment, and he, though an 'insect' compared to 'this creature', is another standard against which the now dehumanized Napoleon falls short. Yet again, the language used to make the comparison is that of Shakespearean drama, this time *Richard III*:

> Slave, I have set my life upon a cast
> And I will stand the hazard of the die. (v. iv. 9–10)

Byron weighs up Napoleon's career in anticipation of the 'historian's pen' and in his play of evaluations contrasts epigrammatic generalizations – 'a crown may not be worth dying for' – with specific detail – 'Yet to outlive *Lodi* for this!!!' He frames Bonaparte's career according to the philosophical plots of Juvenal's *Satires*, – quoting *Satire* x in Latin – and Johnson's imitation of it, *The Vanity of Human Wishes*. Yet Byron finds these generalized plots conflicting with his own systems of belief, and, as a result, his own voice enters the passage – 'I knew . . .', 'but I thought . . .'. He then turns from these preordained patterns to a more poetic and imagistic response presenting Napoleon as a flawed 'imperial diamond'. Byron is again thinking of the effect Napoleon will have on posterity as an inspirational or talismanic force. At present, this effect is negligible.

But Byron ends his journal entry by turning to Shakespeare:

> Psha! 'something too much of this.' But I won't give him up even now; though all his admirers have, 'like the Thanes, fallen from him'. (*BLJ* III, 257)

The Shakespearean quotations – from *Hamlet* (III. ii. 74) and *Macbeth* (v. iii. 51) – bring the passage to a rhetorical close and draw attention to the element of self-dramatization in the whole entry. Yet they also mark an important development in Byron's response to events as he shifts from the ironic, 'antic' language of Hamlet he had used in the opening of the entry – 'Excellent well' – to Macbeth's fifth-act language of defiance. By equating Napoleon and Macbeth, Byron is once again able to reaffirm his support and to recast Napoleon in the role of the Shakespearean tragic hero.

A 'NEW NAPOLEON': BYRON'S 'ODE'

Byron's prose scribblings illustrate both his accumulating investment in certain images of Napoleon and the way in which Napoleon's career repeatedly called these images into question. However, the individual entries often reveal a shift from a cathartic expression of disappointment over Napoleon's failure to enact his script to a more positive, redramatizing use of him. Despite Napoleon's failure to enact the heroic role, Byron refuses to 'give him up even now' (*BLJ* III, 257). In his 'Ode to Napoleon Buonaparte', which he wrote on the day after he made this vow, he makes a similar shift from catharsis through writing to reinvestment in Napoleon, though now enacted in public and using the transformative powers of myth rather than of Shakespearean drama.

Despite Byron's repeated assertions in early 1814 that he had renounced poetry,[33] Napoleon's abdication was an occasion he could not resist. He explained this reversal to Moore on 20 April by stating that there 'was a mental reservation in my pact with the public, in behalf of *anonymes*; and, even had there not, the provocation was such as to make it physically impossible to pass over this damnable epoch of triumphant tameness' (*BLJ* IV, 100). Throughout 1813 and 1814, Byron had represented writing as a purgative, cathartic mode of debate and discussion (*BLJ* III, 184), describing poetry as the 'lava of the imagination whose eruption prevents an earthquake' (*BLJ* III, 179) and writing that 'All convulsions end with me in rhyme' (*BLJ* III, 184). Over the previous six months, Byron's prose writing on Napoleon had increased, not only in quantity, but in intensity and drama of style, straining towards Shakespearean and histrionic soliloquy. The culmination of this crescendo was the more formalised, controlled and public strain of the 'Ode' – the eruption that prevented the earthquake.[34]

Byron's letter to Moore of 20 April reveals that Napoleon's abdication marked an important stage in the poetry–action debate that had been a feature of his writing on Napoleon over the previous six months. In this letter Byron describes Napoleon's abdication as a 'cursed business' which causes him to reverse his normal hierarchy of vocations: 'after all, I shall think higher of rhyme and reason, and very humbly of your heroic people' (*BLJ* IV, 100). Previously, Byron as poet had always felt himself to be overshadowed by Napoleon as the heroic man of action. Yet the abdication called into question the validity of the heroic mode and prompted a re-evaluation of 'rhyme', its dialectic opposite. Because the heroic life of action is now questioned, poetry can no longer be defined as simply something that fritters away time that could be better spent in active pursuits. Rather, as something 'higher' it provides the natural and appropriate form for a critique of the 'heroic'. However, even here Byron is incapable of writing off either Napoleon or the heroic mode, and continues: 'till – Elba becomes a volcano, and sends him out again. I can't think it all over yet' (*BLJ* IV, 100). Byron looks to the future when Napoleon may redeem himself and reinstate the heroic. The 'Ode' itself is similarly open-ended. While criticizing Napoleon's failure to exit gloriously, Byron's 'rhyme' – itself the 'lava of the imagination' – can transform and compensate for it.

This transformation of Napoleon emerges from a series of tensions apparent throughout the 'Ode'. Byron proceeds through analogy with other historical, literary or mythical figures (many of whom, such as Milo, Sulla and Charles V, he had already used in his prose). After an opening in which Byron addresses Napoleon, contrasting the remembered, prelapsarian glory of 'yesterday' with the present reality of 'now', he shifts to treating Napoleon in the third person:

> Is this the man of thousand thrones,
> Who strew'd our earth with hostile bones,
> And can he thus survive?
> Since he, miscall'd the Morning Star,
> Nor man nor fiend hath fall'n so far. (lines 5–9)

Byron draws the theme, language and imagery of these five lines from the apocalyptic vision of Isaiah: '*How art thou fallen from heaven, O Lucifer, son of the morning! how art thou cut down to the ground which did weaken the nations?* . . . They that see thee shall narrowly look upon thee, and consider thee, saying, *Is this the man that made the earth to tremble, that did shake kingdoms*' (14: 12–16, my italics). Like Satan, who, as Byron reminds us, had lost the name of Lucifer, 'the Morning Star', Napoleon has become a 'nameless thing' (line 3). He too has been 'miscall'd the Morning Star' in that he has failed to fulfil his potential as a 'light-bringer' or enlightenment ruler.

But Byron is again mythologizing Napoleon. While he pours scorn on the anti-climactic act of abdication, he nonetheless represents Napoleon's fall in the grandest available literary and historic terms, prefacing the 'Ode' with an epigram from Gibbon's *Decline and Fall of the Roman Empire*. The act of abdication may itself be 'shameful', like that of Emperor Nepos, but Byron still makes it part of an epic historical scheme, comparable to Gibbon's. It is the same elevation of Napoleon that underpins Byron's Satanization of him as he draws upon Isaiah's model of the fall of Satan to represent Napoleon's fall in universal and archetypal terms. Hyperbole is the dominant note of this opening stanza – 'thousand thrones', 'strewed our earth'. While Byron sustains his scornful tone in the opening nine stanzas of the 'Ode', then, he nonetheless seeks to transform Napoleon's career into something significant. He refuses to allow Napoleon to be 'pared away to gradual insignificance' (*BLJ* III, 218). As in his prose, Byron projects Napoleon onto a vast stage that is both literary and historic. He draws on Attila's harangue to his army in stanza 4 – 'The rapture of the strife' – and again turns to Isaiah – 'Thus saith the Lord, the heaven is my throne, and earth is my footstool' (66: 1) – for hyperbole:

> To think that God's fair world hath been
> The footstool of a thing so mean; (lines 79–80)

Throughout the 'Ode', Byron both inflates and deflates Napoleon. His 'want' of a 'hero' and his investment in Napoleon as the most dazzling candidate for this role contests with his belief that in abdicating Napoleon may have proved that 'he is not the true one' (*Don Juan* I, 1). Thus, while Byron criticizes Napoleon for not exiting from the world stage in the dramatic manner of Lucius Sylla, who 'threw down the dagger – dared depart, / In savage grandeur, home' (lines 58–9), he does so in terms that seem more suitable to admiration, or even adoration:

> But thou – from thy reluctant hand
> The thunderbolt is wrung – (lines 73–4)

Byron's representation of Napoleon here anticipates his description of him in *Childe Harold's Pilgrimage III* as 'the Thunderer of the Scene' (stanza 36) and in *Don Juan* as 'Jupiter' and 'the modern Mars' (XI, 83: X, 58). Even while castigating Napoleon, Byron deifies him.

As in his prose, Byron is struggling both to come to terms with and to shape Napoleon's career, keenly aware of its effect on posterity:

> If thou hadst died as honour dies,
> Some new Napoleon might arise,
>   To shame the world again – (lines 95–7)

Through dramatic death Napoleon could have ensured his place in the pantheon of inspirational literary and historical heroes. But his abdication has made his example as a role-model questionable:

> But who would soar the solar height,
> To set in such a starless night? (lines 98–9)

In the 'Ode' Byron weighs Napoleon in the balance and finds him wanting, and this again prompts an aphoristic comment that draws on the poem's epigram from Juvenal:

Weigh'd in the balance, hero dust
Is vile as vulgar clay. (lines 100–1)

Yet these lines, like the reference to Juvenal, once again stress that it is '*hero* dust' that is being weighed. Byron's commitment to the example of the heroic, albeit now called into question, re-emerges in the rest of the stanza:

But yet methought the living great
Some higher sparks should animate,
To dazzle and dismay,
Nor deem'd Contempt could thus make mirth
Of these, the Conquerors of the earth. (lines 94–8)

Byron brilliantly resolves these contradictions and tensions in the final stanza of the 'Ode'. Throughout, his renunciation of Napoleon as a result of the abdication has been somewhat undercut by his investment in a grand and heroic representation of him that he still cannot relinquish. By abdicating, Napoleon had failed to play the part of the Shakespearean tragic hero that Byron had scripted for him. The 'Ode' projects several possible models for what appeared to be this act of abject surrender – the domestic submission of Dionysius the Younger (lines 125–6), the brooding captivity and, by implication of Marlowe's play, the suicide of Bajazeth (lines 126–30) and the madness of Nebuchadnezzar (lines 131–5). These are scornful and contemptuous parallels. But in the final stanza Byron suddenly introduces a new possibility:

Or like the thief of fire from heaven,
Wilt thou withstand the shock?
And share with him, the unforgiven,
His vulture and his rock!
Foredoom'd by God – by man accurst,
And that last act, though not thy worst,
The very Fiend's arch mock;
He in his fall preserved his pride,
And, if a mortal, had as proudly died! (lines 136–44)

The 'Ode' has been described as a poem which attacks the failure of the Promethean spirit in Napoleon,[35] but it is surely the very opposite. Byron specifically offers Napoleon the possibility of Promethean status – 'Wilt thou . . .'. He scripts a new heroic role for Napoleon, mythologizing him in Aeschylean terms. In so doing he transforms Napoleon's abdication, turning an act of surrender into one of defiance, reformulating not only Napoleon but history itself.

Of course, Byron was aware of the different characters and backgrounds of Napoleon and Prometheus, as his first draft of the poem reveals:

> He suffered for kind acts to men
> Who have not seen his like again,
>   At least of kingly stock.
> Since he was good, and thou but great
> Thou canst not quarrel with thy fate.[36]

He distinguished between the two even more clearly in a quatrain he attatched to his fifth proof, on 25 April:

> Unlike the Offence, though like would be the fate –
> *His* to give life, but *thine* to desolate,
> He stole from Heaven the flame, for which he fell,
> Whilst *thine* was stolen from thy native Hell.[37]

But in the 'Ode' it is the equivalence of 'fates' that Byron invokes, rather than the differing natures of the 'Offence'. He rejects his earlier insistence on the Shakespearean tragic plot with its defiant conclusion, and discovers a new type of heroism as well as a 'new Napoleon' in the stoic resistance of Prometheus.

In moving towards this vision of a 'new Napoleon', Byron seems to have been heavily influenced by a letter from Leigh Hunt of 2 April 1814.[38] This letter was a response to one from Byron which, in turn, was stimulated by some 'remarks' of Hunt's, possibly in the *Examiner.* Though Byron's letter either no longer exists, or is still to be rediscovered, much of its subject-matter can be deduced from Hunt's reply, particularly as Byron seems to have repeated the predominant themes of his prose. It was a 'long letter' in which Byron had evidently given a picture of his hopes for Napoleon. Hunt's reply, which Byron appears to have drawn on for his comments on Wellington in *Don Juan* ('Never had mortal Man such opportunity, / Except Napoleon, or abused it more' (IX, 9)), again stresses the extent to which Napoleon operated as a repository for his political hopes. Hunt replies that 'Your picture of what he might have been, it is almost too painful to contemplate; never had man such opportunities of true glory, or so wantonly threw them away.' Byron again seems to have stressed his desire for an heroic, apocalyptic ending to Napoleon's career. Hunt writes that 'There certainly is a feeling among men of spirit in general, which leads them to prefer this desperate flash-out of a man's career to his quieter and more patient extinction.' Hunt's comments reveal that

Byron felt that in failing to achieve this dramatic climax, Napoleon's behaviour would not 'stand the test of truth and reason' and that he had once again cited the Shakespearean examples of Richard III and Macbeth.

Hunt addresses himself to these ideas. He interprets Richard III and Macbeth as historical figures, not as dramatic characters as Byron had done, and dismisses them as 'ruffians'. Instead he offers a very different model of how he believes Napoleon should conduct himself in defeat. He writes:

> To be sure, it is rather late in the day for Bonaparte to set up for a philosopher, but if he would do it at all, it is clear he must do it in this manner, and not, as it were, run his head impatiently against his hard fortune . . . Bonaparte has had, or pretended to have, 'great views' for society at large, – he has affected a certain great and speculative philosophy; and perhaps may have really juggled with his conscience by promising himself to do mighty things for us, as soon as he had demolished our principles and cut all our throats. He may therefore say to himself 'My views for society have not succeeded; I am suddenly rendered powerless; but as my object was not mere reigning, as I pretend to courage and understanding superior to most men, and above all, as I have undertaken in so many words that adversity shall not be too much for me, I must show myself able to bear my reverses with fortitude' . . . he had no right to imitate the useful desperation of patriotism; – in him, it would have been mere useless bloodshed, and boyish or rather ruffianish obstinacy.

It is a mythic form of this role that Byron offers Napoleon at the climax of the 'Ode'. The conflicts in Byron's attitude towards Napoleon's career, the strophic and antistrophic movement of admiration and criticism, are ultimately replaced by an epode of future possibility. The failure of Satan is transformed into the positive pride of Prometheus, anticipating, and possibly stimulating, Shelley's use of the mythic hero in his drama of the rejuvenation and regeneration of the liberal cause and overthrow of despotic tyranny.[39] In the final couplet, Byron examines the duality of divine and mortal status:

> He in his fall preserv'd his pride,
> And if a mortal, had as proudly died!

Byron acknowledges Prometheus' immortality and Napoleon's mortality, but stresses that Napoleon can still achieve Promethean status through proud death; one achieved by slow and patient suffering and defiance. Man, while aware of his mortality, can begin to take on a Titanic significance. Byron's use of Napoleon anticipates his later use of Prometheus in his lyric of 1816:

Thou art a symbol and a sign
To Mortals of their fate and force;
Like thee, Man is in part divine,
A troubled stream from a pure source. (lines 45–8)

In the mythic figure of Prometheus, then, the subject of Byron's lyric of 1816 and of Shelley's epic drama, Byron found a new heroic role for Napoleon. Unlike the Lakers' demonization or Satanization of Napoleon, Byron sought to establish a new place for him in the public imagination. He reclaims, even redeems Napoleon by turning him into a Promethean figure – a symbol of strength, hope and defiant opposition. Byron's mythologizing act reveals something truly Promethean and defiant in his own nature.

CHAPTER 5

Waterloo: 'The greatest event of modern times'[1]

> Oh, Wellington . . .
> . . . Waterloo has made the world your debtor –
> (I wish your bards would sing it rather better).
>
> Byron, *Don Juan* (IX, 1–3)

The Battle of Waterloo is a landmark in the political and imaginative landscape of English Romanticism. Amidst the national jubilation, Southey and Wordsworth marked the victory over Napoleon with a celebration on Skiddaw, dancing round the bonfire singing 'God save the King' and eating 'roasted beef and boiled plum-puddings' (*SL* IV, 121–2). In more serious though no less patriotic mood, they seized upon the battle as an occasion with which to consummate in verse their teleological plotting of the war; using it to close the complex and deeply troubling history of the period that had dawned with the fall of the Bastille. What is impressive about their major works on Waterloo, *The Poet's Pilgrimage to Waterloo* and the 'Thanksgiving Ode',[2] is that though they use the battle to present a simplified and providential version of history, they do so only after investigations of their own representational strategies and models of history. Byron, however, saw no reason for the historical optimism of the Lakers. In *Childe Harold's Pilgrimage III* he rebukes those who represented Waterloo as a great and decisive event. For him Waterloo was not a 'closing deed magnificent' as it was for Wordsworth or a 'consummation' as it was for Southey.[3] Rather, at the moment and in the place where his identification with Napoleon was at its closest Byron makes the battlefield of Waterloo the starting-point for a figuring of Napoleon that is not only complex and ambivalent, focusing on his 'antithetically mixt' 'spirit' (III, 36), but politically controversial.

To get a clearer picture of these three Napoleonic texts, however, we need to place them in their cultural context as part of the British response to Waterloo, and particularly as part of the phenomenon of the

'Waterloo poem'. It is this context which I have set out to outline in the first section of this chapter, before moving on to explore Southey's, Wordsworth's and Byron's literary responses to the fall of Napoleon at Waterloo.

'NUMEROUS EFFUSIONS ON THAT VICTORY'[4]

The battle of Waterloo vies with the fall of the Bastille for consideration as the most celebrated event of the English Romantic period.[5] The *Morning Post* broke the 'Great and Glorious News' of the battle on 22 June 1815[6], which was immediately represented by the exultant British press as a decisive victory; one that brought about the complete overthrow of Napoleon, ended twenty-three years of almost uninterrupted war in Europe and signalled the end of the revolutionary and Napoleonic periods. *The Times*, for example, began its leader only a week after the news broke with the sort of superlative that would quickly become commonplace, claiming that 'Nothing in ancient or modern history equals the effect of the victory of Waterloo.'[7]

This hailing of Waterloo as a glorious British victory over Napoleon in a single decisive battle was a triumph for British propaganda, however. As David Chandler has shown, the campaign was in fact a pair of double battles, namely Ligny and Quatre-Bras on 16 June, and Waterloo and Wavre two days later.[8] In these battles Napoleon engaged both British and Prussian armies. In British reports of the campaign the British role was inevitably exaggerated: Belgians, Dutch and Hanoverians, who accounted for almost two-thirds of the Allied manpower, often went unmentioned, and the importance of the Prussian intervention was played down. The British press gave the credit for the victory to its own army and, above all, to Wellington. The hyperbolic nature of the accounts of the battle is revealed by a fascinating critique from a most unexpected quarter. In 1816 Wellington himself remarked that 'I am really disgusted with and ashamed of all I have seen of the battle. The number of writings upon it would lead the world to believe that the British Army had never fought a battle before.'[9] In his characteristically matter-of-fact style Wellington implicitly denies the uniqueness that was being claimed for Waterloo. For him it was a battle like any other. Indeed, his own account of it in the official dispatches was so brief and restrained that it caused outrage when published in Great Britain.[10]

As Wellington's comment suggests, the battle prompted an extraordinary explosion of writing on the subject, particularly in the form of poetry. By June 1816, as the *Monthly Review* noted, there had been 'numerous effusions on that victory.'[11] The *Edinburgh Review*'s selective listing of new publications helps to gauge the quantity and type of writing on Waterloo. For the months from July to October 1815 the *Review* lists four works of history giving 'narratives', 'accounts' and 'circumstantial details' of the battle, three long poems on the subject, two first-hand reports of tours of the area and biographies of Blucher and Wellington. The publication of similar quantities of material continued well into 1817, and as late as 1822 Harriet Cope published *Waterloo, a Poem in Two Parts*. Between July 1815 and March 1817 there are at least thirty-two new publications relating to the battle listed by the *Edinburgh Review*. Francis Jeffrey's comment in his review of *Childe Harold's Pilgrimage III* of December 1816 for the *Review* that there had been 'hundreds' of poems on Waterloo is indicative of the proliferation of works on the subject even if – like so much talk of Waterloo – it feels somewhat hyperbolical.[12] David Chandler, however, also puts the number of contemporary accounts in the 'hundreds'.[13] The main modern authority, Betty Bennett, comments only that there was a 'vast number of poems on the subject of Waterloo'.[14]

The context of Scott's *The Field of Waterloo*, Southey's *The Poet's Pilgrimage to Waterloo*, Wordsworth's 'Thanksgiving Ode' and Byron's *Childe Harold's Pilgrimage* is a nation swamped by these 'numerous effusions on that victory'.[15] Their work is part of the cultural phenomenon of Waterloo poems described by Jeffrey: 'All our bards . . . great and small, and of all sexes, ages, and professions, from Scott and Southey down to hundreds without names or additions, have adventured upon this theme.[16] For three of these four writers, Scott, Southey and Byron, the visit to the battlefield was integral to the conception and writing of their poems. There they could examine the important landmarks and question the participants and witnesses. In their poems, they each use the site of the battle as a starting-point for a consideration of its wider issues and consequences, including, of course, their evaluation of Napoleon. Yet each was also aware of the cultural context in which he was working; of other versions of his chosen subject and other celebrations of the scene he intended to celebrate.

Walter Scott, according to Lockhart, was 'among the first civilians who hurried over to see the field of Waterloo'.[17] He visited it in August 1815 with the specific intention of writing a poem on the battle[18] which he started on the first day of his visit and completed while staying in Paris. As one of the vanguard of writers on Waterloo, and the first major writer to adventure on the subject, Scott wasn't faced by competition from other versions. However, the sections of *The Field of Waterloo* on Napoleon are greatly indebted to Byron's 'Ode to Napoleon Buonaparte' to which it directly alludes.[19] In *Paul's Letters to his Kinfolk* we can trace the change in Scott's relationship to his subject and its context. He had conceived this prose account of his visit to Waterloo as a means of defraying the cost of his journey. It took longer to complete than the poem and was not published until early in 1816. By this time Scott had to take into account the fact that Waterloo, the site of 'the greatest event of modern times', had become a 'celebrated scene'.[20] Southey's conception of his poem similarly necessitated the visit to the battlefield which he made in October 1815. As he explained in the opening of his *Journal of a Tour in the Netherlands in the Autumn of 1815*, feeling 'in some degree bound to celebrate the greatest victory in British history, I persuaded myself that if any person had a valid cause or pretext for visiting the field of Waterloo, it was the Poet Laureate'.[21] As this suggests, in *The Poet's Pilgrimage to Waterloo* Southey as Poet Laureate not only celebrates the greatest victory but reflects its glory back on himself to enhance his own special status.

Byron visited the battlefield on 4 May 1816 on his way to exile in Italy. The genesis of what would become the Waterloo passage in *Childe Harold's Pilgrimage III* illustrates a combination of historical and contextual stimuli. On the night of his visit to the battlefield Mrs Pryse Gordon, the wife of Byron's (and previously Scott's) guide round the battlefield, asked him to write some verses in her album. This was the same album in which Walter Scott had already written some lines from his *Field*, a work which Byron had read in the author's presence. Byron countered Scott's account with two stanzas on the same subject, which began:

Stop! – for thy tread is on an Empire's dust. (line 145)

Byron quickly developed these into the forty-four stanzas in the completed canto on the Brussels Ball, Quatre-Bras, Waterloo and Napoleon (III, 12–46).[22]

Of the four poets only Wordsworth did not visit the battlefield before writing his poem, though he did make such a visit part of his continental tour of 1820 – the occasion of another sonnet.[23] Wordsworth's lack of interest in visiting the site is indicative, for his principal concern is not with the battle itself, but with its reception and representation in Britain. The stimulus to write came not with the news of the victory, but seven months later, in January 1816, when the battle was commemorated in

Britain. Wordsworth's acute awareness of the context in which he was writing is revealed in the 'Ode' when, as a means of critique, he parodies the tropes of the standard poetic accounts of the battle.

As a result of the context in which they were working, each of these four writers needed to take into account a reading public which, while keen for more works on Waterloo, was cognizant with – and in danger of being saturated by – the subject. As an anonymous reviewer of Southey's *The Poet's Pilgrimage* wrote in the *Augustan Review*: 'Various travellers, on foot and in vehicles of every incredible description – together with a multitude of prosaic poets, and an host of poetic prose-writers, have combined to celebrate that famous scene, and to familiarise with it the minds of the people of England.'[24] The familiarity of the readership with the details of the battle could, of course, be exploited by the writer. Scott, in the ninth of *Paul's Letters*, uses it to save himself a lot of work:

> I should now, my dear sister, give you some description of the celebrated field of Waterloo. But although I visited it with unusual advantage, it is necessary that I should recollect how many descriptions have already appeared of this celebrated scene of the greatest event of modern times, and that I must not weary your patience with a twice-told tale.[25]

As Scott suggests, the writer was responsible for providing certain details, but by alluding to other texts which had dealt with them could avoid repetition. But such a method of allusion fulfils more than a formal or factual requirement. Waterloo was a subject of international political importance represented almost unanimously in Britain as a British triumph. As a review of Southey's *Poet's Pilgrimage* makes clear, the proliferation of poems that were 'poured forth' on Waterloo were 'all tributes'.[26] Jeffrey, similarly, describes those who wrote on the subject as having 'yielded to the patriotic impulse'.[27] As these comments suggest, a poem on Waterloo was clearly expected to be a 'celebration' and a 'tribute', its martial tones perhaps softened by a note of elegy. By its very nature it would be an expression of a 'patriotic impulse'. The majority of works on the subject shared certain features; features that were expected by the reading public. There was a definite 'matter of Waterloo' in these works; an agenda that was political rather than aesthetic.

Betty Bennett, in her anthology *British War Poetry in the Age of Romanticism: 1793–1815*, includes only one poem on the subject: 'The Battle of Waterloo' by William Thomas Fitzgerald which, she notes, is 'representative of the vast number of poems written on the subject of Waterloo'.[28] As a paradigmatic Waterloo poem, published in three different journals, *The New Monthly Magazine*, *The Gentleman's Magazine* and *The European Magazine*, it can be used to identify what I have termed 'the matter of Waterloo'. Fitzgerald begins with condemnation of Napoleon and lists his 'atrocities' which have prompted cries for retribution (lines 1–17). These cries are satisfied at the battle of Waterloo, in which Britain is given the central role:

> And HEAVEN decreed, in its appointed hour,
> That BRITAIN's arm should crush the TYRANT's power. (lines 18–19)

Praise for 'Great Wellesley' (lines 21–5) is followed by tributes to Brunswick, 'valiant' Picton and Ponsonby (lines 29–30). The centrepiece of the poem is the description of the battle, which focuses on the French cavalry charges of the English squares, represented through the metaphor of the sea crashing against some 'bold, projecting rock'; a metaphor which neatly picks up and redefines the image of the sea and the White Cliffs of Dover that was so frequently used during the invasion crisis (lines 31–62). The arrival of the Prussians is briefly noted before Wellington is credited with ordering the advance which wins the battle (line 60). The battle is compared to Cressy, Agincourt and Blenheim, and Wellington with Edward the Black Prince, Henry V and Marlborough (lines 64–7). The poem ends with a general memorial and thanksgiving and an acknowledgement of the 'Gallant Germans' (line 83). Fitzgerald's tone of exultation is also characteristic, as when he adopts the inexpressibility topos so characteristic of such pieces:

> But where's the BARD, however grac'd his name,
> Can venture to describe GREAT WELLESLEY's fame?
> Such Bard, in strength and loftiness of lays,
> May soar beyond hyperbole of praise,
> And yet not give the tribute that is due
> To BRITONS, WELLINGTON, led on by you!!
> For to the plains of WATERLOO belong
> The magic numbers of immortal song. (lines 20–7)

The exultant tone of these pieces can further be gauged by Fitzgerald's constant use of eulogistic terms: 'valiant', 'honour'd', 'GALLANT', 'GREAT', 'GLORIOUS', 'GLORY', 'triumphant', 'noble' and 'high renown'. 'Gallant', that fine chivalric term, is used three times in the poem. The poem exemplifies John Keegan's comment that 'official thanksgiving determined . . . that the style writers adopted should be heroic and declamatory from the outset'.[29]

In their poems on Waterloo Scott, Southey, Wordsworth and Byron indicate that they feel themselves to be writing for a readership which would expect the 'matter of Waterloo'. This could be done either directly or by referring to other works on the subject. Scott's poem is very much an establishment work. He dedicated it to 'The Duchess of Wellington, Princess of Waterloo' and donated the profits of the first edition to the Waterloo Subscription.[30] It includes all the features of the 'matter of Waterloo'. Southey distinguishes his own task from that of the historian, but only after having devoted 16 stanzas to the features of the battlefield and details of the battle (I, iii, 15–31). Moreover, in so doing he does not fail to provide the standard praise of Wellington:

> Deem not that I the martial skill should boast
> Where horse and foot were stationed here to tell,
> What points were occupied by either host,
> And how the battle raged, and what befell,
> And how our great Commander's eagle eye,
> Which comprehended all, secured the victory.
>
> This were the historian's, not the poet's part . . . (I, iii, 32–3)[31]

Both Wordsworth and Byron acknowledge the type of works that will supply the details they leave out of their poems, but they do so with somewhat affected ingenuousness. Byron, for example, refers the reader to other works – and particularly to Scott's *The Field* – for elegies for those killed in the battle:

> Their praise is hymn'd by loftier harps than mine . . . (line 253)

These comments may appear no more than the sort of gracious acknowledgement found in any number of poems on public affairs. However, Scott's review of Byron's *Childe Harold's Pilgrimage III* for the Tory *Quarterly Review* reveals the political importance of including, or at least alluding to, 'the matter of Waterloo' in works on the subject.[32] Scott praises Byron for his 'beautiful description of the evening which preceded the battle of Quatre-Bras' and the 'beautiful elegiac stanza on Honorable Major Howard'.[33] The latter is, of course, part of 'the matter of Waterloo'. But to Scott's horror Byron 'shuns to celebrate the victory of Waterloo'.[34] Scott criticizes the politics of the poem not only for what Byron says, but for what he fails to say, lamenting that 'we have lost that note of triumph with which his harp would otherwise have rung over a field of Glory such as Britain has never reaped before'.[35] Moreover, Byron leaves out one of the essential ingredients of the genre as a whole, the praise of Wellington. As Scott writes, 'If his lofty muse has soared in all her brilliancy over the field of Waterloo without dropping even one leaf of laurel on the head of Wellington, his merit can dispense even with the praise of Lord Byron.'[36] For Scott, Byron's poem is subversive and regrettable because it chooses the battle as its subject but fails to include the full agenda built in to the 'matter of Waterloo'. His comments reveal how important it is to bear in mind the cultural context of the 'matter of Waterloo' when considering the works on the subject by Southey, Scott and Byron, a context that becomes all the more important when considering the political implications of the various representations of Napoleon.

'CHRISTIAN THANKFULNESS' AND 'BRITISH PRIDE':[37] SOUTHEY'S *PILGRIMAGE*

In *The Poet's Pilgrimage To Waterloo* Southey celebrates Waterloo not only as a glorious British victory but as the triumphant vindication of his own anti-Napoleonic crusade:

> I, who with faith unshaken from the first,
>   Even when the Tyrant seem'd to touch the skies,
> Had look'd to see the high-blown bubble burst,
>   And for a fall conspicuous as his rise,
> Even in that faith had look'd not for defeat
> So swift, so overwhelming, so complete. (I, i, 5)

Here, as throughout the poem, Southey makes Waterloo the culmination of the moralistic plot of rise and fall which he had exploited to persuade and reassure the British public in works as various as the allegorical epic-romance *The Curse of Kehama*, the satirically apocalyptic ballad 'The March to Moscow'[38] and the sublime political 'Ode, written during the Negotiations with Buonaparte, in January, 1814'. In these pieces Southey had continued to represent the war in terms of political and moral polarities; as the struggle between liberty and tyranny, good and evil. For psychological and propagandist reasons, he ruthlessly subordinated historical and political complexity to this simple and convenient plot.

Unlike Napoleon's first abdication in 1814, which disappointed Southey because it failed to fulfil his hopes for a final catastrophic conclusion to Napoleon's career – he confessed to Scott that his 'first feeling' on hearing the news 'was not a joyous one' (*SL* IV, 69) – the battle of Waterloo was unmistakably a momentous event in world history. As he wrote exultingly to his friend John Rickman, 'Was there ever such a land battle in modern times?' (*SL* IV, 119). With the news of Waterloo, Southey was able to reclaim with renewed vigour the apocalyptic tone of his letters on Spain, the 'Ode' and the 'Carmen Triumphale' of 1814 with its refrain 'Glory to God, deliverance for mankind' (line 9). He described his feelings exultingly to Grosvenor Bedford: 'Our bells are ringing as they ought to do; and I, after a burst of exhilaration at the day's news, am in a state of serious and thoughtful thankfulness for what, perhaps, ought to be considered as the greatest deliverance that civilized society has experienced since the defeat of the Moors by Charles Martel' (*SL* VI, 117). Through the parallel with Martel's victory over the Moors in 732 Southey aligns Waterloo with the battles of Christianity against the infidel. He transforms it into another victory in the crusade of Christianity against impiety and evil.

In *The Poet's Pilgrimage to Waterloo* Southey represents the battle as a single, decisive event; a 'defeat / So swift, so overwhelming, so complete' (I, i, 5) in which Napoleon received his 'great and total overthrow' (I, iii, 31). He again draws the analogy with Martel's victory, as well as with the battle of Platea, to underline the world-historical significance of the modern battle in the opening of the first part of the poem:

> Our world hath seen the work of war's debate
>   Consummated in one momentous day
> Twice in the course of time; and twice the fate
>   Of unborn ages hung upon the fray: . . .
>
> Such was the danger, when that Man of Blood
>   Burst from the iron Isle, . . .
> Such too was our deliverance, when the field
> Of Waterloo beheld his fortunes yield. (I, i, 1 and 4)

Through the analogies Southey presents Waterloo as a battle in which Christian and civilized values ('Art, Science, Freedom' (I, i, 2)) triumph over barbarism, despotism and impiety. Yet despite the general and universal nature of these forces Southey presents as triumphant at Waterloo, and despite some acknowledgement of the Germans' role in the battle (I, iii, 25), he repeatedly asserts the central role of Britain in the defeat of Napoleon. Napoleon received 'his meed / From Britain and the outstretched arm of God' (II, I, 25). Britain and God, not Britain and Prussia, are the principal allies that defeat Napoleon.

The Poet's Pilgrimage to Waterloo is a 'matter of Waterloo' poem that seeks to transcend its status. It is an unusual mix of historical detail, first-hand reportage, personal recollection, elegiac meditation, allegory and universal philosophizing. In the first of the two parts, Southey recounts his own journey through Flanders to Brussels and the field of Waterloo itself. Though he frequently stresses that his account of the battlefield is a personal one, and not that of the 'historian' (I, iii, 33), he still manages to include all the features that I have identified as the 'matter of Waterloo': condemnation of Napoleon and listing of his atrocities (II, i, 22–42; II, iv, 13–22; I, iv, 5–23, 36–9); the placing of Britain in the central role (passim, esp. II, iv, 22); praise of Wellington (I, iii, 12, 22–4, 32); elegies, both for individuals (I, iii, 49; I, iv, 25) and general (I, ii, 8–11); description of the battle and features of the site (I, iii, 15–31); tide/flood metaphor (I, iii, 27); parallel of Waterloo with Blenheim (I, iii, 11–12) and comparisons of Wellington with Marlborough. Yet Southey aimed at a broader treatment of the battle than that afforded by the standard Waterloo poem. In a letter to Walter Scott he outlined the difference between their respective works on the battle: 'My poem will reach you in a few weeks: it is so different in its kind, that however kindly malice may be disposed, it will not be possible to institute a comparison with yours. I take a different point of time and a wider range, leaving the battle untouched, and describing the field only such as it was when I surveyed it' (*SL* IV, 152–3[39]). Southey rather overstates his lack of engagement with the battle in detail. His elegiac survey of the field uses the major sites that were familiar to his readership – Mont St Jean, Belle Alliance, Hougoumont, La Haye Sainte, Pappelotte – to give a fairly detailed account of the action of the battle and its aftermath (I, iii, 15–31, 40–7; I, iv, 14–18, 26, 34–5.) Yet his letter indicates his desire to surpass the standard poetic accounts of the battle and suggests that he has in mind a grand design for his work that will transform the themes and tropes of other Waterloo poems. This aim to elevate the 'matter of Waterloo' – a subject already characterized by its raised diction – is stimulated by his desire to write a poem that will rise to and confirm his laureate status as a spokesman for his country:

> Me most of all it behoved to raise
>   The strain of triumph for this foe subdued,
> To give a voice to joy, and in my lays
>   Exalt a nation's hymn of gratitude,
> And blazon forth in song that day's renown, . . .
> For I was graced with England's laurel crown. (I, i, 6)

Here Southey presents his poem both as a testimony of his own individual position ('Me most of all', 'my lays') and as the expression of the united nation ('a voice', 'a nation's hymn'). Southey aligns his own position, and the status of his poem, with its principal ideological message. Meditating on the site of the battle in the poem he feels:

> A Christian thankfulness, a British pride,
> Temper'd by solemn thought, yet still to joy allied. (I, iv, 2)

By this process of representation, of course, Southey awards the credit of the victory to these patriotic forces.

To achieve this elevated, quasi-epic, quasi-sacred poem Southey invokes a whole tradition of English national poets; poets whose work represents, or could be made to represent, national and Christian values, most notably Chaucer, Spenser, Shakespeare and Milton. For example, he adopts the title and at times the style of Chaucer: 'Certes we were a joyous company' (I, i, 33). Like Wordsworth in *The Convention of Cintra*, he uses the literature of the past to ennoble the historical and poetical present – 'the field of British glory to survey' (I, i, 7). In the 'Proem', Southey invokes the two most important authorities for his poem:

> But when I reach at themes of loftier thought,
> And tell of things surpassing earthly sense,
> (Which by yourselves, O Muses, I am taught,)
> Then aid me with your fuller influence,
> And to the height of that great argument
> Support my spirit in her strong ascent!
>
> So may I boldly round my temples bend
> The laurels which my master Spenser wore;
> And, free in spirit as the mountain wind
> That makes my symphony in this lone hour,
> No perishable song of triumph raise,
> But sing in worthy strains my Country's praise. (Proem, 23–4)

As the last stanza makes plain, Spenser is a key figure who particularly sanctions the allegorical second part of the poem.[40] Yet the penultimate stanza of the Proem indicates a closer involvement with the great national poet for all the Romantics – Milton; the writer used, of course, by Coleridge and Wordsworth to read the Napoleonic period and Napoleon's career. In the final lines of this stanza Southey reworks the invocation to *Paradise Lost* – 'what is low raise and support / That to the height of this great argument' (I, 23–4). Southey highlights the Miltonic model in the final book of the poem in which he advances his orthodox Christian explanation of 'the course of human things' through the allegorical figure of the heavenly teacher. When this figure delivers her justification of history, the war and Waterloo, she does so in Miltonic terms; she 'vindicates the ways of God to Man' (I, iv, I). Directly here, as indirectly throughout the poem, Southey invokes *Paradise Lost* to support him in his 'great argument'. His aim in *The Poet's Pilgrimage* is no less than a Miltonic assertion of eternal providence and a justification of the ways of God to man; a justification he believes is all the more necessary because of the shattering effects of the revolutionary and Napoleonic periods.

As for Wordsworth in *The Convention of Cintra*, *Paradise Lost* provides the literary and ideological framework for Southey's representation of Napoleon in the poem. Through a series of allusions to Milton's epic in part one, Southey insistently equates Napoleon with Satan as an incarnation of evil who has instigated the fall of man from his *ancien régime* Eden. With his first reference to contemporary events, Southey establishes the Miltonic plot which underpins his representation of both Waterloo in general and Napoleon in particular:

> Such was the danger, when that Man of Blood
> Burst from the iron Isle, and brought again,
> Like Satan rising from the sulphurous flood,
> His impious legions to the battle plain:
> Such too was our deliverance, when the field
> Of Waterloo beheld his fortunes yield. (I, i, 4)

From the outset, then, Southey Satanizes Napoleon. He transforms the Napoleonic wars into a Miltonic epic struggle. Waterloo becomes the final triumph of the war in heaven in which the 'impious legions'[41] – another Miltonic formulation – are overcome, presumably by the Good Angels. The stanza establishes one of the central themes of part one of the poem, the world delivered from evil by the defeat of Satan at Waterloo. Again Southey reduces the complication of history to a predetermined plot in which good triumphs over evil; as he says in the 'Argument', 'to the Christian Philosopher all things are consistent and clear'.

Through most of part one, Southey's equation of Napoleon and Satan is somewhat routine – a poetic reworking of Wordsworth's and Coleridge's strategy in their writing on the Peninsular War. Yet in the final book of part one of the poem he uses allusions to Milton and the Miltonic plot of *Paradise Lost* to provide the representation of the whole of the revolutionary and Napoleonic period. Consequently, the vengeance taken on the French in their flight from Waterloo (I, iv, 10) becomes a vengeance taken for the whole of Napoleon's career. At Waterloo:

. . . righteous fate
Brought on the French, in warning to all times,
A vengeance wide and sweeping as their crimes:

Vengeance for Egypt and for Syria's wrong;
For Portugal's unutterable woes;
For Germany, who suffer'd all too long
Beneath these lawless, faithless, godless foes;
For blood which on the Lord so loud had cried,
For Heaven opprest, and Heaven insulted and defied. (I, iv, 22–3)

Southey represents this Napoleonic period of devastation as a fall from the pre-lapsarian age of *ancien régime* rule. He uses the Belgians to present the longing for a return to an Edenic pre-1789 world, remarkably inverting the common use of the same tropes for the world after the fall of the Bastille:

They now look'd back upon their father's times,
Ere the wild rule of Anarchy began,
As to some happier world, or golden age of man. . . .

One general wish prevail'd, . . .if they might see
The happy order of old times restored!
Give them their former laws and liberty,
This their desires and secret prayers implored. (I, iv, 39 & 43)

In other words, Southey represents Waterloo as nothing less than the historical equivalent of the fall. Satanizing Napoleon, Southey makes him the sole instigator. The Belgians describe Napoleon as 'the author of this strife' (I, iv, 5), a phrase which alludes to Milton's descriptions of Satan as 'the Author of all ill' and 'author of evil' (II, 381; VI, 262). More subtly, they claim that 'One man was cause of all this world of woe' (I, iv, 6), a phrase which draws on the Miltonic leitmotif 'all our woe'[42] and conflates in Napoleon the figures of Satan (IX, 225) and Eve (X, 935).

Southey's commitment to presenting the period 1789–1815 as the fall and his anachronistic Satanization of Napoleon prohibit him from making the more nuanced type of historical judgement sometimes inherent in his personal correspondence. For example, in a letter of 15 January 1814 he writes that 'I was a republican; I should be so still, if I thought we were advanced enough in civilization for such a form of society; and the more my feelings, my judgements, my old prejudices might incline me that way, the deeper would necessarily be my hatred of Bonaparte' (*SL* IV, 57). Yet what distinguishes *The Poet's Pilgrimage to Waterloo* from Southey's demonizing of Napoleon in works such as the 'Ode, written during the

Negotiations with Buonaparte, in January, 1814' is that in part two of the poem Southey dramatizes and investigates the leap from an engagement with the problematic and complex 'particulars' of history to a confidently avowed faith in the generalized and Christian model of a progressive and providential history – the major strategy in the Lake poets' writing on the war and Napoleon from 1809 onwards. Southey neatly characterized this favourite strategy for dealing with the complexities of history in a letter to Wynn of 15 December 1815 in which he outlined the structure of *The Poet's Pilgrimage*: 'The Lamentation [II, i–ii] will express a feeling concerning the state of affairs very similar to yours, and the Reproof [II, iii–iv] instead of answering the particulars as it strikes home, will deal in generals and hold out a picture of the hopes of mankind' (*SNL* II, 124–5). Southey embodies these two very different ways of thinking about Waterloo and its results in the two allegorical figures that meet and instruct the poet: the Evil Prophet and the Heavenly Guide. The first of these, initially presenting himself as Wisdom, quickly turns out to be an advocate of earthly 'materialism' – the doctrine of the Revolution that Southey argues is embodied by Napoleon. Though the poet easily counters this doctrine, he is bewildered by the carnage of Waterloo and the Evil Prophet exploits this, presenting history as incoherent and meaningless – 'a thorny maze without a plan!' (II, ii, 19). The failure of the French Revolution, and its bloody climax at Waterloo, are enlisted by the Prophet as the latest examples of this pessimistic model, and he prophesies greater carnage and chaos to come.

There is an obvious propagandist aim in Southey's representation of the clearly Whiggish views of the 'Evil Prophet'. In his 'Argument' Southey makes it clear that he uses the 'Evil Prophet' to present the 'opinion' of a specific group: 'it states the opinion of those persons who lament the restoration of the Bourbons, because the hopes which they have entertained from the French Revolution, have not been realized: and of those who see only evil, or blind chance, in the course of human events'. Indeed, according to Malcolm Kelsall Byron is the specific target here, something that seems more than likely bearing in mind Southey's later attack on the dangerous morals and politics of the 'Satanic School'. Kelsall writes that the 'preface points the finger directly at the Jacobins (or Liberals as they now call themselves). That word Pilgrimage in the title indicates one gloomy Jacobin above all others.'[43] To some extent the historical arguments of the Evil Prophet's 'Lamentation' are set up so that the poet can knock them down. The debate over 'materialism', for example, enables Southey not only to denounce the principle, but to identify it with the French Revolution and Napoleon – 'Such . . . was the Tyrant's creed / Who bruised the nations with his iron rod' (II, i, 25). The strategy both preempts contrary arguments and disarms any opposition to Southey's point of view. Southey gives the impression of tackling the historical questions head on, answering them and so dismissing them, though, in fact, he sidesteps them.

Yet it also seems possible that the nature of the allegory enables Southey to raise and work through the problems of his own historical situation as someone who has lived through the whole revolutionary and Napoleonic epoch; the poem externalizes through allegory an internal debate. The 'Evil Prophet''s lamentation for the failure of the French Revolution and the restoration of the Bourbons (II, ii, 4–7) can be compared to another of Southey's letters of the previous year, in which he wrote that 'As for the Bourbons, I do not wish to see them restored . . . They have been a detestable race . . . I used to think that the Revolution would not have done its work, till the Houses of Austria and Bourbon were both destroyed, – a consummation which the history of both houses has taught me devoutly to wish for' (*SL* IV, 60–1). Through the persona of the poet, Southey expresses disappointment over the fate of Italy, Greece and Spain (II, iii, 8–16) and fears of civil disruption in Britain (II, iii, 17). Indeed, the tone of the opening stanza of part two recalls the searching introspective analysis prompted by the French Revolution in Books IX and X of Wordsworth's *The Prelude*:

> I thought upon these things in solitude,
> And mused upon them in the silent night;
> The open graves, the recent scene of blood,
> Were present to the soul's creative sight;
> These mournful images my mind possess'd,
> And mingled with the visions of my rest. (II, i, 1)

As these lines suggest, Southey seems to have been genuinely shocked by his visit to the battlefield. He wrote in his journal: 'I had never before seen the real face of war so closely and God knows! a deplorable sight it is.'[44] Moreover, Waterloo seems to have led Southey to question his beliefs, as he writes in the poem, 'The shaken mind felt all things insecure' (I, iv, 39).

Once again, these feelings of uncertainty and incomprehension in the face of the 'particulars' of the 'state of affairs' as expressed in the 'Lamentation' (II, i and ii), are countered by the assertion of a providential and divine schema in the 'Reproof' of the Heavenly Guide of (II, iii and iv). After a series of ceremonies which dramatize the poet's induction into the Christian way of thinking (II, iii, 40–52) the Heavenly Guide reels off the doctrines of the 'Christian Philosopher' which, as Southey writes in the 'Argument', make 'all things consistent and clear'. Chiding the poet for not remembering 'that Man is free and God is good' (I, iii, 23), she presents a generalized and Christian model of a progressive and providential history in which nations, like the individual, prosper according to their virtue:

> And in the scale of nations, if the ways
> Of Providence mysterious we may call,
> Yet, rightly view'd, all history doth impart
> Comfort and hope and strength to the believing heart.
>
> For through the lapse of ages may the course
> Of moral good progressive still be seen,
> Though mournful dynasties of Fraud and Force,
> Dark Vice and purblind Ignorance intervene;
> Empires and Nations rise, decay and fall,
> But still the Good survives and perseveres thro' all. (II, iv, 4–5)

Southey's representation of Napoleon within this providential world view again requires a spectacular disengagement from his historical particularity and a conceptualization of him in terms of a moral force. Southey represents Napoleon through the Heavenly Guide as 'that man, in guilt the first, / Pre-eminently bad among the worst' (II, iv, 15). He denies any form of historical, diplomatic or political means of accounting for him:

> Not led away by circumstance, he err'd. (II, iv, 17)

and repeatedly refuses historical models of evaluation and representation:

> For not, like Scythian conquerors, did he tread
> From his youth up the common path of blood;
> Nor like some Eastern Tyrant was he bred
> In sensual harems, ignorant of good; (II, iv, 16)

Rather, Southey asserts, Napoleon can only be understood as evil:

> But from his wicked heart his error came:
> By Fortune to the highest place preferr'd,
> He sought through evil means an evil aim, (II, iv, 17)

Again, this convenient pantomime stereotype of the arch-villain enables Southey to present Waterloo as nothing less than the battle of Good against Evil. As Southey announces in the 'Advertisement', Waterloo can be celebrated as the moment when Europe was finally redeemed after the fall of the revolutionary and Napoleonic periods: 'The contest in which this country was engaged against that Tyrant, was a struggle between good and evil principles, and never was there a victory so important to the best hopes of human nature as that which was won by British valour at Waterloo.'

'A CLOSING DEED MAGNIFICENT':[45] WORDSWORTH'S WATERLOO

As we might expect, when Wordsworth came to celebrate Napoleon's defeat at Waterloo, he resorted initially to the sonnet. Having seized upon a specifically Miltonic version of this form in 1802 as the medium through which he could conduct his critique of Napoleon and his contest with him, Wordsworth had continued to use the sonnet as the principal poetic weapon of his anti-Napoleonic campaigns of 1802–3, 1806–7 and 1808–11. Napoleon's fall at Waterloo offered the obvious opportunity to shape and conclude the narrative of these sequences; to consummate what was both a personal and a general history of nearly the entire Napoleonic career. Yet the three sonnets on Waterloo that Wordsworth wrote between 17 November 1815 and 18 January 1816 – 'Inscription for A National Monument In Commemoration of the Battle of Waterloo', 'Occasioned by the Same Battle, February 1816' and 'February 1816'[46] – fail to transcend their status as pseudo-laureate celebrations of the British victory. Their national and public function – they were published in *The Champion* in February 1816[47] – prohibited the exploration of political and psychological tension, a feature which had been one of the main strengths of the sequence of 1802–3. There is no sense of Wordsworth's own long poetic struggle with Napoleon in these pieces, or of the intensely personal engagement with historical crises that had so energized his writing in *The Prelude* and *The Convention of Cintra*. Instead, he represents Waterloo in predictably pious and patriotic forms, as the war in heaven,[48] the triumph of Christianity over the infidel,[49] and Agincourt.[50]

Indeed, while the sonnet form may have appeared the obvious choice for Wordsworth's celebration of Waterloo, it seems rather at odds with content in these three works. Two of the poems are proleptic in conception. 'Occasioned by the Same Battle' anticipates a poem in which 'The Bard' – a visionary figure 'Assoiled from all incumbrance of our time' – 'Shall comprehend this victory sublime; / And worthily rehearse the hideous rout' (lines 11–12). 'February, 1816' is an invocation in which Wordsworth aspires to write a poem equivalent to the Odes of Filicaia; works on 'contemporary events' of 'celestial aim' and 'saintly rapture' (lines 4–5 and note). Even though, as Wordsworth wrote in a letter, he 'had no design of doing anything more' on Waterloo after he had written these sonnets (*MY* II, 284), both poems suggest an aspiration beyond the limitations of the form to a grander work in which Wordsworth could claim the role of the 'Bard' described in 'Occasioned by the Same Battle', a figure whose visionary power includes a sense of the historical:

> He whose experienced eye can pierce the array
> Of past events, – to whom, in vision clear,
> The aspiring heads of future things appear,
> Like mountain-tops whence mists have rolled away (lines 5–8)

Wordsworth's dissatisfaction with the sonnet form is further suggested by the genre of the works that he alludes to in these poems. Whereas in 1802–3 Milton's sonnets had provided the model for both form and content, Wordsworth now invokes the Miltonic epic *Paradise Lost*, the Shakespearean history play *Henry V*, and the Odes of Filicaia as suitable models for rehearsing the 'victory sublime' of Waterloo. The third of the sonnets, 'Inscription for a National Monument', while obviously in the Romantic tradition of inscription verse,[51] suggests that Wordsworth not only wanted to memorialize the battle but to write something monumental in the sense of 'massive', 'vast' and 'impressive'.[52] Only such a response would be appropriate to the event.

It was by abandoning the sonnet and returning to the sublime lyric mode of the irregular or Pindaric ode that Wordsworth found a form in which he could 'worthily rehearse' the 'hideous rout' of Waterloo.[53] It is in the 'Thanksgiving Ode' – the main text of the 1816 volume of the same name[54] – that Wordsworth creates the real consummation of the sonnet sequence; indeed, of all his writing on Napoleon. In a letter to John Scott of 11 March, 1816, explaining the genesis of the 'Thanksgiving Ode',[55] Wordsworth presented the form as facilitating the sort of expressive spontaneity that was missing in the three sonnets: 'When I wrote the Sonnets inserted in the Champion I had no design of doing anything more. But I could not resist the Temptation of giving vent to my feelings as collected in force upon the morning of the day appointed for a general Thanksgiving. Accordingly, I threw off a sort of irregular Ode upon this subject, which spread to nearly 350 lines' (*MY* II, 284). Similarly, Wordsworth wrote to Crabb Robinson that the ode was 'poured out with much feeling' (*MY* II, 334), though in both letters he also stressed the 'labour' of 'correction' that followed this initial outpouring (*MY* II, 284, 334). To his fellow poet Robert Southey Wordsworth offered a more conscious model of his composition of the ode, describing it as 'a poem composed or supposed to be composed on the morning of the thanksgiving, uttering the sentiments of an individual upon that occasion. It is a dramatised ejaculation' (*MY* II, 324). Wordsworth claims a greater artistry than when writing to Scott and Crabb Robinson, but, as he continues, the 'irregular frame of the metre' he had adopted allowed for 'fervour and impetuosity'. Wordsworth makes an interesting link with his earlier sonnet 'Occasioned by the Same Battle' in which he argued that one of the requisite qualities of the bard was that he should be 'Fervid' (line 3). Unlike the tight and restrictively regular rhymes and rhythms of the sonnet, the irregular ode form allowed Wordsworth a freedom of composition in which he could express his feelings about Waterloo with fervour and impetuosity. The cumulative force of the three sonnets climaxed in the outpouring of the ode; a possibly simulated spontaneous overflow of powerful feelings.

Yet, though Wordsworth presented the ode as a personal and individual expression – describing it as 'of the lyric kind' (*MY* II, 284) and distinguishing it from the 'hymn' form which 'utter[s] the sentiments of a multitude' (*MY* II, 324) – his chosen form had a more public encomiastic function that can be traced back to Pindar. As Carl Ketcham has written, 'Wordsworth clearly felt that the Ode in the heroic tradition was the only response adequate to the victory at Waterloo'.[56] In the 'Advertisement' to the poem, Wordsworth represents himself as the spokesman of a more generalized, national, feeling, writing that 'the present publication owes its existence to a patriotism, anxious to exert itself in commemorating that course of action, by which Great Britain, for some time past, distinguished herself above all other countries'. Indeed, what distinguishes this Pindaric ode from Wordsworth's earlier use of the form in the ode 'There was a time' is his treatment of his subject on the grand scale rather than in terms of detail. He replied to Southey's suggestion that he use a more regular form by listing the 'great objections' 'in respect to a stanza for a grand subject to be treated comprehensively' (*MY* II, 324–5). In the 'Advertisement' he wrote that it had 'fallen within his province to treat [the subject of the battle] only in the mass'.[57] Stephen Gill sees this 'generalizing utterance' as the cause of the poem's lifelessness: 'Wordsworth forsook the very ground of the success of most of his poems, which is that they are realized only in and through the matter-of-fact, the everyday, the human.'[58] Yet to read the poem in this way and to criticize it accordingly is to miss Wordsworth's essential point. While the ode was not literally composed on the day of thanksgiving, it was this commemorative event, rather than the battle itself, which prompted Wordsworth to write it.[59] In it he not only treats a 'grand subject' 'comprehensively', but in doing so provides a critique of the numerous poems on, and accounts of, Waterloo. The ode needs to be placed in the broader context of these works if we are to appreciate Wordsworth's radical approach to the subject and to understand the integrity of his exploration of his own representation of the war against Napoleon.

Wordsworth was well aware of the context of Waterloo poems in which he was working, though many of the comments in which he differentiated his own treatment of the subject are misleading in their apparent respect for such works. He wrote to John Scott, who was also working on a long poem on Waterloo, that 'My short Essays . . . cannot possibly interfere with your own work, as they stand at a distance from the Body of the subject' (*MY* II, 282). Similarly, in the 'Advertisement', Wordsworth alludes to other, more detailed, accounts of the battle when he writes that the 'author has only to add that he should feel little satisfaction in giving to the world these limited attempts to celebrate the virtues of his country if he did not encourage a hope that a subject, which it has fallen within his province to treat only in the mass, will by other poets be illustrated in that detail which its importance calls for, and which will allow opportunities to give the merited applause to PERSONS as well as THINGS'.[60] This dutiful acknowledgement satisfies the criteria of the 'matter of Waterloo'. Wordsworth suggests that while his ode adds another dimension to the treatment of the battle, it does not conflict or counter the more detailed accounts provided elsewhere. Similarly, within the poem itself, when Wordsworth turns to focus on the battle after the apostrophe and invocation of the first two stanzas, he acknowledges these standard accounts of the battle:

> Who to the murmurs of an earthly string
> Of Britain's acts would sing,
> He with enraptured voice will tell
> Of One whose spirit no reverse could quell;
> Of one that mid the failing never failed:
> Who paints how Britain struggled and prevailed,
> Shall represent her labouring with an eye
> Of circumspect humanity

Shall show her clothed with strength and skill,
All martial duties to fulfil,
Firm as a rock in stationary fight;
In motion rapid as the lightning's gleam;
Fierce as a flood-gate bursting in the night
To rouse the wicked from their giddy dream –
Woe, woe to all that face her in the field!
Appalled she may not be, and cannot yield. (lines 67–82)

With its emphasis on the stoic heroism of the personified 'Britain', its employment of the standard imagery of rock and water and its allusion to Livy ('Vae victus' – 'Woe to the vanquished'), Wordsworth's representation of an 'enraptured' account of the battle seems to fall in with the standard treatments of Waterloo.

However, in the next stanza, Wordsworth produces one of the most striking transitions or undercuttings of the ode to reveal his comprehensive approach to the battle:

And thus is missed the sole true glory
That can belong to human story!
At which *they* only shall arrive
Who through the abyss of weakness dive:
The very humblest are too proud of heart:
And one brief day is rightly set apart
To Him who lifteth up and layeth low;
For that Almighty God to whom we owe,
Say not that we have vanquished – but that we survive. (lines 83–91)

Wordsworth abruptly and unexpectedly discredits not only his own representation of the battle in the preceding stanza, but the whole 'heroic', action-based, approach to Waterloo. He shifts the emphasis of his representation completely away from the details of the battle itself and on to a divine level. Wordsworth insists that Napoleon's defeat at Waterloo must be understood primarily not as a British victory, but as an act of 'Almighty God'.

Stephen Gill believes that Wordsworth's representation of Waterloo as the victory of this Old Testament 'Almighty God' is not a product of the public and national function of the ode or a pious knee-jerk reaction, but rather the culmination of Wordsworth's long struggle to comprehend the war. He writes that 'it is fair to say that he had thought about the significance of war and its eventual outcome as seriously as any man and no one could impugn the sincerity of the emotions expressed in the 1816 odes'.[61] In his writing on the Peninsular War, Wordsworth attempted to resolve the tension in his political loyalties through a polarization of the war into a struggle between good and evil. This act of polarization was both a propagandist manoeuvre and a defence against the complex crises of identity as those dramatized in *The Prelude* IX and X. It involved side-stepping more complex, historical issues. Similarly, the Battle of Waterloo offered an event which Wordsworth seized upon to shape Napoleon's career into an apocalyptic plot. But by adopting this clear-cut method of representation in the ode Wordsworth glosses over the complexities of the historical issues raised by the battle. His awareness of these complex issues are seen, for example, in a letter written during the Hundred Days, indeed only a month before the apocalypse of Waterloo, in which Wordsworth considered the European situation:

> If Buonaparte were a man of genuine talents, such is the present state of Italy I am persuaded he might yet atchieve [*sic*] a noble work, which would almost redeem him in my estimation; I mean the making and consolidating the several states of that divided kingdom into one; and if this were done the independence [of] that people would be established – one of the most desirable political events that could possibly take place. The Italians have been abominably used, in being transferred to Austria, to the king of Sardinia and the rest of those vile Tyrants. B.'s is a strange adventure, he must doubtless have very many adherents in France, but I must be in deplorable ignorance of the facts, if it is possible that such an Enterprise should succeed. (*MY* II, 219–20).

In this private letter Wordsworth engages with contemporary events in a manner that the public and 'comprehensive' nature of his ode would make impossible. Despite his hesitancy to speak favourably of Napoleon, his opinion is much more ambivalent than we might expect having read *The Convention of Cintra* or the 'Thanksgiving Ode'. As the three 'if's indicate, he considers hypothetical historical questions and his tone is always equivocal. Like Southey, Wordsworth was disappointed by the treatment of Italy in the Allied restoration of 1814. Moreover Austria, Napoleon's enemy and Britain's ally, is one of the 'vile Tyrants' rather than a providential embodiment of the workings of the Deity. Wordsworth, though he acknowledges he is not entirely sure of the facts, shows his awareness of the complexities of the European situation and this prevents him from being anything other than ambivalent. His uncertainty is conveyed most fully in the phrase 'B.'s is a strange adventure'. Here Wordsworth stands back questioningly to view Napoleon's career, but finds himself unable to express anything other than a romantic sense of wonder.

Yet the 'Thanksgiving Ode', antithetical as it is in its treatment of history and the self to the probing narrative of *The Prelude*, marks the culmination of Wordsworth's transformation of the war against Napoleon into an apocalyptic struggle, a manoeuvre that side-stepped historical complexity. Accordingly, in his ode Wordsworth adopts the apocalyptic register of Isaiah and Revelation for his representation of the Napoleonic career and the battle of Waterloo. Once again Napoleon is demonized, and the war viewed as a battle of the Deity against 'That Soul of Evil . . . from Hell let loose' (line 95). Wordsworth portrays Napoleon's career as a world-wide war waged against spiritual values as well as natural objects. Wordsworth's apocalyptic representation of the war is not only visionary, but revisionary, enabling him to consummate the plot of the war that he had developed in *The Convention of Cintra* – one very different from that of *The Prelude* or even the sonnets of 1802–3. In his writing on the Peninsular War, Wordsworth had gone as far as he could go at this time and he had to wait for Waterloo to enact the triumphant finale of his providential plot. Yet the standard 'matter of Waterloo' poems failed to see the battle in these terms, they 'missed the sole true glory / That can belong to human story!'. Wordsworth responded by reasserting the 'Deity' as the primary agent in the victory over Napoleon. Yet Wordsworth refuses to rest contented with this pious and orthodox sentiment, investigating its full implications in the infamous climax of the twelfth stanza:

> Nor will the God of peace and love
> Such martial service disapprove
> . . .
> For thou art angry with thine enemies!
> For these, and for our errors,
> And sins that point their terrors,
> We bow our heads before Thee, and we laud
> And magnify thy name, Almighty God!
> But thy most dreadful instrument,
> In working out a pure intent,
> Is Man – arrayed for mutual slaughter, –
> Yea, Carnage is thy daughter. (lines 260–1, 274–82)

Ketcham writes of this passage:

> Look for a moment, Wordsworth is saying to his audience, at where your assumptions have led you. If Waterloo was a just and good event, then God (who also has his uses for tornadoes and earthquakes) of course approved of the means as well as the result. This is the darker side of the general thanksgiving: a view of the sterner aspect of the Deity which Wordsworth will not let us ignore . . . Wordsworth, never one to shrink from an effect because it was startling, halts

his readers in mid-celebration, forcing them to inspect the total implications of their rejoicing.[62]

Ketcham attempts to save and justify the lines that startled Shelley and Hazlitt[63] by presenting Wordsworth as testing and questioning the assumptions of his readers. Yet in the context of Wordsworth's own account of the 'Thanksgiving Ode' as a personal and individual statement, these lines need also to be seen as Wordsworth pushing to the extreme his own conclusion. In them he tests for himself the full implications of his strategy of dealing with both the Battle of Waterloo and the war as a whole by representing it as a battle of the 'Deity' against 'That Soul of Evil'. Wordsworth comes to terms with the physical destruction, the 'slaughter' of the battle and the war of the last twenty-three years by making it a part of the divine plan, akin to natural disasters. The representation of this God is thus the final logical step in Wordsworth's working out of his own world view. Once this step has been made he can hymn his God as the victor of the battle and the restorer of peace:

> To THEE – To THEE –
> On this appointed Day shall thanks ascend,
> That Thou hast brought our warfare to an end,
> And that we need no further victory! (lines 289–92)

Yet for Wordsworth Waterloo was not only a historical apocalypse, but an apocalypse of the 'Imagination' itself. With the defeat of Napoleon:

> Imagination, ne'er before content,
> But aye ascending, restless in her pride,
> From all that man's performance could present,
> Stoops to that closing deed magnificent,
> And with the embrace is satisfied. (lines 163–7)

In these extraordinary lines Wordsworth hyperbolically rewrites the history of his 'Imagination' and makes his contest with Napoleon central to that history. That the 'Imagination, ne'er before content' is 'satisfied' only at the moment of Napoleon's defeat suggests that despite its attempts to transcend human performance, the 'Imagination' has been constantly engaged with the threat and challenge of Napoleon himself. The lines make it possible to redefine Wordsworth's 'Imagination' not as passive, retiring and quietist, as Abrams represents it, but as militantly active; a force that fought its major battles with Napoleon in the sonnet sequences, the 'Alps' passage of Book VI of *The Prelude* and *The Convention of Cintra*. Wordsworth's 'Imagination' is a product not only of the failure of the French Revolution but of his epic struggle against the Satanic usurper, Napoleon Bonaparte.

'BLOODY AND MOST BOOTLESS': BYRON'S WATERLOO

When, in the mock-heroic *The Vision of Judgement* Byron has the self-applauding 'Bard Southey' cite a few of his works, the juxtaposition of 'Rhymes on Blenheim – Waterloo' (line 768) devastatingly exposes the dramatic shift in the Poet Laureate's treatment of 'famous victories'. In 'The Battle of Blenheim', which was first published in the *Morning Post* in 1798, Southey had skilfully undermined the myth of the great and decisive battle through the figure of Old Kaspar who, despite his insistent refrain, ''twas a famous victory', is unable to say why the battle was fought or what good came of it.[64] By 1816, however, as we have seen, Southey was seeking to re-establish this myth in *The Poet's Pilgrimage*, presenting Waterloo as a decisive event in a progressive and providential model of history. He even went so far as to re-evaluate Blenheim itself, and to use it as an analogy:

> And even our glorious Blenheim to the field
> Of Waterloo and Wellington must yield. (I, iii, 12)

There is no evidence to suggest that Byron had read *The Poet's Pilgrimage* before writing *Childe Harold's Pilgrimage III*. Yet it is tempting to suggest that he would have been aware of this latest example of 'cant' 'political' and 'poetical', particularly as it had provocatively usurped his own notion of 'Pilgrimage' and yoked it to a poem which sought to legitimize not only the social and political establishments of restoration Europe, but the writer's own position as Poet Laureate. Similarly, it seems unlikely that Byron was familiar with Wordsworth's 'Thanksgiving Ode' at this stage, though he later invoked it in *Don Juan* – ' "Carnage" (so Wordsworth tells you) "is God's daughter" ' (VIII, 9).[65] Yet it was against the establishment interpretation and religious justifications of Waterloo that Byron would later find exemplified by *The Poet's Pilgrimage* and the 'Thanksgiving Ode' that he counterattacked in the third canto of his own 'Pilgrimage' poem.

In the first of the two stanzas which Byron wrote in Mrs Gordon's album on the night of his visit to the battlefield – which became stanza 17 of canto III – Byron builds to a powerful rhetorical climax in which he startlingly questions the British interpretation of Waterloo as a historical event:

Stop! – for thy tread is on an Empire's dust!
An Earthquake's spoil is sepulchered below!
Is the spot mark'd with no colossal bust?
Nor column trophied for the triumphal show?
None; but the moral's truth tells simpler so,
As the ground was before, thus let it be; –
How that red rain hath made the harvest grow!
And is this all the world hath gained by thee,
Thou first and last of fields! king-making victory?

Here, Byron invokes and dismisses the standard methods of commemorating the battle as part of his critique of the British response. As early as November 1815 Wordsworth had written his sonnet which purported to be an 'Inscription for a National Monument in commemoration of the battle of Waterloo'. Such monuments were, in fact, erected on the battlefield within a few years – the Gordon Monument in 1817, the Hanoverian memorial in 1818, the Prussian Monument in 1818 and the Lion Mound from 1821.[66] Yet Byron condemns all such tributes at a time when they must already have been in the planning or subscription stage. Because the Battle of Waterloo has changed nothing, Byron argues, the field of Waterloo should itself remain unchanged. Using the same tactic, he appropriates a trope of the 'matter of Waterloo' and inverts its meaning. As Carl Woodring has shown, Scott and Southey had each 'noted, and worked into stanzas, the paradoxical renewal of vegetation, a sense of the power of Nature in restoring ripeness in the autumn, greenness in the Spring'.[67] Yet they had used this imagery metaphorically as a means of assimilating the battle within a natural, organic and progressive model of history. Byron, however, refuses the metaphorical dimensions of this imagery. His exclamatory statement:

How that red rain hath made the harvest grow! (line 151)

is horrifyingly blunt. Waterloo means nothing more than a richer harvest. In the culminating couplet of the stanza Byron drives his point home. The insistent monosyllabic questioning of the first line:

And is this all the world hath gained by thee, . . . (line 152)

switches the address from Harold to a personification of the battle itself:

Thou first and last of fields! king-making Victory? (line 153)

Not only had Waterloo restored the Bourbon monarchy to the throne of France, and returned Europe to the pre-1789 position, but it had strengthened monarchical power throughout Europe. The 'Crowning Carnage, Waterloo' (line 38) as Byron called it in his quasi-apocalyptic attack on Southey's *The Vision of Judgement*, again invoking Wordsworth's 'Thanksgiving Ode', brought about a return to what he labelled in his journal the 'king-times' (*BLJ* VIII, 26).

Byron continues to question the purpose and results of Waterloo in stanzas 19 and 20. He still acknowledges and condemns Napoleon's tyranny which has caused 'death, depopulation, bondage, fears' (III, 20), but he denies that the victorious restored monarchs are themselves anything other than tyrants. His allusion to Harmodius' assassination attempt on Hippias and Hipparchus makes it clear that Waterloo was not a blow struck for freedom.[68] The implication of stanza 20 is that while one despot has fallen others have taken his place, a pattern that anticipates one of his most striking formulations of the historical dilemma of his time:

> Can tyrants but by tyrants conquered be,
> And Freedom find no champion and no child . . .
> (*Childe Harold's Pilgrimage* IV, 96)[69]

The suffering of the struggle to resist and defeat Napoleon has been in vain because his final defeat has changed nothing. As Byron lamented in his Popean satire on the Congress of Verona *The Age of Bronze*, Waterloo was both 'bloody and most bootless' (line 223).

Byron made his boldest and bluntest expression of his political reaction to Waterloo after he had visited the battlefield in May 1816. He wrote to the Bonapartist Hobhouse: 'The plain at Waterloo is a fine one – but not much after Marathon and Troy – Cheronea – & Platea. – Perhaps there is something of prejudice in this – but I detest the cause and the victors – & the victory – including Blucher and the Bourbons' (*BLJ* V, 76). Byron reuses this technique of distinguishing Waterloo from the battles of the past to reinforce his political point in *Childe Harold's Pilgrimage III*. He writes:

> While Waterloo with Cannae's carnage vies,
> Morat and Marathon twin names shall stand;
> They were true Glory's stainless victories,
> Won by the ambitious heart and hand
> Of a proud, brotherly, and civic band,
> All unbought champions in no princely cause
> Of vice-entail'd Corruption; they had no land
> Doom'd to bewail the blasphemy of laws
> Making kings' rights divine, by some Draconian clause. (III, 64)

In his note to these stanzas, McGann emphasises that Waterloo and Cannae were conflicts of states which sought dominion over each other rather than victories of men fighting for liberty, such as Morat and Marathon.

In Britain in 1816 such a statement was shocking. Even though Byron cunningly shapes his political sentiments in *Childe Harold III*, putting them much less directly than he does in his letters, Sir Walter Scott, for one, detected the underlying politics of the poem. He protested that 'to compare Waterloo to the battle of Cannae, and speak of the blood which flowed on the side of the vanquished as lost in the cause of freedom [was] contrary not only to plain sense and general opinion'[70] but also to the condemnation of Napoleon as 'Gaul's vulture' in the first canto. Yet Scott himself goes some way towards explaining this inconsistency when he astutely comments on Napoleon's redeemed political status:

> Childe Harold saw the scenes which he celebrates, – and does he now compare to the field of Cannae the plain of Waterloo, and mourn over the fall of the tyrant and his military satraps and slaves whose arms built his power, as over the fall of the cause of liberty? We know the ready answer which will be offered by the few who soothe their own prejudices, or seek to carry their own purposes by maintaining this extravagant proposition. They take a distinction: Buonaparte, according to their creed, fell a tyrant in 1814, and revived a deliverer in 1815. A few months' residence in the Isle of Elba had given him time for better thoughts, and had mortified within his mind that gorging ambition . . . [71]

It is, however, precisely because Byron 'shuns to celebrate the victory of Waterloo',[72] to use Scott's phrase, and because of his Republican, anti-legitimist political convictions, that he is able to engage with Napoleon in a way impossible for Wordsworth, Southey and Scott. Their propagandist aims necessitated a crude vilification of Napoleon. Scott's review makes it clear that Byron deliberately frustrated the expectations of his readership in order to make a political statement. One can go further and say that he subverts these expectations as a means of appropriating the subject-matter to his own highly individual myth. More than any other poet, Byron makes Napoleon's Waterloo his own.

Byron's use of Napoleon to figure a characteristically Byronic predicament in stanzas 36–45 has often been remarked on. The passage is a paradigm of the process which McGann has characterized as central to *Childe Harold's Pilgrimage III*, whereby 'the various historical characters in the poem are all used as "figurae" expressing one or another aspect of Byron's central attitudes of mind, quality of character, or circumstances of life'.[73] Byron's shift from his closely focused analysis of Napoleon – 'There sunk the greatest, nor the worst of men' (line 316) – to the more generalized investigation of the 'unquiet things' – 'Conquerors and Kings / Founders of sects and systems, to whom add / Sophists, Bards, Statesmen' (lines 380–2) – may appear to be a move away from the political critique of Waterloo with which he began. His portrayal of Napoleon's 'antithetically mixt' 'spirit' and his representation of him as 'Extreme in all things' (lines 317, 320) recall the 'Byronic heroes' of the Oriental Tales such as Lara:

> In him inexplicably mixt appeared
> Much to be loved and hated, sought and feared: . . .
> (*Lara*, stanza 17, lines 1–2)

Moreover, there is a strong sense of autobiography in these stanzas on Napoleon. As McGann has commented, the 'shift into self-analysis is all but explicit from l. 338'.[74] Byron certainly saw a parallel between his own 'overthrow', as he self-dramatically termed his fall from grace in English society in his 'Epistle to Augusta' (lines 22–3), and Napoleon's overthrow at Waterloo. When he decided to leave England in 1816 he modelled his own exile on Napoleon's, extravagantly commissioning a copy of Napoleon's coach for his journey.[75] This gesture of identification anticipates Byron's later adoption of the initials N. B. (Noel Byron)[76] and his description of himself in *Don Juan* as 'The grand Napoleon of the realms of rhyme' (xi, 55). If there is a Byronic vision of Napoleon, then there is also a Napoleonic Byron.

Yet Byron's public merging of his own history with Napoleon's in *Childe Harold's Pilgrimage III* is a highly polemical, political act. Marilyn Butler has described the heroes of the Oriental Tales as a 'focus for contemporary fantasies' and added that 'not the least element of guilty complicity is that they echo the French cult of Napoleon'.[77] In *Childe Harold's Pilgrimage III* Byron makes a spectacular gesture of this 'guilty complicity'. He assimilates Napoleon within the cult of the Byronic hero, embodying in him the spiritual condition of the entire canto. He thus gives the misanthropy and duality of the Byronic hero a specific historical and political dimension, incorporating it within the poem's anti-legitimate stance. It becomes an expression of the political gloom of the post-Waterloo world, one which powerfully counters the triumphalism of other accounts of Waterloo.

The contemporary response to this merging of the Napoleonic and the Byronic cults emphasizes the political resonances of these stanzas. In their reviews, both Jeffrey and Scott identified the portrait of Napoleon as being at the heart of their criticisms of the canto's politics. Jeffrey describes the passage as 'splendidly written' but adds that 'we trust it is not true'.[78] He strives to demystify Byron's portrait of Napoleon, and particularly to disassociate him from the Byronic cult of gloominess and 'misanthropy', arguing that 'from Macedonia's Madman to the Swede – from Nimrod to Napoleon, the hunters of men have pursued their sport with as much gaiety, and as little remorse, as the hunters of other animals – and have lived as cheerily in their days of action, and as comfortably in their repose, as the followers of better pursuits'.[79] Walter Scott takes issue with Byron's presentation of Napoleon as self-defeated, the victim of his own 'just habitual scorn of men and their thoughts'.[80] Such a view of Napoleon, while incorporating Napoleon within the Byronic cult, denies Britain the credit of the victory at Waterloo. Instead Scott offers an alternative view of Napoleon as a Machiavellian politician.[81] As these responses indicate, Byron's public identification with Napoleon is not merely an exercise in autobiography, but a strikingly radical pose. He transforms the gloominess he had done so much to make fashionable in his earlier works[82] into a political attitude that both incorporates Napoleon and broods over his fall.

Whereas Southey and Wordsworth used Waterloo to bring to a close the revolutionary and Napoleonic periods, with their devastating historical and political complexity, Byron used it to reopen an engagement with the figure of Napoleon that controversially merged the political and the personal. At Waterloo, the Lakers had defined and legitimized their own positions: Southey as the official spokesman for his own country; Wordsworth as a poet whose 'Imagination' had fought with Napoleon throughout his career. Yet Byron, while himself in exile, refuses to exile Napoleon from the Romantic Imagination. In a headnote to his 'Ode (From The French)' in the *Morning Chronicle* he had drawn attention to alternative national perceptions of the battle, commenting that 'The French have their *Poems* and *Odes* on the famous battle of Waterloo as well as ourselves.'[83] In his own account of the battle, Byron counters the patriotic and religiously orthodox interpretation of European affairs with a vision of contemporary history that is itself European. While he uses Napoleon to figure a series of individual and general predicaments, in all these forms Napoleon remains a powerful political symbol who can be used to resist the Southean and Wordsworthian visions of history that cantingly legitimized the myth of the English establishment.

CHAPTER 6

'A proud and full answer':[1] Hazlitt's Napoleonic riposte

> As active partisans, we must take up with the best we can get in the circumstances, and defend it with all our might against a worse cause . . .
>
> 'On the Spirit of Partisanship' (XVII, 40[2])

> He always vindicates Bonaparte not because he is insensible to his enormous crimes, but out of spite to the Tories of this country and the friends of the war of 1792.
>
> Crabb Robinson of William Hazlitt[3]

GIVING 'THE DEVIL HIS DUE'

The radical William Hazlitt, like the conservative Lake poets, saw the Napoleonic contest in Europe as a re-enactment of the Miltonic epic struggle. However, he read both *Paradise Lost* and the war in a Blakean way as a supporter of the 'Devil's party'[4] – a textual re-appropriation that anticipates his more famous political reading of Caliban, itself a response to Coleridge's anti-Jacobinism.[5] In 'On Shakespeare and Milton', one of the *Lectures on the English Poets* first published in 1818, Hazlitt offers an interpretation of Satan as 'the most heroic subject that was ever chosen for a poem' in which he makes him not only represent opposition and defiance of the 'Almighty' but the drive to equality (V, 63). While such a revolutionary reading of *Paradise Lost* reflects eighteenth-century critical trends, and anticipates the 'Satanism' of Shelley and Byron, it must nevertheless have startled a contemporary audience more than likely familiar with Coleridge's demonizing use of it in his lecture on Milton of 1814 and his *Lay Sermon* of 1816 and certainly cognizant of the propagandist association of Satan and Napoleon.[6] Dorothy George, for example, has argued that George Cruikshank's *Boney's meditations on the Island of St Helena – or – The Devil addressing the Sun* (plate 9), in which he represents Napoleon as Satan of Book IV of *Paradise*

9 George Cruikshank, *Boney's meditations on the Island of St. Helena – or – The Devil addressing the Sun* (London, 1815).

Lost, was the 'most famous' caricature on the subject of St Helena.[7] It is while characterizing the particular suitability of *Paradise Lost* for political appropriation and re-appropriation that Hazlitt explicitly acknowledges the analogy that was by this time well established in newspapers, pamphlets, poetry and caricatures:[8]

> What proves the truth of this noble picture in every part, and that the frequent complaint of want of interest in it is the fault of the reader, not of the poet, is that when any interest of a practical kind takes a shape that can be at all turned into this (and there is little doubt that Milton had some such in his eye in writing it), each party converts it to its own purposes, feels the absolute identity of these abstracted and high speculations; and that, in fact, a noted political writer of the present day has exhausted nearly the whole account of Satan in *Paradise Lost* by applying it to a character whom he considered as after the devil, (though I do not know whether he would make even that exception) the greatest enemy of the human race. (v, 66)

In this climactic passage, Hazlitt invites his audience to reread his heroically defiant Satan as Napoleon himself, dismissing the Lakers' analogy of Satan and Napoleon based on the simple formula 'evil be thou my good'. His strategy achieves an empowering interchange of historical and literary authority, seen even more explicitly in the passage from the essay of 1827, 'On Means and Ends', used as the epigraph to my introduction, where Hazlitt redraws the analogy with a similar political aim. Hazlitt's debunking and subversive re-appropriation of *Paradise Lost* – his conversion of it to his 'own purposes' – enables him to eulogize Napoleon and to suggest alternative ways of reading his career to that didactically imposed by the Lakers. By playing devil's advocate, Hazlitt reinvokes the text as a riposte to those who had used the analogy with Satan for simple demonization.

Hazlitt's powerful counter-reading of both *Paradise Lost* and 'the greatest enemy of mankind' neatly illustrates his tenacious determination to give 'a proud and full answer' to the forces of cultural and political conservatism that he felt held sway in the post-Waterloo world. This 'proud and full answer' – a phrase he uses in the Preface to *The Life of Napoleon Buonaparte* (XIII, ix) – he came increasingly to embody in Napoleon. The Miltonic model of politics and writing which he outlines in this lecture, however, provides a useful introduction to his own practices. Hazlitt supports his revolutionary interpretation of *Paradise Lost* in his lecture by representing the republican Milton as a 'political partisan' who embodied his beliefs in his characters; a common idea in the period, as M. H. Abrams has observed, writing that 'Romantic critics were unanimous that, without complication of objectivity and mannerless to veil his image, John Milton, as Coleridge put it, "himself is in every line of *Paradise Lost*".'[9] In 'On Genius and Common Sense' Hazlitt puts this idea succinctly:

Milton has by allusion embodied a great part of his political and personal history in the chief characters and incidents of *Paradise Lost.* He has, no doubt, wonderfully adapted and heightened them, but the elements are the same; you trace the bias and opinions of the man in the creations of the poet. (VIII, 42)

In his lecture 'On Shakespeare and Milton' Hazlitt explores this notion in greater detail. Explaining Milton's decision not to present Satan as 'physically deformed' he writes:

He relied on the justice of his cause, and did not scruple to give the devil his due. Some persons may think that he has carried his liberality too far and injured the cause he professed to espouse by making him [Satan] the chief person in his poem. Considering the nature of his subject, he would be equally in danger of running into this fault, from his faith in religion, and his love of rebellion; and perhaps each of these motives had its full share in determining the choice of his subject. (V, 65)

Milton's 'love of rebellion', Hazlitt suggests, is embodied in the character of Satan; the 'liberality' of his representation of him is perhaps a covert expression of his own liberalism. Hazlitt unites Milton's and Satan's rebellious causes and implies that both are, in fact, just ones. Continuing this argument in the following paragraph, Hazlitt presents the speeches in Hell as an expression of Milton's political beliefs:

There is a decided manly tone in the arguments and sentiments, an eloquent dogmatism, as if each person spoke from thorough conviction; an excellence which Milton probably borrowed from his spirit of partisanship, or else his spirit of partisanship from the natural firmness and vigour of his mind. In this respect Milton resembles Dante, (the only modern writer with whom he had anything in common) and it is remarkable that Dante, as well as Milton, was a political partisan. That approximation to the severity of impassioned prose which has been made an objection to Milton's poetry, and which is chiefly to be met with in these bitter invectives, is one of its great excellences. (V, 65)

Hazlitt concludes his discussion of Satan with the analogy with Napoleon as proof that the poem was written to be interpreted politically – 'there is little doubt that Milton had some such in his eye when writing it'. He implies that like himself, Milton was a true poet, and of Napoleon's party without knowing it.[10]

This Miltonic model of partisanship is an important one for Hazlitt not only as a literary critic, but as a historian and author of *The Life of Napoleon Buonaparte*, the massive four-volume epic to which he dedicated his final years and hoped would be remembered as his 'sterling work' (VIII, 325–6). The implication of his reading of *Paradise Lost* is that his own interpretation of it is an expression of his own 'political and personal history': you trace the bias and opinions of the man in the interpretations of the critic. As we have seen, in his lecture 'On Shakespeare and Milton' Hazlitt is explicit about the fact that contemporary history, just like literature, is not fixed but is 'turned' to endorse the 'purposes' of the writer. This process is at the heart of Hazlitt's epic biography. Robert E. Robinson's exhaustive yet meticulous research into the sources of *The Life* has spectacularly revealed Hazlitt's process of 'turning' history, particularly in the form of documentary source material, to conform with what Robinson terms his 'too-firmly established convictions'.[11] Just as Milton's hero Satan is an expression of his creator's own 'political and personal history', so is Hazlitt's hero Napoleon. In *The Life* you trace the bias and opinions of the man in the creation of the historian.

Indeed, Hazlitt's writing on Napoleon in his biography, his journalism and his essays is unmistakably the 'impassioned prose' and 'eloquent dogmatism' of the 'political partisan'. As is implicit in his polemical defence of his own political method in the essay of 1820 'On the Spirit of Partisanship', Napoleon was the best Hazlitt could get in the circumstances, and he would defend him with all his rhetorical might against the worse cause of 'Legitimacy' (XVII, 40). In this essay Hazlitt proffers the Napoleonic cause as a prime example of the need for 'partisanship'. He berates those whose self-righteous scrupulousness – 'They will not, "to do a great right, do a little wrong"' (XVII, 36) – prevented them from supporting Napoleon:

> They will not take their ready stand by the side of him who was 'the very arm and burgonet of man', and like a demi-Atlas, could alone prop a declining world, because for themselves they have some objection to the individual instrument . . . (XVII, 37)

Hazlitt makes it plain in this essay that he was aware that his own championing of Napoleon – his use of him as an instrument to prop up the cause of the Revolution – involved some sacrifice or compromise of his own principles. Yet he believed such a minor sacrifice was necessary when 'everything . . . dear and valuable to man' was felt to be at stake; 'when there is but the one dreadful alternative of entire loss, or final recovery of truth and freedom, it is no time to stand upon trifles or moot-points; the great object is to be secured first, and at all hazards' (XVII, 37). To use another of Hazlitt's definitions of 'partisanship' from this crucial but strangely neglected essay, Napoleon was a figure for whom he actively developed 'a passionate attachment founded on an abstract idea' (XVII, 34) – namely opposition to the arbitrary power of 'Legitimacy'. Though a devastating critic of idolatry, he conspicuously fostered Napoleon as 'the God of mine idolatry' in both his writing and his conversation (VII, 10). There was certainly something deeply personal in his attachment to Napoleon, as the history of the 'little bust' of Bonaparte in *Liber Amoris* suggests,[12] but this 'idolatry' was no simple exercise in hero-worship. It was rather a highly public and polemical gesture; one which, as Stanley Jones has observed, 'troubled certain among his friends'.[13] Hazlitt was keenly aware of the ideological impact of the written word, as his own remarks on Shakespeare and Burke reveal.[14] He comments near the conclusion of his lecture on *Coriolanus* that 'We may depend upon it that what men delight to read in books, they will put in practice in reality' (IV, 216), and he realized that if men were to delight in his representation of Napoleon, and particularly in what he made Napoleon represent, he needed to make him appeal to the 'imagination', a faculty which, as he wrote in his 'Letter to William Gifford', 'delights in power, in strong excitement, as well as in truth, in good, in right' (IX, 37). To use the categories of his lecture on *Coriolanus*, Hazlitt sought to combine in Napoleon an appeal to the 'imagination' with one to the 'understanding' (IV, 214). He uses Napoleon to represent 'abstract right', but he dresses him out in 'pride, pomp, and circumstance'. In Napoleon, as in Satan, Hazlitt found a figure who could be converted into a hero, a figure of greatness, and made to represent not only 'power' and 'poetry', but also 'the cause of the people' – Hazlitt's own ideological cause or 'purpose'.[15]

A 'PROPER THEATRICAL HATRED'

John Kinnaird has described Hazlitt as 'the historian's classic example of the English Jacobin turned Buonapartist'.[16] Brought up in the Dissenting tradition – his father was a Unitarian minister – Hazlitt passionately committed himself to the cause of the French Revolution and was fond of uniting its history with his own. In 'On the Feeling of Immortality in Youth', for example, he writes:

For my part, I set out in life with the French Revolution, and that event had considerable influence on my early feelings, as on those of others. It was the dawn of a new era, a new impulse had been given to men's minds, and the sun of Liberty rose upon the Sun of Life in the same day, and both were proud to run their race together. Little did I dream, while my first hopes and wishes went hand in hand with those of the human race, that long before my eyes should close, that dawn would be overcast, and set once more in the night of despotism – 'total eclipse!' Happy that I did not. I felt for years, and during the best part of my existence, *heart-whole* in that cause, and triumphed in the triumphs over the enemies of man. At that time, while the fairest aspirations of the human mind seemed about to be realized, ere the image of man was defaced and his breast mangled in scorn, philosophy took a higher, poetry could afford a deeper range. (XVII, 196–7)

Noticeably here, unlike many of his contemporaries, including Coleridge and Wordsworth – whose 'Immortality Ode' is so obviously invoked and politicized in this passage – Hazlitt does not distinguish between the Revolutionary and Napoleonic wars. Rather he sees Napoleon as maintaining the principles of the Revolution, triumphing 'over the enemies of man', another neat rhetorical inversion in which Hazlitt takes the popular term for Napoleon, much favoured by Coleridge, and reapplies it to the Allied powers. It was Napoleon's fall at Waterloo, a battle which Hazlitt describes in *The Life* as 'the greatest and most fatal in its consequences that was ever fought in the world' (XV, 269), that signalled the 'total eclipse' of Hazlitt's political hopes. His most recent biographer, Stanley Jones, picks up Hazlitt's own Wordsworthian language and imagery and applies it to Hazlitt's later career, writing that that 'dawn was far in the past; it had merged in the long day of the Napoleonic epic, and now [the time of Waterloo] he was forced to acknowledge that the sun of Austerlitz that had illumined the day had finally set'.[17] The battle of Waterloo certainly had a devastating effect on Hazlitt, particularly after the renewed hopes of the return from Elba. Talfourd describes Hazlitt's disappointment:

He was staggering under the blow of Waterloo. The reappearance of his imperial idol on the coast of France and his triumphal march to Paris, like a fairy vision, had excited his admiration and sympathy to the utmost pitch; and though in many respects sturdily English in feeling, he could scarcely forgive the valour of the conquerors; and bitterly resented the captivity of the Emperor in St. Helena, which followed it, as if he had sustained a personal wrong.[18]

Haydon's description confirms this picture of desolation when he writes that 'it is not to be believed how the destruction of Napoleon affected him; he seemed prostrated in mind and body, he walked about unwashed, unshaven, hardly sober by day, and always intoxicated by night, literally, without exaggeration, for weeks'.[19] Hazlitt's support of Napoleon had been as long-standing as his pre-Waterloo journalism – most importantly the 'Illustrations of Vetus' and 'Whether the Friends of Freedom . . .' (VII, 39–72, 79–85) – and his reaction to the battle make clear. But Waterloo and the restoration of the Bourbons enacted his brother-in-law Stoddard's reactionary rallying-cry 'Europe as it was in 1788' against which he had railed with increasing vigour in his articles of 1814.[20] It hardened his conception of himself as a 'political partisan'. As he wrote in 'A Farewell to Essay-Writing', 'my conviction of right was only established by the triumph of the wrong' (XVII, 316). Moreover, Jones sees this failure of Hazlitt's public hopes coinciding with a period in which his private hopes also failed with the collapse of an unknown love affair. In 1815 Hazlitt 'lamented the loss of general liberty in the same way as he bewailed the loss of his personal happiness'.[21]

But Waterloo, as Kinnaird has pointed out, marks the beginning of the period in which Hazlitt 'accomplish[es] his best and most distinctive work'.[22] To quote again from 'On the Feeling of Immortality in Youth', Hazlitt writes of the period after Waterloo that '"That time is past with all its giddy raptures". Since the future was barred to my progress, I have turned for consolation to the past, gathering up the fragments of my early recollections, and putting them in a form that might live' (XVII, 197). Here the world of memory and of creation out of memory replaces that of action, an aspect of Hazlitt's development as a writer that Stanley Jones has stressed in his biography.[23] But Hazlitt's practice is not always as elegiacally nostalgic as this passage suggests, or as Jones presents it. In 'A Farewell to Essay-Writing', Hazlitt again describes his commitment to the French Revolution and describes the effect of Napoleon's fall at Waterloo:

> One great ground of confidence and support has, indeed, been struck from under my feet; but I have made it up to myself by proportionable pertinacity of opinion. The success of the great cause, to which I had vowed myself, was to me more than all the world: I had strength in its strength, a resource which I knew not of, till it failed me the second time. (XVII, 316)

In this essay of 1828, otherwise one of his most nostalgic pieces, Hazlitt retrospectively sees himself as having compensated for Napoleon's second fall at Waterloo with 'proportionable pertinacity of opinion'. His essays, to which he is bidding farewell, and his *Life*, the massive work on which he was engaged at this time, were the expressions of this pertinacity; the battlefields where Hazlitt continued the Napoleonic struggle against the arbitrary rule of 'Legitimacy' even after Napoleon had fallen at Waterloo.

In *The Plain Speaker* Hazlitt writes that 'One thing exists and has a value set upon it only as it has some foil in some other; learning is set off by ignorance, liberty by slavery, refinement by barbarism' (XII, 332). In Hazlitt's work, Napoleon exists and has a value set upon him as a foil to the absolute rule of legitimate monarchy. Crabb Robinson testifies to this in a diary entry of 1815, which, as Jones notes, is a 'valuable statement, evidently scrupulously exact, of Hazlitt's declared position at this time':[24]

> Hazlitt and myself once felt alike on politics, and now our hopes and fears are directly opposed. Hazlitt retains all his hatred of kings and bad governments, and believing them to be incorrigible, he from a principle of revenge rejoices that they are punished. I am indignant to find the man that might have been their punisher become their imitator, and even surpassing them all in guilt. Hazlitt is angry with the friends of liberty for weakening their strength by going with the common foe against Buonaparte, by which the old governors are so much assisted, even in their attempts against the general liberty. I am not shaken by this consequence, because I think, after all, that should the governments succeed in the worst projects imputed to them, still the evil would be infinitely less than what would arise from Buonaparte's success. I say destroy him at any rate and take the consequences. Hazlitt says: 'Let the enemy of old tyrannical governments triumph, I am glad, and I do not much care how the new government turns out'. Not that either I am indifferent to the government which the successful kings of Europe may establish or that Hazlitt has lost all love for liberty. But his hatred, and my fears, predominate and absorb all weaker impressions. This I believe to be the great difference between us.[25]

Crabb Robinson's assertion that Hazlitt's principal political motivation was a 'hatred of kings and bad governments' rather than an admiration for Napoleon, is borne out in Hazlitt's own writing. In the opening of the Preface to his *Political Essays*, published in 1819, Hazlitt makes his most explicit declaration of his political position, stating that 'I am no politician, and still less can I be said to be a party-man: but I have a hatred of tyranny, and a contempt for its tools; and this feeling I have expressed as often and as strongly as I could' (VII, 7). For Hazlitt 'tyranny' was exemplified in the slogan 'the right divine of kings to govern wrong' (VII, 81). The vital 'question', he continues in the Preface, is 'between . . . natural liberty and hereditary slavery, whether men are born free or slaves, whether kings are the servants of the people, or the people the property of kings . . .' (VII, 7). This hatred of legitimate monarchy – 'To be a true Jacobin, a man must be a good hater' Hazlitt writes elsewhere (VII, 151) – is at the centre of Hazlitt's political writing, and is something which he frequently reasserts, making it the basis of his argument in the Preface to *The Life*.[26] He even uses it with a degree of self-mocking irony to define himself in 'On People with One Idea', reminiscing that 'I myself at one period took a pretty strong turn to inveighing against the Doctrine of Divine Right, and am not yet cured of my prejudice on that subject' (VIII, 62).

Moreover, after Waterloo Hazlitt felt himself to be living in a culture that remorselessly reinforced this pre-revolutionary doctrine both directly and indirectly. He writes in the Preface to the *Political Essays* that 'kings at present tell us with their swords, and poets with their pens' that the people 'have no rights, that they are their property, their goods, their chattels, the live-stock on the estate of Legitimacy' (VII, 10). In his polemic, Hazlitt fights not only against the restored monarchs but against the coercive power of the reigning political and cultural conservatism exemplified for him by the 'righteous apostacy' of the Lake poets.[27] The Lakers, of course, had had a powerful political and aesthetic influence on Hazlitt in his youth, as his essay 'My First Acquaintance with Poets' memorably recalls. But their writing towards the end and after the war – Wordsworth's *The Excursion* and 'Thanksgiving Ode', Southey's *Carmen Seculare* and *Lay of the Laureate* and Coleridge's *Lay Sermon* – looked to Hazlitt like proof of their falling in with arbitrary power. His comment in 'A Modern Tory Delineated' that 'a Tory . . . reads no poetry but birthday Odes and verses in celebration of the battle of Waterloo' (XIX, 175) reveals his opinion of the political purpose of the recent compositions by Southey and Wordsworth that I examined in the previous chapter. He wrote of Coleridge's 'daily prose' in 1816 that it was 'dedicated to the support of all that courtiers think should be supported'.[28] His critique of these writings as part of the coercive power of conservatism is well illustrated by the vitriolic attack with which he ends the first part of his 'Observations on Mr. Wordsworth's Poem *The Excursion*', first published in the *Examiner* and republished in the *Round Table*. Again Hazlitt laments the defeat of the Revolution:

> The dawn of that day was suddenly overcast; the season of hope is past; it is fled with other dreams of our youth, which we cannot recal [*sic*], but has left behind its traces, which are not to be effaced by Birth-day and Thanks-giving odes, or the chanting of *Te Deums* in all the churches in Christendom. To these hopes eternal regrets are due; to those who maliciously and willfully blasted them, in the fear that they might be accomplished, we feel no less than we owe – hatred and scorn as lasting! (IV, 120)

Much of the power of this passage is derived from Hazlitt's appropriation of Wordsworth's 'Intimations Ode' from which he has already quoted, and his politicization of it as a revolutionary text which registers the 'glad dawn of the day star of liberty'. Hazlitt constructs the Wordsworth canon as a history of the French Revolution – one which begins with the levelling muse of the early poetry and ends with the apostasy and cultural conservatism of the 'Thanksgiving Ode'. Hazlitt's individual attacks on the Lakers are numerous, but he frequently takes on all three together. Indeed, in an article for *The Examiner* of September 1816 in which Hazlitt's main target is Ferdinand of Spain, he added Stoddard to their ranks and so, like Cavanagh, 'played four capital players together, and beat them':

> Ferdinand . . . is an honest King. He is a tyrant both by profession and practice. He has but one idea in his head, like the Editor of the Times, that a king can do no wrong, and he acts up to it, as the Doctor raves up to it, or as Mr Coleridge cants up to it, or as Mr Southey rhymes up to it, or as Mr Wordsworth muses up to it. (XIX, 164)

In his writing Hazlitt strove to counter this raving, canting, rhyming, musing conservatism. Napoleon, as the object of so much of the Lakers' abuse, offered a powerfully symbolic figure in which Hazlitt could controversially embody his hatred of legitimacy and his political and cultural heterodoxy. He writes in *The Life* that Napoleon 'was the only resource of those who had . . . the proper theatrical hatred of the Bourbons' (XV, 211) and his use of the Burkean term 'theatrical' is indicative. Like his political counter-readings of *Paradise Lost* and *The Tempest* as revolutionary texts, Hazlitt could employ Napoleon to act out the struggle between 'liberty' and 'legitimacy' on a world-wide stage. While *The Life* is certainly an epic text – as Barton R. Friedman has shown it importantly invokes the *Iliad*[29] and also alludes to the *Odyssey* (XV, 229–30) – it is also dramatic and frequently Shakespearean. I shall return to this in greater detail with particular reference to *Coriolanus* – both the play and Hazlitt's lecture on it – but an example will illustrate my point here. In one of the most dazzling and poetic – words I use deliberately and will examine further – passages of *The Life*, Hazlitt describes Napoleon's return to France during the Hundred Days:

> It was the greatest instance ever known of the power exerted by one man over opinion; nor is this difficult to be accounted for, since it was one man armed with the rights of a people against those who had robbed them of all natural rights and gave them leave to breath their charter. Therefore Buonaparte seemed

from his first landing to bestride the country like a Colossus, for in him rose up once more the prostrate might and majesty of man . . . (XV, 230)

Hazlitt's imaging of Napoleon as a 'Colossus' – drawn from *Julius Caesar* (I. ii. 136–7) – seems initially to give suitably vast proportions to the republican hero, to make him a figure of Hazlitt's 'theatrical hatred'. Yet the allusion is deeply ambivalent, and highlights the ambivalence of *The Life* as a whole. Within the play the phrase is used by Cassius as part of his critique of the Caesar as someone who is shifting from republican to imperial status:

> Why, man, he doth bestride the narrow world
> Like a Colossus, as we petty men
> Walk under his huge legs, and peep about
> To find ourselves dishonourable graves. (I. ii. 136–39)

Hazlitt's Shakespearean representation of Napoleon as one who towers above men while certainly making him more grandiose, at the very least calls into question his representation of figuring him as a representative of the 'rights of the people'. The paradoxical and twisted logic of Hazlitt's representation of Napoleon which this passage illustrates is at the very heart of his defence of him.

'THE CHILD AND CHAMPION OF THE REVOLUTION'

Hazlitt uses Napoleon to give 'a proud and full answer' to the 'vital question' of 'whether mankind were, from the beginning to the end of time, born slaves or not?' in two main ways. The first of these is to represent him as an individual of genius who has taken the career open to talent, an attractive model for Hazlitt in terms of class and ambition. Hazlitt makes Napoleon symbolize the potentiality of all mankind and so belie the doctrine of 'divine right'.[30] Hazlitt writes in his Preface to *The Life* that his support of Napoleon was influenced by 'the wish to see personal merit prevail over external rank and circumstances' (XIII, x). He concludes, 'I felt pride (not envy) to think there was one reputation in modern times equal to the ancients, and at seeing one man greater than the throne he sat upon' (XIII, x). Napoleon, he argues, realized his position through his own 'merits'. He was 'nothing, he could be nothing but what he owed to himself' (XIII, ix). This point Hazlitt makes throughout *The Life*, for example, describing Bonaparte as having 'himself raised the platform of personal elevation on which he stood' (XIV, 240). Hazlitt makes Napoleon a symbol for all mankind; as Kinnaird has neatly put it, he shows 'to men everywhere that the source of all power, in politics as in art and culture, lies nowhere but in themselves'.[31] Hazlitt illustrates this point in his description of the Treaty of Tilsit in *The Life*:

> If Buonaparte here rose to a height imperial, and thought it no robbery to be equal with Kings and Caesars, neither should he: he rose to that height from the level of the people, and thus proved that there was no natural inferiority in the one case, no natural superiority in the other. He confounded and annulled the distinction between the two classes of men, which it has been wished to keep sacred, making unceasing war upon and arrogating to himself with a high hand their personal claims and prerogatives. It was a satisfactory and noble demonstration that greatness was not the inheritance of a privileged few, and that kings and conquerors sprung from the earth, instead of being let down from Heaven to it. (XIV, 302)

Like Satan's 'endeavouring to be equal with the highest' (V, 66), Napoleon's equality with 'Kings and Caesars' does not set him above 'the people', but rather shows to them that they too can be equal with kings and Caesars.

Indeed, as a symbol of human potentiality Hazlitt makes Napoleon as powerful as the example of 'Art' itself, strikingly evoked in the passage in *The Life* on Napoleon's art collection at the Louvre. Hazlitt's visit to the Louvre in 1802 confirmed his faith in the Revolution and in *The Life* he uses it to symbolize the freeing of art from the clutches of the *ancien régime*:

> These works, instead of being taken from their respective countries, were given to the world, and to the mind and heart of man from whence they sprung . . . Art, no longer a bondswoman, was seated on a throne, and her sons were kings. The spirit of man walked erect, and found its true level in the triumph of real over factitious claims. (XIII, 212)

The Louvre, Hazlitt concludes, was a 'a great moral lesson' (XIII, 213) – a phrase that again inverts an earlier use of it by Wellington for the dispersal of the art treasures[32] – because it 'disallowed all distinction that could insult or interfere with those of truth, nature and genius' (XIII, 213). Throughout his writing Hazlitt puts Napoleon to the same use, making him 'a great moral lesson' because 'With him, the state of man rose exalted too' (VII, 12) and 'in him rose up once more the prostrate might and majesty of man' (XV, 229). He makes Napoleon stand as a symbol of democratic meritocracy and, as a political and aesthetic hero, of an art open to the people.

Indeed, when Hazlitt is forced to concede a point of criticism about Napoleon, he uses this essential distinction between Napoleon and the monarchy of the *ancien régime* as a means of reasserting his support. In the Preface to the *Political Essays*, for example, he writes that:

If he was ambitious, his greatness was not founded on the unconditional, avowed surrender of the rights of human nature. But with him, the state of man rose exalted too. If he was arbitrary and a tyrant . . . he was not, nor could he not become, a tyrant by divine right. Tyranny in him was not sacred: it was not eternal: it was not instinctively bound in league of amity with other tyrannies: it was not sanctioned by all the laws of religion and morality. There was an end of it with the individual . . . (VII, 12)[33]

It is because of this, as Hazlitt argues in the Preface to *The Life*, that Napoleon's rule in France still maintains the principle of the French Revolution:

Whatever fault might be found with them, they did not proceed upon the avowed principle, that 'millions were made for one', but one for millions; and as long as this distinction was kept in view, liberty was saved, and the Revolution was untouched.(XIII, x)

In part, then, this is what Hazlitt means in his Preface to *The Life* when he writes that 'what chiefly attracted me to him, was his being, as he had been long ago designated, "the child and champion of the revolution"' (XIII, ix). Again Hazlitt takes up a term of abuse, this time from Pitt and Coleridge, and transforms it into one of approbation. By depicting Napoleon as a figure who has risen through his own merit, Hazlitt uses him to embody the revolutionary principle. But it is by presenting Napoleon as the 'champion of the revolution' that Hazlitt gives the second of his 'proud answers' to the 'vital question'. In the Preface to *The Life* he writes that 'as long as he was *a thorn in the side of kings* and kept them at bay, his cause rose out of the ruins and defeat of their pride and hopes of revenge' (XIII, ix). Like Byron, Hazlitt triumphed in Napoleon's triumphs over the enemies of man. He writes in the Preface to the *Political Essays* that 'If Buonaparte was a conqueror, he conquered the grand conspiracy of kings against the abstract right of the human race to be free; and I, as a man, could not be indifferent which side to take' (VII, 12). In *The Life* Hazlitt aligns the Napoleonic war with what we have seen to be his main political principle, arguing that 'the war was never a national quarrel, but a struggle between the different classes and races of men, whether one should be considered as an inferior order of beings to the other . . . the real gist of the argument is . . . between the natural rights and the hereditary and lasting bondage of the people' (XIV, 182). Hazlitt conceives Napoleon as 'the assertor of the people's rights against those who say they have no rights' (VII, 10). With the string of battles 'of Marengo, of Austerlitz, of Jena, of Wagram, of Friedland, and of Borodino' he 'triumphed in the triumphs over the enemies of man' (XVII, 197) in which Napoleon 'put down the rabble of kings' (VIII, 196) – yet another neat rhetorical inversion.

'POETRY', 'POWER' AND THE 'IMAGINATION'

Yet the underlying paradox of Hazlitt's championing of Napoleon is illustrated by the Preface to the *Political Essays* (1819). Initially Hazlitt presents Napoleon as a figure who stoically resists the forces of legitimacy:

> He withstood the inroads of this new Jaggernaut, this foul Blatant Beast, as it strode forward to its prey over the bodies and minds of a whole people, and put a ring in its nostrils, breathing flame and blood, and led it in triumph, and played with its crowns and sceptres, and wore them in its stead, and tamed its crested pride, and made it a laughing-stock and a mockery to the nations. He, one man, did this, and as long as he did this, (how, or for what end, is nothing to the magnitude of this mighty question) he saved the human race from the last ignominy, and that foul stain that has so long been intended, and was at last, in an evil hour and by evil hands, inflicted on it. (VII, 10)

In his representation of the arbitrary power of legitimacy here Hazlitt draws upon the language and imagery he had used in a number of earlier pieces, particularly the connected critiques of 'power', 'poetry' and 'imagination', in his essay 'The Times Newspaper: On the Connection between Tyrants and Toad-Eaters' and his lecture on *Coriolanus*, both of 1817. In the first of these two pieces of bitter invective, Hazlitt had satirically illustrated the way in which man's innate 'love of power' – something he had explored in the two essays of 1815, 'On the Love of Life' and 'On Mind and Motive' – makes most men slaves rather than tyrants because they satisfy it vicariously through 'idolatry'. 'Arbitrary power' holds such sway, he argues, because it appeals to 'the grossness of the imagination which is seduced by outward appearances from the pursuit of real ultimate good' (VII, 145–6):

> Power is the grim idol that the world adore [*sic*]; that arms itself with destruction, and reigns by terror in the coward heart of man; that dazzles the senses, haunts the imagination, confounds the understanding, and tames the will, by the vastness of its pretensions, and the very hopelessness of resistance to them. (VII, 149)

It is from a passage in this essay that Hazlitt draws much of the imagery he uses in the Preface:

> Power . . . pursues its steady way, its undeviating, everlasting course, 'unslaked of motion', like that foul Indian idol, the Jaggernaut, and crushes poor upstart poets, patriots, and philosophers (the beings of an hour) and the successive never-ending generations of fools and knaves, beneath its feet; and mankind bow their willing necks to the yoke, and eagerly consign their children and their children's children to be torn in pieces by its scythe, or trampled to death by the gay, gaudy, painted, blood-stained wheels of the grim idol of power! (VII, 147)

Similarly, in his use of 'crowns' and 'crested pride' in the Preface Hazlitt recalls the lecture on *Coriolanus.* In this lecture he famously argued that 'The language of poetry naturally falls in with the language of power' (IV, 214). He cited as an example the notorious line from the 'Thanksgiving Ode', 'Carnage is its daughter' (IV, 214), implicating Wordsworth, as a representative of the Lakers, in the reinforcement of the prevailing reactionary ideology. The 'cause of the people', Hazlitt argues in this lecture, is 'little calculated as a subject for poetry' because poetry, which appeals to the 'aristocratical' 'imagination', is an anti-levelling force that both expresses and reinforces the hold of arbitrary power (IV, 214). It is in his description of 'poetry' that Hazlitt links it with the images he reuses in the Preface, writing that 'Poetry . . . presents a dazzling appearance. It shows its head turretted, *crowned* and *crested*' (IV, 214; my italics).

In the Preface, then, drawing on his earlier writing, Hazlitt represents legitimacy as a sublimely powerful force analogous to, and reinforced by, poetry in its appeal to the imagination. Initially, Hazlitt uses Napoleon to show up the forms and trappings of legitimacy, to make the sublime appeal of monarchy ridiculous: 'He . . . makes a mock of this Doctrine . . . He . . . made it a laughing stock and a mockery to the nations' (VII, 10). Yet Hazlitt's representation of Napoleon as the 'tamer' of the Blatant Beast suggests that he also conceives Napoleon in another role, that of the romance hero, Calidor, of Spenser's *Faerie Queene* (V, XII), who muzzled the Blatant Beast and drew him with a chain to Fairy-land. The *Faerie Queene* itself provides the verb 'taming' (V, XII, 38). By portraying Napoleon in this guise, Hazlitt attempts to satisfy the necessity, which David Bromwich has identified, of countering Burke by finding an 'intensely vivid "example"' with which to present his cause. Bromwich argues that 'To overthrow the Queen [Marie Antoinette] in the minds of his readers as well as in fact, some hero or heroine from romance would have to be fitted to the cause of the people themselves'.[34] Though Bromwich does not extend his analysis to offer Napoleon as this 'intensely vivid "example"', he was an obvious candidate who would have satisfied the need for the association of an essentially unpoetic popular cause with a hero who could captivate the minds of his readers. Napoleon can thus be represented as the 'saviour' of the cause of the French Revolution and so as the 'saviour' of the human race. For this Hazlitt makes him 'the God of my idolatry' (VII, 10).

But even in this seemingly straightforward passage Hazlitt's representation of Napoleon is ambiguous, even paradoxical. The force of his assertion of Napoleon depends upon his individuality and uniqueness: 'He who did this for me, and for the rest of the world, and who alone could do it, was Buonaparte . . . He, one man, did this' (VII, 10–11). In this stress on Napoleon's individuality, Hazlitt seeks to appeal to the imagination. As he writes in *The Life*, 'the imagination can only be appealed to by individual objects and personal interests' (XIV, 274). But in so doing Hazlitt's representation of Napoleon inevitably falls in with the language of power and of poetry. As he wrote in 'On the Connection . . .', 'Man is naturally a worshipper of idols and a lover of kings. It is the excess of individual power, that strikes and gains over his imagination' (VII, 149). Hazlitt's own idolatry of Napoleon is heavily implicated in his critique of power and poetry. The stress on Napoleon as 'one man' echoes his insistence in the lecture on *Coriolanus* on 'a single man':

> There is nothing heroical in a multitude of rogues not wishing to be starved, or complaining that they are like to be so: *but when a single man comes forward* to brave their cries and to make them submit to the last indignities, from mere pride and self-will, our admiration of his prowess is immediately converted into contempt for their pusillanimity. (IV, 215; my italics)

This perilous intertwining of Hazlitt's mythologization of Napoleon and his critique of power is even more complex. Hazlitt's phrasing, and his use of 'alone', 'did this', 'do it', echo the lines in *Coriolanus* that he had singled out to recall Kemble's playing of the role:

> Like an eagle in a dove-cote, I
> Flutter'd your Volscians in Corioli,
> Alone I did it . . .[35]

Moreover, Hazlitt also quoted this passage when writing of the prose style of Edmund Burke, a figure who, as John Whale has shown, as a praiseworthy prose stylist but an apostate from the revolutionary cause prompted a conflict for Hazlitt between aesthetic and political power.[36] Hazlitt wrote that 'Burke's style was forked and playful as the lightning, crested like the serpent. He delivered plain things on plain ground; but when he rose, there was no end of his flights and circumgyrations – and in the very Letter [*Letter to a Noble Lord*], "he, like an eagle in a dove-cot, fluttered *his* Volscians" (the Duke of Bedford and the Earl of Lauderdale) in Corioli' (XII, 228). So while Hazlitt presents Napoleon as a figure who withstands the inroads of power, to do so he appropriates the Shakespearean language of poetry and of power that is equally applicable to Burke's prose style. Napoleon is at once a symbol of opposition to power and its embodiment.

As Hazlitt develops his argument in the Preface, his representation of Napoleon becomes increasingly active:

> He put his foot upon the neck of kings, who would have put their yoke upon the necks of the people: he scattered before him with fiery execution, millions of hired slaves, who came at the bidding of their masters to deny the right of others to be free. (VII, 11)

Hazlitt's imagery here is of course biblical,[37] but once again he is re-appropriating for Napoleon the language and imagery that he had used for legitimacy in the essay and lecture of 1817. But as Hazlitt reapplies this language to Napoleon, Napoleon also now begins to duplicate the activities of the *ancien régime* monarchs. The construction of the sentence parallels Napoleon with the monarchs – 'He put upon the neck of . . . who would have put their yoke upon the necks of . . .'. Napoleon 'scattered before him' just as the monarchs had 'shattered hopes'. He had tamed the monster that was 'breathing flame', but now he himself scatters those before him with 'fiery execution'. This rhetorical strategy of inversion is again biblical, but it involves a significant change in Hazlitt's representation of Napoleon. Having earlier been conceived of as a saviour, a romance hero and the tamer of the sublime force of the Blatant Beast, Napoleon now himself becomes the creator of such a sublime force in making France a terror:

> The monument of greatness and glory he erected, was raised on the ground forfeited again and again to humanity – it reared its majestic front on the ruins of the shattered hopes and broken faith of the common enemies of mankind. If he could not secure the freedom, peace, and happiness of his country, he made her a terror to those who by sowing civil discontent and exciting foreign wars, would not let her enjoy those blessings. (VII, 11)

Again the ambiguous presentation of Napoleon is suggested by the 'majestic front' of his creation. As in the *Faerie Queene* the Blatant Beast would seem to have 'broke his yron chain, / And got into the world of liberty again' but has now taken on the shape of Napoleon. Napoleon, once the romance hero, has now become the maker of the monster. The grim idol of power is superseded by another idol of power, Napoleon Bonaparte, 'the God of my idolatry' (vii, 10).

Of course, it would be possible to argue that Hazlitt's political defence of Napoleon is simply a method of licensing or legitimizing his own 'idolatry' of Napoleon, and so of exempting himself from the critique of hero-worship and political fantasy that he carries out so devastatingly in 'The Times Newspaper: On the Connection between Toad-Eaters and Tyrants' and 'Coriolanus'. Hazlitt could be seen to be 'aggrandizing [his] own vain glory at second hand' (xix, 255–6) as he puts it in 'On the Spirit of Monarchy', without needing to worry about the political implications of such a self-projecting psychological practice. Yet given Hazlitt's self-knowledge, the process being enacted in the Preface is surely a more complicated one. What the underlying ambiguities in his representation of Napoleon suggest is that while Hazlitt seized upon him as a figure who could be made to embody his hatred of legitimacy, Hazlitt was aware that writing as a 'political partisan' he needed to satisfy the idolization of power and the 'logic of the imagination and the passions' that he repeatedly argued were inherent in the human mind. He fought to convert Napoleon into a suitable object for popular idolatry, an object that by its very nature was ambiguous, like Satan in *Paradise Lost.* In his 'impassioned prose' he seeks to make him into an 'idol that the world adore . . . that dazzles the senses, haunts the imagination' (vii, 149), but that still represents an 'abstract idea' (xvii, 34). Hazlitt turns Napoleon into a Coriolanus figure, with all the imaginative appeal of power, but who still represents the 'cause of the people'.

As the analogies with Satan suggest, Hazlitt frequently presents Napoleon's career in heroic terms. He writes in *The Life* that it 'was the admiration inspired by the person and the enterprise that carried him through, and made all sanguine, anxious, full of interest for him as for the hero of some lofty poem or high-wrought romance' (xv, 230). Indeed, as Kinnaird writes, 'The *Life* is more "poetry" than "history"; it is less a biography than a hero-epic in prose.'[38] Yet Napoleon's 'heroic' status in *The Life* is complex and ambivalent; he is no mere defender of the principles of the Revolution. Rather, Hazlitt strives to make him a compelling figure – like Satan, 'the most heroic subject that was ever chosen for a poem' (v, 63) – by making him 'sublime'; a word he uses for both Napoleon and Satan (v, 63; xvii, 220–1; xv, 230).

The sublimity of Hazlitt's conception of these two heroes is clear in the analogy made in 'On Means and Ends' (xvii, 221). In terms of the 'imagination' they are 'stupendous'; in terms of reality 'fearful and imposing' (xvii, 221). In the language of Burke, they astonish and terrify. Hazlitt's sublime conception of Napoleon is perhaps best illustrated by the use he makes of what had become the principal paradigm of the sublime in *Paradise Lost*, a passage referred to by Blake and Keats[39] and which Wordsworth had drawn on for his Satanic representation of Napoleon in *The Convention of Cintra*. In section iv of *A Philosophical Enquiry into the Origin of our Ideas of the Sublime and Beautiful*, Edmund Burke had written:

We do not anywhere meet a more sublime description than this justly celebrated one of Milton, wherein he gives the portrait of Satan with a dignity suitable to the subject.

He above the rest
In shape and gesture proudly eminent
Stood like a tower; his form had yet not lost
All her original brightness, nor appeared
Less than archangel ruin'd, and th' excess
Of glory obscured: as when the sun new ris'n
Looks through the horizontal misty air
Shorn of his beams; or from behind the moon
In dim eclipse disastrous twilight sheds
On half the nation; and with fear of change
Perplexes monarchs.

Here is a very noble picture; and in what does this poetical picture consist? in images of a tower, an archangel, the sun rising through mists, or in an eclipse, the ruin of monarchs, and the revolutions of kingdoms.[40]

That Hazlitt's conception of both Satan and Napoleon seeks to exploit this Burkean notion of the sublime is suggested by his use of the phrase 'noble picture'. Hazlitt begins his analogy of Satan and Napoleon: 'What proves the truth of this *noble picture*' (v, 66; my italics). In his descriptions of Satan and Napoleon Hazlitt draws heavily upon 'images of a tower'. Satan 'stood like a tower' (v, 63), Napoleon has a 'towering spirit' (xiii, 20) and 'his majestic stature towered above thrones and monuments of renown' (xii, 166). Hazlitt discusses the use of this tower imagery in the first of the *Lectures on the English Poets*, 'On Poetry in General':

We compare a man of gigantic stature to a tower; not that he is anything like so large, but because the excess of his size beyond what we are accustomed to expect, or the usual size of things of the same class, produces by contrast a greater feeling of magnitude and ponderous strength than another object of ten times the same dimensions. The intensity of the feeling makes up for the disproportion on the objects. Things are equal to the imagination, which have the power of affecting the mind with an equal degree of terror, admiration, delight or love. (v, 4)

Hazlitt sees Milton using such imagery to evoke the sublimity of Satan in *Paradise Lost*, again stressing the 'gigantic' stature, which, he writes, 'is illustrated with the most striking and appropriate images: so that we see it always before us, gigantic, irregular, portentous, uneasy, and disturbed – but dazzling in its faded splendour, the clouded ruins of a god' (v, 64).

Hazlitt, by his own confession, conceived *The Life* as a work that would present Napoleon as a figure of 'gigantic stature', or a 'Colossus'. In 1825 he told Medwin that he planned to write 'a life of Napoleon, though it is yet too early: some have a film before their eyes, some want magnifying-glasses – none have seen him as he is, in his true proportions' (xiii, 356). In *The Life* and elsewhere, Hazlitt conceives Napoleon, like Satan, in terms of the visual sublime. This is not only a question of scale, though Hazlitt certainly stresses this – Napoleon is 'raised to . . . a gigantic and glorious height' (vii, 203) and 'rose to a height imperial' (xiv, 302). It is also a matter of the sort of brightness that confounds the understanding. Napoleon's 'exploits' are 'dazzling' (viii, 106); his career 'astonishing' and 'brilliant' (xiii, 326, 226); his actions produce a 'dazzling glare', they are 'stunning' and stimulate 'admiration' and 'awe' (xiii, 317–18).

What this analogy with Milton's Satan reveals is the ambiguity of Hazlitt's sublime conception of Napoleon. Hazlitt, like Milton, describes Napoleon with striking and appropriate images, and he does so not only to produce a figure who is 'gigantic' but one who is 'irregular', 'uneasy' and 'disturbed' and who will gratify the 'logic of the imagination and the passions'. In terms of his critique of 'poetry' in 'Coriolanus', Hazlitt's Napoleon is unmistakably 'aristocratic' and 'poetic', presenting a 'dazzling appearance'. This can be seen in the continuation of the 'Colossus' passage of *The Life* from which I have already quoted. As I have already argued, Hazlitt's representation of Napoleon as a 'republican' hero was somewhat undermined by his Shakespearean allusion. In *Julius Caesar* the 'Colossus' is the man who may betray republicanism. As Hazlitt continues, however, Napoleon's appeal becomes that to the 'imagination' and not to the 'reason':

The implied power to serve and buckler up the state was portentous: if it was fear and personal awe that threw a spell over them in spite of themselves, and turned aside all opposition, though it might take from the goodness of the cause, it would not lessen the power and the reputation of the man. Even if the French had forgot themselves and him, would not their former sentiments be revived in all their force by his present appearance among them, so full of the bold and the marvellous? The very audacity of the undertaking, as it baffled calculation, baffled resistance to it, as much as if he had returned from the dead. Its not seeming ridiculous stamped it sublime . . . (XV, 230)

In this passage the earlier emphasis on the 'goodness of the cause' becomes of secondary importance. Hazlitt prioritizes Napoleon's sublime appeal as the main reason for his success. The ambivalence of this appeal is revealed by the fact that it is not just terrifying in the tradition of the Burkean sublime, producing 'fear and personal awe', but enchanting – it 'threw a spell over them', and was 'full of the marvellous'.

It is at the end of this passage that Hazlitt writes that the 'admiration inspired by the person and the enterprise . . . made all sanguine, anxious, full of interest for him as for the hero of some lofty poem' (XV, 230). A pursuit of the analogy with Satan, the hero of another 'lofty' poem (V, 63), as well as with Coriolanus, who is 'a conqueror and a hero' (IV, 215) like Napoleon, reveals the extent to which Hazlitt draws upon the rhetoric of the imagination in his character of Napoleon. While Hazlitt uses these two characters to represent opposite ends of the political spectrum – Satan as a figure who challenges Almighty power, Coriolanus as one who reinforces it – both have sublime imaginative appeal and both are driven by the same motivations. Coriolanus acts from 'mere pride and self-will' (IV, 215) and shows the 'insolence of power' (IV, 215). Satan, Hazlitt writes, is the 'abstract love of power, of pride, of self-will personified' (V, 64). Similarly Napoleon, who acts from the 'very genius of heroic daring and lofty ambition' (XIV, 181) – phrases which once again recall Satan's own 'lofty ambition' (XVII, 221) – is driven by the love of power, pride and will. Hazlitt describes him as a 'monster . . . of power' (XIX, 25) and argues that with him 'we feel the presence of a power which we have never felt before, and which we can never forget' (XIX, 25–6). His character is 'mixed . . . courage and pride' (XIX, 203), he is driven by his 'excessive perversity of self-will' (XIV, 125) and Hazlitt writes that 'to contrive and to will were the first necessities of his soul' (XIV, 22).[41] On the subject of Napoleon's intervention in Spain, obviously one of the more problematic moments of Napoleon's career for Hazlitt, he brings together Napoleon's love of power, his ambition and his self-will, arguing that 'He beheld an immense engine of power within his reach, and conceived a strong desire to snatch it from the baby-hands that knew not how to wield it. In this there was, it is true, a sort of natural justice, which gave an indirect warrant to the dictates of his ambition and self-will'

(XIV, 315). To some extent all three of these characters are embodiments of what Hazlitt argued were fundamental principles of the human mind in the early pieces 'An Essay on the Principles of Human Action', 'On the Love of Life' and 'On Mind and Motive'. In the second part of the last of these, for example, he writes that 'Our passions in general are to be traced more immediately to the active parts of our nature, to the love of power, or to the strength of will' (XX, 49). It is because they figure these principles that Satan, Coriolanus and Napoleon are so compelling, and gratify the passions and the imagination. Yet as the lecture on *Coriolanus* implies, the gratification of these faculties generally reinforces the sway of legitimacy. How then does Hazlitt reconcile Napoleon's imaginative appeal with his status as a representative and upholder of the Revolution?

Hazlitt argues in *The Life* that Napoleon is driven not by any love of liberty or of France, or by any desire to prolong the cause of the French Revolution, but rather by the Satanic or Coriolanian characteristics of the love of power and self-will. It may seem surprising when, in 'On the Pleasure of Hating', Hazlitt writes that he has 'seen all [his hopes] undone by one man, with just glimmering of understanding enough to feel that he was a king, but not to comprehend how he might be king of a free people' (XII, 136). Hazlitt's tone reflects the bitterness of the whole essay, but his point is not at odds with the argument of *The Life*. Napoleon, he argues, does not want to be the king of a free people. To adopt the terms of the 'Coriolanus' lecture (IV, 215–16), though 'great and powerful' he does not have the 'beneficence and wisdom of the Gods', or a 'knowledge of what is good for the people', or 'as great a care for their interests as he has for himself'. He does not 'sympathize with their welfare' and 'bestow his benefits as free gifts on them'. Rather, Hazlitt argues in *The Life*, he is driven by a desire for 'personal aggrandisement' (XIV, 182) and 'has never acted but from motives of glory and a sense of superiority' (XV, 79). He 'was fonder of organizing than emancipating' (XIV, 293) and 'he was fonder of power than of liberty!' (XV, 46). 'Napoleon at no time had that proper theatrical hatred of the Bourbons' (XV, 211). Hazlitt illustrates and develops such epigrammatic statements throughout *The Life*. For example, of the Egyptian expedition he writes that 'So far from propagating new principles of civilization in the East, it was his object to crush and neutralize them at home; and instead of commencing and giving full scope to an era in society, to patch up and lengthen out the old one, which had fallen in pieces from its own imperfection and infirmity' (XIV, 30).

Hazlitt argues that Napoleon attaches himself to the Revolution not out of any love for its ideas, but because he associates it with his own success. It is a vehicle for his own 'vision of ambition and power' (XIII, 318) and is then forgotten in his 'own projects of aggrandisement and selfish policy' (XIII, 319). But it is because Napoleon needs a strong France to ensure his own power that, in spite of himself, he upholds the principle of the French Revolution; a typically twisted piece of logic. 'Buonaparte clearly identified the fortunes, well-being and glory of France with his own' (XIV, 172), and so 'the great principle of the Revolution found its firmest support and most unflinching ally in personal aggrandisement and soaring ambition' (XIV, 235). Napoleon 'could not but save the principle of the Revolution, while he saved himself' (XIV, 176). So though Napoleon's 'personal aggrandisement and soaring ambition' may seem at odds with the upholding of the Revolution, Hazlitt argues with paradoxical defiance that the end is the same: 'Buonaparte . . . taking the reins into his own hands, and giving unity and stability to the State . . . thus secured the great principle of the Revolution, the right of changing her existing government for one more congenial to it' (XIV, 161). It is in this way that Hazlitt connects Napoleon 'with the cause of the Revolution' 'in spite of himself' (VII, 9), and argues that he could not 'divest himself of the character' of 'the child and champion of the French Revolution' even though he had wished it (XII, ix). Hazlitt's argument in *The Life* elucidates the parenthesized qualification in the Preface of the *Political Essays*:

> He, one man, did this, and as long as he did this (how, or for what end, is nothing to the magnitude of this mighty question) . . . (VII, 10–11)

Furthermore, Hazlitt argues, even though Napoleon has acted out of ambition, he could not have done otherwise because of the circumstances in France. 'In fact, Buonaparte was not strictly a free agent':

> He could hardly do otherwise than he did, ambition apart, and merely to preserve himself and the country he ruled. France was in a state of siege; a citadel in which Freedom had hoisted the flag of revolt against the threat of hereditary servitude; and that in the midst of distraction and convulsions consequent on the sentence of ban and anathema passed upon it by the rest of Europe for having engaged in this noble struggle, required a military dictator to repress internal treachery and headstrong factions, and repel external force. (XIII, x)

In this manner, Hazlitt utilizes France's circumstances as a means of justifying Napoleon's actions.[42]

Indeed, Hazlitt argues that the internal and external circumstances of

France demanded a character such as Napoleon's to uphold the Revolution. Hazlitt binds together his political argument with his depiction of Napoleon's character traits:

> To contend with any chance of success against the armed prejudice, pride, and power of Europe, something more than mere good-nature, moderation, and a belief in external professions was necessary, whatever might be the danger or the inconvenience on the opposite side, instead of fastidious scruples or Quaker morality, it required the very genius of heroic daring and lofty ambition . . . to make head against it. Everyone will allow that Buonaparte came up to these conditions. (XIV, 181)

Hazlitt's writing on Napoleon Bonaparte, then, was no simple indulgence of his own idolatry, but a calculated campaign of imaginative terrorism undertaken by a 'political partisan'. His Bonapartism was less an embarrassing personal flaw than a powerful and controversial expression of his unyielding radicalism. His writing has often been seen as involved in a dialogue with the apostates Wordsworth, Coleridge, Southey and Burke.[43] By championing Napoleon and inverting the Lakers' Satanic myth of him, Hazlitt was able to give 'a proud and full answer' to these advocates of cultural and political conservatism and so to sustain his own polemical attack on what he saw as the reactionary forces that propped up the post-Waterloo world.

Conclusion: 'The Age of Bronze'

Hazlitt's notion of 'partisanship' is one that can be used to characterize the extensive body of writing on Napoleon in the period. Bonaparte himself becomes a battlefield – the site of a series of political and aesthetic contests in a larger ideological war conducted between the different writers or groupings of writers. Their engagement with Napoleon stresses the extent to which they remain directly, even obsessively, concerned with their own historical experience and with their own roles as interpreters and transformers of that experience.

It is the writers' obsession with Napoleon's powerful hold over the 'Imagination' which most strikingly illustrates how critical he is to our understanding of the cultural politics and poetics of the Romantic period. Perhaps the most startling result of this early engagement with the figure of Napoleon was Wordsworth's description of the 'Imagination' in Book VI of *The Prelude*, a passage which can be seen as the culmination of the two-year period during which he had been obsessed with Napoleon. But as the Lakers' political vision of Napoleon changed – both in response to contemporary historical events and as part of their well-documented shift from radicalism to conservatism – they came to regard his hold over the contemporary 'imagination' as dangerous, even treacherous. Rather than turning away from the sphere of political affairs, they repeatedly committed themselves to it in a series of literary and Miltonic interventions. Napoleon's pre-eminence and his sway made it impossible for the 'Imagination' to shun its historical responsibility – to ascend 'from all that man's performance could present' ('Thanksgiving Ode', line 165). The 'Imagination' could only be 'satisfied' by direct political action and the apocalyptic defeat of Napoleon in the 'Imagination' was only achieved with his actual defeat at Waterloo.

If the Lakers strove to drive Napoleon from his 'strong-holds in the imagination' (*CoC* 261), however, Hazlitt fought to represent him in such a way that he would regain his position there. In this way he used Napoleon to champion the cause of the Revolution even after Napoleon's death. Though this strategy involved some paradoxical and twisted logic, he made Napoleon stand as a symbol of democratic meritocracy and, as a political and aesthetic hero, of an art and poetry open to the people.

Byron, whose paradoxical or antithetical formulations of Napoleon encapsulated his ambivalence towards him, used him in an equally polemical fashion, as a symbol of his 'proper theatrical hatred of the Bourbons', to use another phrase of Hazlitt's (*HCW* xv, 211). His provocative merging of the private and the political in his representation of Napoleon in *Childe Harold III* anticipates his later use of him, be it in the flaunted ironic identification of *Don Juan* or the detailed analysis of Napoleon's character and career in *The Age of Bronze*. In the latter, a satire on the Congress of Verona written in 1822–3, two years after Napoleon's death and a year before his own, Byron grants Napoleon a symbolic status as a mascot of opposition to the 'pious unity' of the Holy Alliance (line 398). The poem, which testifies to Byron's continuing interest in Napoleon long after Waterloo, is to some extent a rewriting of the 'Ode to Napoleon Buonaparte' for the post-Waterloo age. Returning to the Popean heroic couplets of his early Satires, Byron once again presents the 'antithetical' figure of Napoleon:

> Yes! where is he, the champion and the child
> Of all that's great or little, wise or wild . . .
> The king of kings, and yet the slave of slaves,
> Who burst the chains of millions to renew
> The very fetters which his arm broke through . . .
> (lines 49–50, 255–755[1])

As in his prose of 1813–14, Byron places Napoleon on a world-historical stage as 'the modern, mightier far' (line 43), comparing him to Alexander (line 31), Sesostris (line 45), Julius Caesar (line 137), Cambyses (line 143), Charles XII (line 172), Washington (line 234) and Hannibal (line 239). For all the paradoxes and flaws that Byron highlights in Napoleon, he again transforms him into Prometheus:

> Hear! hear Prometheus from his rock appeal
> To earth, air, ocean, all that felt or feel
> His power and glory, all who yet shall hear,
> A name eternal as the rolling year; . . . (lines 227–30)

This manoeuvre replays the defiant conclusion of the 'Ode to Napoleon Buonaparte'. As in that work, Byron's mythologizing of Napoleon turns him into a powerful symbol of the liberal cause:

That name shall hallow the ignoble shore,
A talisman to all save him who bore . . . (lines 105–6)

In *The Age of Bronze* Byron envisions the French carrying Napoleon's bones into battle (line 128), and like them he transforms Napoleon into a 'talisman' of liberty, an important weapon in his 'war . . . in words' against 'Tyrants and Sycophants' (*Don Juan* IX, 24). Byron arrogates Napoleon to his own cause, assimilating him within his own stance as a militant poet who has 'sworn' 'downright detestation / Of every despotism in every nation' (*Don Juan* IX, 24). Behind his mock-heroic self-coronation as 'the grand Napoleon of the realms of rhyme' and his comic comparison between their two careers stands an avowed antagonism to the established political and poetic order.

But Byron was never fully satisfied with the role of poet. In 1813 he had hoped that Bonaparte would drive the Turks out of Greece[2] and a decade later he set out to offer what assistance he could in furtherance of the same cause. In this final attempt to realize his ambition in the heroic sphere of 'action' and of 'war' he seems once again to have had a Napoleonic model in mind. In his 'Journal in Cephalonia' he compares his own attempt to help liberate Greece with Napoleon's first Italian campaign about which he was reading in the recently published *Le Memorial de Sainte Hélène*:

I have advanced the sum above noted to pay the said Squadron – it is not very large – but it is double that with which Napoleon the Emperor of Emperors – began his campaign in Italy, withal – vide – Las Cases – passim vol I (tome premier) . . . (*BLJ* XI, 34)

Byron's mixture of poignant realism ('it is not very large') and ironic self-aggrandizement ('double that with which Napoleon the Emperor of Emperors . . .') is characteristic, but there is something fitting about the paradoxical reversal of roles here. While Napoleon, the epitome of the 'man of action' spent his final years creating the Napoleonic legend in his epic and heroic memoirs, Byron ensured his own legendary status by putting aside his own ironic epic and answering the trumpet call of liberty (*BLJ* XI, 34). He brought his own lifelong performance to a close with the final theatrical gesture of the expedition to Greece. Having transformed Napoleon into a Promethean symbol of liberty, he himself took on this role. In doing so he ensured a place in the European consciousness on a par with that of his 'pagod' (*BLJ* III, 256).

Notes

INTRODUCTION: THE POETS AND THE CONQUEROR

1. Richard Whately, *Historic Doubts Relative to Napoleon Bonaparte*, ed. and with a critical introduction and notes by Ralph S. Pomeroy (Berkeley and London: Scolar Press, 1985), pp. 21, 18.
2. See Marilyn Butler, *Romantics, Rebels and Reactionaries: English Literature and its Background 1760–1830* (Oxford University Press, 1981), p. 2.
3. *Letters of John Keats: A New Selection*, ed. Robert Gittings (Oxford University Press, 1970), p. 164.
4. *Letters of John Keats*, p. 212.
5. Unless otherwise stated, all quotations from Byron's poetry are from *The Complete Poetical Works of Lord Byron*, ed. Jerome McGann (Oxford: Clarendon Press, 1980–91). References to *Childe Harold's Pilgrimage* and *Don Juan* are by canto and stanza, unless otherwise stated.
6. Unless otherwise stated, all quotations from Wordsworth's poetry are taken from *William Wordsworth*, ed. Stephen Gill, in the Oxford Authors series (Oxford University Press, 1984; rpt with corrections 1986).
7. Unless otherwise stated, all quotations from this work are from the 1805 text in the Norton edition, *The Prelude 1799, 1805, 1850*, ed. Jonathan Wordsworth, M. H. Abrams, Stephen Gill (New York and London: W. W. Norton and Co., 1979).
8. Leslie Marchand, *Byron: A Portrait*, 3 vols. (London: John Murray, 1957), II, 569. Marchand quotes Augusta: 'before our dinner [Byron] said he considered himself "the greatest man existing". G. [George Leigh] said, laughing, "except Bonaparte". The answer was, "God, I don't know that I do except even him".'
9. *HCW* XI, 87; V, 162.
10. Line 56. Unless otherwise stated, all quotations from Coleridge's poetry are from *The Poetical Works of Samuel Taylor Coleridge*, 2 vols., ed. Ernest Hartley Coleridge (Oxford University Press, 1912, rpt 1983).
11. '*Calais*, August 15th, 1802', line 2.
12. Hayden White, *The Tropics of Discourse* (Baltimore: Johns Hopkins University Press, 1978), p. 82.
13. For an interesting discussion of these issues, see Barton R. Friedman,

Fabricating History: English Writers on the French Revolution (Princeton University Press, 1988).

14. Claude Lévi-Strauss, *The Savage Mind* (University of Chicago Press, 1966), p. 257.
15. Edward Said, *Orientalism* (London: Routledge, 1978), p. 21.
16. Linda Colley, *Britons: Forging the Nation 1707–1837* (New Haven: Yale University Press, 1992), p. 5.
17. Theresa Kelley, 'J. M. W. Turner, Napoleonic Caricature, and Romantic Allegory', *ELH*, 58, 2 (Summer 1991), p. 354.
18. *The Examiner*, 4 July 1821, quoted by E. Tangye Lean in *The Napoleonists: A Study in Political Disaffection 1760-1960* (Oxford University Press, 1970), p. 266.
19. See Carl Woodring's introduction to *Leigh Hunt's Political and Occasional Essays*, ed. Lawrence Huston Houtchens and Carolyn Washburn Houtchens (New York and London: Columbia University Press, 1962), p. 47.
20. Elizabeth Longford, *Wellington: The Years of the Sword* (London: Weidenfeld & Nicolson 1969, rpt Panther, 1972), p. 422.
21. *The Letters of Sir Walter Scott* ed. H. J. C. Grierson, 12 vols. (London: Constable, 1932–7), x, 261.
22. Quoted by J. G. Lockhart in *The Life of Sir Walter Scott* (London: Adam and Charles Black, 1893), p. 657.
23. Ponsonby in fact claimed that 'he is the greatest man that has ever appeared on the face of the earth. I speak not of his moral character; I speak of the strengths of his faculties and of the energies of his mind.' *Cobbett's Parliamentary Debates*, vol. XVII, 1810, p. 233.
24. 'Great Men have been among us', lines 3–4.
25. *The Poet's Pilgrimage to Waterloo* II, iv, 15. Southey's poetry is quoted from *Poems of Robert Southey*, ed. Maurice H. Fitzgerald (Oxford University Press, 1909).
26. Ronald Paulson, *Representations of Revolution (1789–1820)* (New Haven and London: Yale University Press, 1983), p. 5.
27. Stephen Prickett, ed. *England and the French Revolution* (London: Macmillan Education, 1989).
28. Marilyn Butler, 'Telling it Like a Story: The French Revolution as Narrative', *SiR*, 28, 3 (Fall 1989), pp. 345-64.
29. Stephen C. Behrendt, 'History, Mythmaking and the Romantic Artist', in Stephen C. Behrendt, ed., *History and Myth: Essays on English Romantic Literature* (Detroit: Wayne State University Press, 1990).
30. Paul Fussell, *The Great War and Modern Memory* (Oxford University Press, 1975).
31. Paul Fussell, *Wartime: Understanding and Behaviour in the Second World War* (Oxford University Press, 1989).
32. 'Telling it Like a Story', pp. 347–8.
33. *CoC* 256; *SNL* I, 222; *EoT* I, 322, 325; *F* II, 215.

34. *EoT* I, 311–39, II, 371; Byron, *The Age of Bronze*, line 137; Byron, *Childe Harold's Pilgrimage* IV, 90.
35. Epigram to Byron's 'Ode to Napoleon Buonaparte'.
36. *BLJ* III, 256, IV, 93; 'Ode to Napoleon Buonaparte' line 55.
37. *BLJ* III, 256.
38. Ibid.
39. Ibid.
40. Ibid.; 'Ode to Napoleon Buonaparte', line 64.
41. *F* II, 161; *EoT* II, 368.
42. *BLJ* III, 256; 'Ode to Napoleon Buonaparte' line 46.
43. *The Age of Bronze* line 45.
44. Ibid., line 144.
45. *BLJ* IV, 302,; *The Age of Bronze* line 239; Epigram to 'Ode to Napoleon Buonaparte'; *EoT* II, 138: *CNB* III, 3845.
46. *BLJ* IX, 155; 'Ode to Napoleon Buonaparte' line 127; *CoC* 242; *LoL* II, 328.
47. 'Ode to Napoleon Buonaparte' line 127.
48. *EoT* II, 57.
49. *EoT* III, 139.
50. *CoC* 256.
51. Ibid., 256.
52. *F* II, 62; *EoT* II, 37, 224–5; *HCW* XIX, 25.
53. *EoT* II, 349–55.
54. *The Age Of Bronze*, line 172.
55. *CoC* 242; 'Ode to Napoleon Buonaparte' line 27; *Marino Faliero* V, III, 99.
56. *F* I, 443.
57. *BLJ* I, 228.
58. *EoT* I, 209, 373n; *CoC* 256.
59. *EoT* II, 199.
60. 'Ode to Napoleon Buonaparte' st. 17-19; *EoT* I, 222, II, 74; *The Age of Bronze* line 234.
61. *EoT* I, 207, 219, 346, III, 27.
62. *EoT* II, 347–8.
63. *Don Juan* IX, 9.
64. Wordsworth, 'Rob Roy's Grave', lines 95–8.
65. *BLJ* III, 257, IV, 27, 93; *LoL* I, 137, 537, 545–6.
66. *BLJ* IV, 27.
67. *HCW* XV, 230.
68. *HCW* VII, 9–13 (Napoleon as the Tamer of the 'Blatant Beast').
69. *The Age of Bronze* line 227; 'Ode to Napoleon Buonaparte', line 136; *CL* IV, 964.
70. *EoT* II, 128.
71. *Don Juan* xi, 83.
72. Ibid.
73. Ibid., x, 58.
74. *EoT* I, 56.

75. Ibid., 76.
76. Ibid., 112.
77. *F* II, 271.
78. Ibid., 158.
79. Ibid., 158.
80. Ibid., 234; *LS* 66.
81. 'Ode to Napoleon Buonaparte' line 100.
82. Ibid., line 131.
83. *LS* 65–6; *SL* III, 144.
84. *Don Juan* xi, 55–6; Keats, *Letters of John Keats*, p. 163.
85. 'History, Mythmaking and the Romantic Artist', p. 14.
86. Ibid.
87. D. G. Wright, *Napoleon and Europe* (New York and London: Longman, 1984), p. 95.
88. Jean Tulard, *Le Mythe de Napoléon* (Paris: Armand Collin, 1971); Pieter Geyl, *Napoleon: For and Against* (London: Penguin in association with Jonathan Cape, 1949 rpt 1965).
89. Betty Bennet, *British War Poetry in the Age of Romanticism 1793–1815* (New York and London: Garland, 1976).
90. John Ashton, *English Caricature and Satire on Napoleon I* (London: Chatto and Windus, 1888).
91. A. M. Broadley, *Napoleon in Caricature: 1795–1821* (London: Bodley Head, 1911), II, 291–349.

1 A 'CONQUEROR OF KINGS' AND 'A DELIVERER OF MEN': THE REVOLUTIONARY FIGURE OF NAPOLEON IN THE WRITING OF COLERIDGE, SOUTHEY AND LANDOR

1. For an examination of Abrams's idealizing project in the context of the Kennedy era, see two articles by Jon Klancher, 'English Romanticism and Cultural Production', in *The New Historicism* ed. H. Aram Veeser (New York and London: Routledge, 1989), pp. 77–88, and 'Romantic Criticism and the Meaning of the French Revolution', *SiR*, 28, 3 (Fall 1989), 463–91, and see also Jonathan Arac, *Critical Genealogies* (New York: Columbia University Press, 1987) pp. 77–9.
2. M. H. Abrams, 'English Romanticism: The Spirit of the Age' in *The Correspondent Breeze: Essays on English Romanticism* (New York and London: W. W. Norton & Co, 1984), p. 47.
3. In M. H. Abrams, *Natural Supernaturalism: Tradition and Revolution in Romantic Literature* (New York and London: W. W. Norton & Co., 1973), Napoleon is not indexed, and mentioned only in passing on pp. 336, 340, and in the quotation from Auden's 'New Year Letter', p. 333.
4. Ibid. p. 328.
5. *England and the French Revolution*, p. 19.
6. *Natural Supernaturalism*, p. 339.

7. De Selincourt annotates Wordsworth's sonnet 'Thought of a Briton on the Subjugation of Switzerland' with 'Napoleon's first invasion of Switzerland was in 1798', *Poetical Works*, second edition, 5 vols. (Oxford University Press, 1952–9), III, 454. In *Blake, Prophet against Empire: A Poet's Interpretation of the History of his own Times* (Princeton University Press, 1954), Erdman writes that 'Wordsworth and Coleridge announced their disillusionment' with 'this new Orc [Napoleon]' . . . 'upon the invasion of Switzerland in 1798' (p. 280).
8. Carl Woodring, *Politics in the Poetry of Coleridge* (Madison: University of Wisconsin Press, 1961), p. 25.
9. Carl Woodring, *Politics in English Romantic Poetry* (Cambridge, Massachusetts: Harvard University Press, 1970), p. 14.
10. J. C. Maxwell, 'Wordsworth and the Subjugation of Switzerland', *MLR*, 65, 1 (January 1970), 16–18.
11. Ibid., p. 18.
12. Alan J. Bewell, 'The Political Implications of Keats's Classicist Aesthetics', *SiR*, 25, 2 (Summer 1986), p. 225. On the combination of the scientific interest and the military and economic objectives of this expedition, see Jean Tulard, *Napoleon: The Myth of the Saviour*, trans. Teresa Waugh (London: Methuen & Co., 1985), p. 67. For a full description of the campaign see David G. Chandler, *The Campaigns of Napoleon* (London: Weidenfeld and Nicolson, 1966), pp. 205–49.
13. Quotations and references are from the King James Bible (Oxford University Press, 1953).
14. See Richard Holmes, *Coleridge, Early Visions* (Harmondsworth: Penguin, 1990), pp. 162–8.
15. Ibid., p. 166.
16. *Coleridge's Verse: A Selection*, ed. William Empson and David Pirie (London: Faber and Faber, 1972), pp. 248–9.
17. Norman Rudich, '"Kubla Khan": A Political Poem', *Romanticisme*, 8 (1974), pp. 36–53. Jerome J. McGann includes an examination of this article in his chapter 'Coleridge, "Kubla Khan", and the Later Poetry' in *The Romantic Ideology: A Critical Investigation* (Chicago University Press, 1983), pp. 95–107, esp. pp. 101–4.
18. Ibid., p. 39, restated on p. 52.
19. Quoted in Geoffrey Carnall, *Robert Southey and his Age: The Development of a Conservative Mind* (Oxford: Clarendon Press, 1960), p. 478.
20. Ibid., p. 55.
21. *CL* I, 294, 298; *SL* II, 26.
22. *EoT* I, lxxxvi. For Erdman's analysis of these recantations and fears, see *EoT* I, lxxiv-lxxxv, and for two famous examples see 'France: An Ode' and Coleridge's letter to Wordsworth *circa* 10 September 1799 proposing 'a poem, in blank verse, addressed to those, who, in consequence of the failure of the French Revolution, have thrown up all hopes of the amelioration of mankind' (*CL* I, 290).

23. David Pirie describes this entry as 'ironic', *Coleridge's Verse: A Selection*, p. 249, and Carl Woodring as 'jesting', *Politics in the Poetry of Coleridge*, p. 26 – but seen in the context of the correspondence with Southey, and of the positive English view of the Egyptian expedition, the comments, while not unequivocal, deserve to be taken seriously.
24. *EoT* I, 207, 219–26, and see Holmes, *Coleridge, Early Visions*, p. 269.
25. *EoT* I, xci.
26. Quoted in *SL* II, 44.
27. See particularly the articles 'On the French Constitution, I–IV', 7–31 December 1799; 'France, I–III', 1–14 January 1800; 'On Peace, II–IV', 2–6 January 1800; 'Bonaparte, I–III', 11–15 March 1800; 'Washington', 27 January 1800 and 'Pitt', 19 March 1800, in *EoT* I, 36–220. For a summary and an analysis of these essays, see John Colmer, *Coleridge: Critic of Society* (Oxford: Clarendon Press, 1959) pp. 54–71, and Erdman's introduction to *EoT*, esp. I, lxxxvi–xcvii.
28. *EoT* I, 212, xci. For Coleridge's ambivalence towards Napoleon see the three essays 'Bonaparte', *EoT* I, 207–16, and esp. 210–11.
29. *EoT* I, xc, 212–16. On the editorial line of the *Morning Post* during this period as anti-Pitt, anti-ministerial and anti-war, see David V. Erdman, 'Coleridge as Editorial Writer' in *Power and Consciousness*, ed. Conor Cruise O' Brien and William Dean Vanech (University of London Press; New York University Press, 1969), pp. 189–90.
30. 'Coleridge as Editorial Writer', p. 190.
31. This letter includes a fascinating critique by Southey of the satires and vilification of Napoleon, which he describes as 'the rankest and most virulent abuse of Bonaparte'.
32. Introduction to *EoT*, I, cv.
33. Ibid, *CNB* I, 1166.
34. See also his comment of 13 December 1796: 'I would rather be an expert, self maintaining Gardener, than a Milton, if I could not unite both' (*CL* I, 163).
35. *BL* 31–3. My definitions of these terms are taken from Engell's and Bate's notes to this passage. John Beer, in *Coleridge the Visionary* (London: Chatto and Windus, 1959) makes this equation and repeats it in his notes to the poem in *S.T. Coleridge: Poems*, Everyman's Library (London: Dent, 1963), pp. 163–6. See also Stephen Bygrave, *Coleridge and the Self: Romantic Egotism* (New York: St Martins Press, 1986), pp. 188–91, and David Calleo, 'Coleridge on Napoleon' in *Yale French Studies*, 26 (1960–1), pp. 83–93.
36. *The Poetical Works of Walter Savage Landor*, ed. Stephen Wheeler, 3 vols. (Oxford: Clarendon Press, 1937).
37. Brian Wilkie, *Romantic Poets and Epic Tradition* (Madison and Milwaukee: University of Wisconsin Press, 1965), p. 30.
38. Quoted in Raymond Dexter Havens, *The Influence of Milton on English Poetry* (New York: Russell and Russell, 1961), p. 296.
39. R. H. Super, *Walter Savage Landor: A Biography* (London: John Calder, 1957), p. 11.

40. Malcolm Elwin, *Landor: A Replevin* (London: Macdonald, 1958), p. 39.
41. Super, *Walter Savage Landor*, p. 11–12.
42. Elwin, *Landor*, pp. 39, 42.
43. Ibid., pp. 39–41.
44. Ibid., pp. 47–8.
45. Ibid., p. 48.
46. Super, *Walter Savage Landor*, p. 16.
47. Elwin, *Landor*, p. 42.
48. Ibid., p. 59.
49. Wheeler, *The Poetical Works of Walter Savage Landor*, III, 444–51.
50. *CPW* I, pp. 89–90, 'To Lord Stanhope: On Reading his late Protest in the House Of Lords', lines 3 and 5, 'To Earl Stanhope', line 14.
51. See Elwin, *Landor*, p. 60 and Super, *Walter Savage Landor*, p. 27.
52. Super, *Walter Savage Landor*, p. 16.
53. Wheeler, *The Poetical Works of Walter Savage Landor*, III, 435–6.
54. See Stuart Curran, *Poetic Form and British Romanticism* (Oxford University Press, 1986), pp. 98–108.
55. Super, *Walter Savage Landor*, p. 26.
56. Elwin, *Landor*, p. 67.
57. See also lines 91–100 for a more extended passage of satire on this theme.
58. For the history of Landor's composition of the poem, and for details of his source, see Elwin, *Landor*, pp. 63–6, Super, *Walter Savage Landor*, pp. 38, 40, 42.
59. Super writes 'since the earliest date we know for Landor's friendship with Rose Aylmer is 1796 . . . *Gebir* was probably written in the autumn of that year', *Walter Savage Landor*, p. 38. Keith Hanley, the most recent editor of Landor's work, agrees with this dating of the poem: 'It was probably written in its first form in autumn 1796', *Walter Savage Landor: Selected Poetry and Prose* (Manchester: Carcanet Press, 1981), p. 215.
60. Landor oversaw the printing of *Gebir* at Ipsley Court in the late spring of 1798. See Super, *Walter Savage Landor*, p. 40.
61. See Elwin's description of Landor's preference for the story of Gebir and Charoba to that of 'The Phocaeans' on which he was already working as a more dramatic medium for the theme of the futility of military conquest, *Landor*, p. 95.
62. See Curran, *Poetic Form and British Romanticism*, pp. 168–9 and Wilkie, *Romantic Poets and Epic Tradition*, pp. 30–58.
63. Wilkie, *Romantic Poets and Epic Tradition*, p. 57.
64. Curran, *Poetic Form and British Romanticism*, p. 168.
65. *The Eclogues, Georgics and Aeneid of Virgil*, trans. C. Day Lewis (Oxford University Press, 1966).
66. See Elwin, *Landor*, p. 68 and Wheeler, *The Poetical Works of Walter Savage Landor*, I, 477.
67. Quoted in Elwin, *Landor*, p. 68.
68. Pierre Vitoux, '*Gebir* as an Heroic Poem', *TWC*, 7, 1 (Winter 1976), p. 54.

69. Curran, *Poetic Form and British Romanticism*, p. 168.
70. Elwin, *Landor*, p. 64.
71. There is some confusion as to whether or not Landor intended to publish this extract. Wheeler, *The Poetical Works of Walter Savage Landor*, II, 549, writes 'One or two copies, if not more, of the 1800 *Poems* contain at the end what is called "Extract from the French Preface". Whether this was cancelled in publication or added in some cases afterwards, is uncertain. The extract was doubtless meant to be taken as a translation from a preface to a volume in which Landor professed to have found his specimens of Oriental poetry. Even if that were so, the half-veiled allusion to George III, in the pretended extract, might have led to a charge of sedition. Warned of this risk Landor may have cancelled both his Extract and the notes.'
72. Ibid., II, 549.
73. See David Chandler, *The Campaigns of Napoleon*, pp. 53–130.
74. Philip J. Haythornwaite, *The Napoleonic Source Book* (London: Arms and Armour, 1990), p. 18.
75. Elwin writes that at the time of Landor's writing of *Gebir* he saw Napoleon as 'a soldier of the people whose influence had stopped the excesses of the Terror and would enable the French to uphold the cause of democratic liberty in every European country', *Landor*, p. 48. Unfortunately, Elwin gives no source for this information, and as there is no edition of Landor's early letters and little record of his conversations at this time, it is hard to verify. However, such an interpretation, excluding the termination of the Terror, does seem to fit with the picture of Napoleon as I shall argue for it in *Gebir*.
76. Wheeler, *The Poetical Works of Walter Savage Landor*, II, 550.
77. Broadley, *Napoleon in Caricature*, I, 24.
78. Chandler, *The Campaigns Of Napoleon*, p. 130.
79. *Catalogue of Political and Personal Satires Preserved in the Department of Prints and Drawings in the British Museum* ed. Mary Dorothy George (London: British Museum, 1942), vol. VII, 1793–1800, no. 8997.
80. Quoted in Broadley, *Napoleon in Caricature*, I, 104.
81. Quoted in Clive Emsley, *British Society and the French Wars 1793–1815* (London: Macmillan, 1979), p. 66.
82. George, *Catalogue of Political and Personal Satires*, VII, number 9189.
83. Ibid., number 9217.
84. Quoted in F. J MacCunn, *The Contemporary English View of Napoleon* (London: G. Bell and Sons, 1914), p. 14.
85. Dorothy George, *Catalogue of Political and Personal Satires*, VII, no. 9194.
86. Quoted in *Burke, Paine, Godwin and the Revolution Controversy*, ed. Marilyn Butler (Cambridge University Press, 1984), p. 218.
87. Wheeler, *The Poetical Works of Walter Savage Landor*, II, 550.
88. See Curran, *Poetic Form and British Romanticism*, p. 168.
89. Super, *Walter Savage Landor*, p. 40.
90. Wilkie, *Romantic Poets and Epic Tradition*, p. 54.

91. I have produced a 1798 text here, incorporating Wheeler's textual notes on the 1798 variants into his 1803 main text; see Wheeler, *The Poetical Works of Walter Savage Landor*, I, 44.
92. Elwin, *Landor*, p. 94; see pp. 94–5 for a commentary on the politics of this poem.
93. Super, *Walter Savage Landor*, pp. 6, 8, 57 and 68.
94. I am using the C. Day Lewis translation in *The Eclogues, Georgics and Aeneid of Virgil.*
95. E. R. Curtius, *European Literature and the Latin Middle Ages*, trans. Willard R. Trask (London: Routledge and Kegan Paul, 1953), pp. 159–62.
96. Ibid., pp. 51–2.
97. Super, *Walter Savage Landor*, p. 69.
98. See James D. Garrison, *Dryden and the Tradition of Panegyric* (California University Press, 1975), p. 34.
99. For example, Wheeler, *The Poetical Works of Walter Savage Landor*, III, 19.
100. *Oxford English Dictionary* (Oxford: Clarendon Press, 1933 rpt 1961) XI, 366.
101. See Edward Tripp, *Dictionary of Classical Mythology* (London and Glasgow: Collins, 1970 rpt 1988), p. 560.
102. See, for example, the 'triple chains' of Coleridge's 'To a Young Lady With A Poem On The French Revolution', *CPW*, p. 64, line 18. I am grateful to John Birtwhistle for introducing me to the political resonance of these various 'triples'.
103. G. M. Matthews, 'A Volcano's Voice in Shelley', *ELH*, 24, 3 (September 1957), 191–228.
104. Wheeler, *The Poetical Works of Walter Savage Landor*, II, 550.
105. Matthews, 'A Volcano's Voice', p. 222.
106. Abrams, 'English Romanticism: The Spirit of the Age', p. 51.
107. Curtius, *European Literature and the Latin Middle Ages*, pp. 183–202.
108. Curran, *Poetic Form and British Romanticism*, p. 92.
109. Wheeler, *The Poetical Works of Walter Savage Landor*, III, 419. I have here amended what I take to be a typographical error in the printing of 'Let' for 'Lest' in line 93.
110. Vitoux, '*Gebir* as an Heroic Poem', p. 56.
111. Tripp, *Dictionary of Classical Mythology*, p. 230.
112. See J. M. Thompson, *Napoleon Bonaparte: His Rise and Fall* (Oxford and New York: Basil Blackwell, 1988), p. 88.
113. Wheeler, *The Poetical Works of Walter Savage Landor*, I, 45, 46.
114. M. C. J. Putnam, *Virgil's Pastoral Art: Studies in the Eclogues* (Princeton University Press, 1970), p. 145.
115. Curran, *Poetic Form and British Romanticism*, p. 88.
116. Quoted Geoffrey Carnall, *Robert Southey and His Age*, p. 55.
117. Super, *Walter Savage Landor*, p. 45, Elwin, *Landor*, p. 82.
118. Super, *Walter Savage Landor*, p. 63.
119. Elwin, *Landor*, p. 91.
120. Super, *Walter Savage Landor*, p. 65.

121. Elwin, *Landor*, p. 42.
122. Ibid., p. 92.
123. Quoted in Wheeler, *The Poetical Works of Walter Savage Landor*, I, 479.
124. For a detailed account of Southey's shifting allegiances during this period, see Carnall, *Robert Southey and His Age*, pp. 54–60.
125. *EoT* I, 75, 88, 123, 176, 212–16.
126. Quoted Colmer, *Coleridge: Critic of Society*, p. 68.
127. *EoT* I, 428. See Chandler, *The Campaigns of Napoleon*, pp. 320–1.
128. *EoT* I, 310, 341, 346, 348, 349, 386, 393, 396, 428; *SNL* I, 299.
129. *EoT* I, 311–39.
130. Ibid., cvi.
131. Ibid., 376–99. For Erdman's discussion of these letters, see *EoT* I, cix–cxi.
132. Ibid., 314.
133. Geyl, *Napoleon: For and Against*, p. 32.
134. Ibid., p. 33.
135. Quoted in Ernest J. Lovell, Jr. *His Very Self and Voice: Collected Conversations of Lord Byron* (New York: Octagon Books, 1980), p. 567.
136. Charlotte Brontë, *Shirley*, ed. Herbert Rosengarten and Margaret Smith (Oxford: Clarendon Press, 1979), p. 47.

2 'IN SUCH STRENGTH OF USURPATION': WORDSWORTH'S NAPOLEONIC IMAGINATION

1. *The Prelude*, VI, 532–3. All quotations from this work are from the 1805 version in the Norton edition, ed. Jonathan Wordsworth, M. H. Abrams, and Stephen Gill unless otherwise stated. All quotations from Wordsworth's other poetry are from *William Wordsworth*, The Oxford Authors, ed. Stephen Gill, unless otherwise stated.
2. See M. H. Abrams 'English Romanticism: The Spirit of the Age', p. 64, and *Natural Supernaturalism*, pp. 452–3; Geoffrey Hartman, *Wordsworth's Poetry, 1787–1814* (New Haven and London: Yale University Press, 1964) – 'perhaps the most significant in *The Prelude*', p. 16; Alan Liu, 'Wordsworth: The History in "Imagination"' *ELH* 51 (Fall 1984) – 'one of the handful of paradigms capable by itself of representing the poet's work', p. 506; Paul de Man, 'Wordsworth and Hölderlin', *The Rhetoric of Romanticism* (New York: Columbia University Press, 1984), pp. 55–9.
3. *Chambers Twentieth Century Dictionary* ed. A. M. Macdonald (Edinburgh & London: W. R.Chambers, 1972), p. 1495.
4. 'English Romanticism: The Spirit of the Age', pp. 62–6; *Natural Supernaturalism*, pp. 452–3.
5. Alan Liu, 'Wordsworth: The History in "Imagination"', pp. 505–48.
6. Alan Liu, *Wordsworth: The Sense of History* (Stanford University Press, 1989).
7. 'The History in "Imagination"', p. 531.
8. For the dating of the composition of this book, see the Norton *Prelude*, p. 519.

9. *Nineteenth Century Literature*, 45, 2 (Sept. 1990), pp. 245, 246. Haydon cites *The Sense of History*: 'My working premise is that ideas are always after-the-fact in the process by which historical context emerges in literary texts. A poet first "senses" context in the form of highly charged and concrete phenomena that are prior to thinkable "ideas" because they mark a constitutive – if morally or otherwise unacceptable – differentiation, contradiction or contest in the historical contest itself . . . Historical sense becomes poetic sensibility when, through a second-order differentiation implicating the poet in his attempt to distance or deny that context, the literary text emerges as a tissue of internal contradictions or ambiguities covered by its own ideology of unity.' Peter Manning, in his review of the book for *SiR*, 28, 3, (Fall, 1989), pp. 514–22, writes that 'Liu's trumping of both the poet and his most influential modern critic [Hartman] rests on the larger argument that "the literary text is not just the displacement but the overdetermined and agonic *denial* of historical reference". The task of *Wordsworth: The Sense of History* is to reconstruct "the shaped *absence* of context". . .' p. 517.
10. David Simpson, reviewing *Wordsworth: The Sense of History* in his essay 'Recent Studies in the Nineteenth Century', *Studies in English Literature 1500–1900* 30, 4 (Winter 1990) writes that 'Wordsworth may be an imaginative Bonaparte, but he is a Bonaparte nonetheless in his fashioning of a "Romantic Self" which is a "testament of social denial" (p. 304). This is also the thesis expounded by McGann and Levinson', p. 723.
11. See his essay 'The Power of Formalism: The New Historicism', *ELH* (1989), 721 and his review of David Simpson's *Wordsworth's Historical Imagination: The Poetry of Displacement* in *TWC* 19, 4 (Autumn 1988), 172–81.
12. McGann, *The Romantic Ideology*, p. 82.
13. Marjorie Levinson, *Wordsworth's Great Period Poems: Four Essays*, (Cambridge University Press, 1986), pp. 1–2, 3, 4.
14. While my overall argument thus seeks to propose an alternative view to Liu's of Wordsworth's treatment of history, I am nonetheless indebted to his work. Liu analyses the Napoleonic diction and allusions of the Simplon Pass passage with great skill, and I have concurred with his analysis of 'usurpation' and the 'Nile', as will be seen. Similarly while I agree that Wordsworth's use of landscape in Book VI of *The Prelude* takes into account military manoeuvres, whereas Liu identifies these as Napoleon's campaigns of 1796 and 1800, I interpret Wordsworth as referring to those of 1798 and 1802, a crucial distinction given the different meanings of the Italian and the Swiss campaigns. I would not go as far as Liu in his identification of all things as Napoleonic, for example his reading of 'cloud' as St Cloud.
15. Stephen Gill, *William Wordsworth: A Life* (Oxford University Press, 1990), p. 45.
16. See M. H. Abrams, *The Mirror and the Lamp: Romantic Theory and the Critical Tradition* (Oxford University Press, 1953), pp. 57–8.

17. *Milton: Complete Shorter Poems*, ed. John Carey (London and New York: Longman, 1968).
18. Quoted from the Alexander Text (London and Glasgow: Collins, 1951 rpt 1985).
19. To give such weight of meaning and importance to a single word may seem insubstantial for the construction of an overall argument, but again this has become a familiar and accepted technique in criticism. It has been written of Professor Marilyn Butler that 'she brings her impressive historical erudition to bear on the most innocent aspects of the work: *a word*, a character type, a narrative *donnée*. By recovering and elucidating the polemical meaning of these representations and procedures in their originary context, she gives her readers a more authentic and immediate relation to the literature'. Levinson, *Wordsworth's Great Period Poems*, p. 8.
20. Paul Hamilton, *Wordsworth*, Harvester New Readings (Brighton, Sussex: Harvester Press, 1986), p. 118.
21. 'The History in "Imagination"', pp. 533–4.
22. Ibid., p. 528.
23. Gill, *William Wordsworth: A Life*, p. 45.
24. Ibid., p. 719.
25. J. R. Watson, *English Poetry of The Romantic Period* (London and New York: Longman, 1985), p. 32.
26. *The Letters of William and Dorothy Wordsworth: The Later Years, Part I 1821–1828*, 2nd ed., revised by Alan G. Hill from the first edition by Ernest de Selincourt (Oxford: Clarendon, 1978), p. 97.
27. Maxwell, 'Wordsworth and the Subjugation of Switzerland', pp. 16–18.
28. Ibid., p. 16.
29. MacCunn, *The Contemporary English View of Napoleon*, p. 58.
30. Ibid., p. 60.
31. Quoted in Bennett, *British War Poetry in the Age of Romanticism*, p. 282.
32. Ibid., p. 289.
33. Ibid., p. 301.
34. Ibid., p. 337.
35. Liu writes of this passage that 'There is a muted story of predation here, of some spoilation or usurpation in the area of Chamounix that the 1805 book 6 (still without the Convent of Chartreuse excursus) must prettify.' 'Wordsworth: The History in "Imagination"', p. 528.
36. 'The wolf also shall dwell with the lamb, and the leopard shall lie down with the kid; and the calf and the young lion and the fatling together . . .' Isaiah 11. 6.
37. J. Hall, *Dictionary of Subject and Symbol in Art* (London: John Murray, 1984).
38. As well as Wordsworth's treatment of Venice, one can think of Byron's 'Ode to Venice', *Childe Harold's Pilgrimage* Canto IV, 1–17, and his *Marino Faliero* (with Napoleon as the 'bastard Attila' (V. 3. 49–99)) and Shelley's 'Lines Written Among The Euganean Hills' (lines 115–205).
39. Carlos Baker has termed this Wordsworth's 'double-exposure technique'

in 'Sensation and Vision in Wordsworth', rpt in *English Romantic Poets*, ed. M. H. Abrams (Oxford University Press, 1960 rpt 1973), p. 106. See also 'Structure and Style in the Greater Romantic Lyric' in M. H. Abrams, *The Correspondent Breeze*, pp. 76–108.

40. Gill, *William Wordsworth: A Life*, p. 59.
41. However, as E. P. Thompson writes, in 'Disenchantment of Default: A Lay Sermon', 'Wordsworth has told us that his first great crisis came, not with the Revolution – this seemed in the course of "nature" – nor with the Terror, but with the opening of hostilities between England and France in 1793' (in *Power and Consciousness*, ed. Conor Cruise O'Brien and William Dean Vanech, p. 169 (see x, 229–89)).
42. Gill, *William Wordsworth: A Life*, p. 88.
43. Maxwell, 'Wordsworth and the Subjugation of Switzerland', pp. 16–18.
44. Ibid., pp. 16–17.
45. Ibid., p. 17.
46. Ibid., p. 18.
47. *The Letters of William and Dorothy Wordsworth: The Later Years*, I, 97.
48. Maxwell, 'Wordsworth and the Subjugation of Switzerland', p. 17.
49. *CoC* I, 319, 323, 329, 380.
50. *Leigh Hunt's Political and Occasional Essays* ed. Lawrence Huston Houtchens and Carolyn Washburn Houtchens, pp. 115–16.
51. The two main points of view on this period, that of Abrams and that of Thompson, are neatly summarised by Levinson, *Wordsworth's Great Period Poems*, pp. 6 and 9.
52. See Norton *Prelude*: 'the likelihood is that completion of Book VI in late April 1804 was followed by composition of IX, 18–293, 566–end, plus a version of x, 1–566, and that at a final stage ca. early June (or conceivably at the beginning of October) IX, 294–55 were inserted. To move on from describing unpolitical response to the Revolution in 1790, to an account of increasing awareness and final identification in 1791–94, might anyway seem natural; but there is also the interesting possibility that the two and a half French Books were composed in a single manuscript, now lost', p. 519.
53. George, *Catalogue of Political and Personal Satires*, VII, number 9426.
54. Quoted MacCunn, *The Contemporary English View of Napoleon I*, p. 19.
55. Ibid., pp. 20–1.
56. Ibid., p. 21.
57. *The Oxford Classical Dictionary* (Oxford: Clarendon Press, 1949 rpt 1961), p. 521.
58. Thompson, 'Disenchantment or Default? A Lay Sermon', p. 153.
59. See Gill, *William Wordsworth*, The Oxford Authors, p. 267.
60. 'Milton! Thou should'st be living' *TWC* 19 (1988), pp. 2–8, pp. 2 and 4. Not only does Erdman's false assumption about sympathetic grief lead to a misunderstanding of the sonnet based on two historical moments (Erdman posits the Battle of the Nile as the occasion for grief) but his interpretation is littered with historical errors. He writes that 'Napoleon's elevating himself

to kingship, then to Emperor, crowned by a Pope, collapsed any remaining hope in the hearts of republicans like Blake and Wordsworth. Wordsworth saw that his grief for Buonaparte had been unthinking . . . [and] in the first of his "Sonnets Dedicated to Liberty", dating it "May 21, 1802" put paid to his grief for Buonaparte as having been "vain" and "unthinking".' The preponderance of surface errors here almost distracts from the fallaciousness of Erdman's overall argument. By 21 May, 1802, Napoleon had become Consul and President of the Cisalpine Republic, but was not King of Italy until 26 May, 1805, or emperor until 2 December 1804, twenty months after this event 'put paid' to Wordsworth's grief for Napoleon. (Erdman makes a similarly elementary mistake when he writes, paraphrasing a later entry in *The Prelude* (x, 938), 'When Englishmen were rushing to see a Pope crown an Emperor, Wordsworth and his sister went to France also.' Wordsworth and Dorothy were in France in the summer of 1802, when, on 15 August, Napoleon was proclaimed Consul for Life. He was not crowned emperor for another sixteen months.) Furthermore, it is from Dorothy's journal entry for 21 May 1802 ('William wrote two sonnets on Buonaparte'), combined with a later statement by William (' I took fire, and produced three sonnets the same afternoon . . . Of these three the only one I distinctly remember is "I grieved for Buonaparte"' (Moorman, *Wordsworth: Early Years*, 565)) that we can ascertain this as the date of composition. Wordsworth never dated it as such: in the quote above he refers to the year as 1801, but the contemporary nature of Dorothy's comment is obviously corrective. Indeed, when Wordsworth did publish the sonnet as the fourth (not the first, as Erdman states, though it was the first written) of the 'Sonnets Dedicated to Liberty', he dated it as 1801. Erdman's interpretation of the sonnet as sympathetic grief followed by a correction of that grief causes him to look for two specific moments. Unfortunately, he finds one of them eighteen months after the poem was written.

61. For the dating and composition of these books, see Norton *Prelude*, pp. 514–20.
62. Most editors normally use this date as the earliest at which Wordsworth wrote this passage (e.g. Norton). Yet the Senate declared Napoleon Emperor on 18 May 1804, and it had been rumoured long before. Speculation about the nature of the coronation was rife through the rest of the year. Whether or not the pope would crown Napoleon was something of a talking-point in the months before the coronation.
63. David Wakefield, *Stendhal: The Promise of Happiness* (Bedford: The Newstead Press, 1984), p. 18.
64. Beethoven's reaction to Napoleon, like that of most others, was more complex than this single event can testify (Fritz Spiegel on the 'Eroica' Symphony, BBC Radio 3, 3 June 1990). Three months after this event the composer was still hawking the symphony to publishers as dedicated to Napoleon – 'Its real subject is Bonaparte'. In 1807, Beethoven was considering the possibility of becoming Napoleon's Kapellmeister.

65. George, *Catalogue of Political and Personal Satires*, VIII, number 9892.
66. See Paulson, *Representations of Revolution*, pp. 48–9, 102.
67. See Ashton, *English Caricature and Satire on Napoleon I*, pp. 242–8 for contemporary depictions of the 'pantomimic business' of the coronation. Wordsworth's word 'Opera' would have had more of an association with pantomime than with opera as we know it today.
68. See Zera Fink, 'Wordsworth and the English Republican Tradition', *Journal of English and German Philology* (1948), 107–26; Erdman, 'Milton! Thou should'st be living', pp. 3, 4, 7; Levinson, *Wordsworth's Great Period Poems*, p. 157; John Williams, *Wordsworth: Romantic Poetry and Revolutionary Politics* (Manchester University Press, 1983), *passim* ('Wordsworth's political views were the products of a tradition of British political thinking that predates the impact of French Revolutionary political philosophy', p. 1); Mary Moorman, *William Wordsworth: A Biography: The Early Years: 1770-1803* (Oxford University Press, 1965), 207 ff; Gill, *William Wordsworth: A Life*, pp. 208–9, 569, 570.
69. Gill, *William Wordsworth*, The Oxford Authors, p. 706.
70. See Norton *Prelude*, p. 519.
71. For details of Wordsworth's visit to France and the subsequent sonnet sequence, see Gill, *William Wordsworth: A Life*, pp. 207–9. For an analysis of the sequence as a whole see Curran, *Poetic Form and British Romanticism*, pp. 45–9.
72. Abrams, *Natural Supernaturalism*, p. 334.
73. Thompson, 'Disenchantment or Default? A Lay Sermon', p. 174.
74. Carlos Baker, 'Sensation and Vision in Wordsworth', rpt in M. H. Abrams (ed.) *English Romantic Poets*, p. 106.
75. John Purkis, *The World of the English Romantic Poets: A Visual Approach* (London: Heinemann, 1982), p. 74.
76. Woodring, *Politics in English Romantic Poetry*, p. 124.
77. Moorman, *Wordsworth: Early Years*, p. 602.
78. Ibid.
79. On Wordsworth's youthful desire to be a soldier, and his interest in military heroes, see Eric C. Walker, 'Wordsworth, Warriors and Naming', *SiR*, 29, 3 (Summer 1990) 224–40.
80. Wilfred Spiegelman, *Wordsworth's Heroes* (Berkeley, Los Angeles and London: California University Press, 1985), p. 13. See also Walker, 'Wordsworth, Warriors and Naming', who argues that in both *The Prelude* and the larger body of *Recluse* texts, 'warrior and poet . . . are twin selves', p. 239.
81. Moorman, *Wordsworth: Early Years*, 152.
82. Erdman, 'Milton! Thou should'st be living', p. 5.
83. Williams, *Wordsworth: Romantic Poetry and Revolutionary Politics*, p. 39.
84. Gill, *William Wordsworth: A Life*, p. 4.
85. Ibid., p. 6.
86. Williams, *Wordsworth: Romantic Poetry and Revolutionary Politics*, p. 40.

87. Spiegelman, *Wordsworth's Heroes*, pp. 17–18.
88. Quoted Gill, *William Wordsworth: A Life*, p. 60.
89. See Gill, *William Wordsworth*, The Oxford Authors, p. 707.
90. Hartman, *Wordsworth's Poetry, 1787–1814*, p. 16.
91. Gill, *William Wordsworth: A Life*, p. 47.
92. Abrams, 'English Romanticism: The Spirit of the Age', p. 65.
93. See Liu, 'Wordsworth: The History in "Imagination"', p. 537.
94. Hartman, *Wordsworth's Poetry, 1787–1814*, p. 17.
95. Gill, *William Wordsworth:* The Oxford Authors, p. 652.
96. Gill, *William Wordsworth: A Life*, p. vii.
97. Quoted Moorman, *Wordsworth: Early Years*, 602.
98. Liu, 'The History in "Imagination"', p. 537.
99. Colin Pedley, 'Anticipating Invasion: Some Wordsworthian Contexts,' *TWC*, 21, 2 (Spring 1990), 64–75, p. 65.
100. Abrams, 'English Romanticism: The Spirit of the Age', p. 58.
101. Jonathan Bate, *Romantic Ecology: Wordsworth and the Environmental Tradition* (London and New York: Routledge, 1991), pp. 3–6. Interestingly, both Jonathan Bate and David Simpson have seen Liu's book as a complex restatement of Abrams's basic argument, mediated through McGann. Bate describes *Wordsworth: The Sense of History* as 'a sophisticated revision of a very old accusation . . . Wordsworth developed a creed of the all-powerful, redeeming poetic Imagination . . . as a kind of compensation for his political disillusionment or even apostasy', p. 23. Simpson writes that 'Liu's important earlier essays are here refigured into a narrative that is, in its bare essentials, surprisingly close to M. H. Abrams now "classic" account of Wordsworth's turn from politics and history to nature, autobiography, and the image of the imagination. But where Abrams saw this as a process of right-minded moral enlightenment, Liu sees deeper and murkier narratives founded in repression', 'Recent Studies in the Nineteenth Century', p. 723.

3 'HISTORIOGRAPHER(S) TO THE KING OF HELL': THE LAKE POETS' PENINSULAR CAMPAIGN

1. I have taken this phrase from Coleridge's note to 'Ode to the Departing Year', in which he applies it to Catherine the Great, *CPW* 163.
2. For a clear summary of the events in the Peninsula up to the Convention, see volume I of *The Prose Works of William Wordsworth*, ed. W. J. B. Owen and Jane Worthington Smyser, 3 vols. (Oxford: Clarendon Press, 1974), pp. 194–8, and Gordon Kent Thomas, *Wordsworth's Dirge and Promise* (Lincoln: Nebraska University Press, 1971), chapter I. The latter, which gives the best general account of Wordsworth's tract, also usefully documents the contemporary reaction to the Convention in chapters I and II. For general information on the Peninsular War see Philip J. Haythornwaite, in *The Napoleonic Source Book*: 'Bibliography; Peninsular War', p. 371.

3. See Gill, *William Wordsworth: A Life*, p. 275.
4. See Curran, *Poetic Form and British Romanticism*, pp. 48–9, for an analysis of the 'inner division' of this sequence.
5. Wellesley, for example, 'had been sent as a deliverer – as an asserter and avenger of the rights of human nature' (*CoC* 251), but signally failed to fulfil this role.
6. See John Derry, 'Opposition Whigs and the French Revolution, 1789–1815' in *Britain and the French Revolution*, ed. H. T. Dickinson (Basingstoke and London: Macmillan Education, 1989), p. 56, for the Whigs' use of the Convention to attack the government.
7. Quoted by F. M. Todd, *Politics and the Poet: A Study of Wordsworth* (London: Methuen & Co., 1957), p. 137.
8. See MacCunn, *The Contemporary English View of Napoleon*, p. 92.
9. George, *Catalogue of Political and Personal Satires*, VIII, number 10371.
10. Ibid., number 10518.
11. For a similar view, see Paulson's discussion of Elizabeth Inchbald in *Representations of Revolution*, p. 286.
12. George, *Catalogue of Political and Personal Satires*, VIII, no.11010.
13. Wordsworth, Abrams, and Gill, eds., *The Prelude*, p. 410.
14. R. J. White, *Political Tracts of Wordsworth, Coleridge and Shelley* (Cambridge University Press, 1953), p. xxxii.
15. Peter J. Manning, *Reading Romantics: Texts and Contexts* (Oxford University Press, 1990), p. 186.
16. Gill, *William Wordsworth: A Life*, p. 59.
17. Quoted by Carnall, *Robert Southey and his Age*, p. 59.
18. For Virgil see *CoC* 265, for Dante, 331, Sidney, 339, Petrarch, 342, Plutarch, 335, Paul 227–8, Daniel 334, Acts 299, Matthew, 292, 295.
19. See Gill, *William Wordsworth: A Life*, p. 276.
20. Quoted from *Milton: Paradise Lost*, ed. Alastair Fowler (London: Longman, 1968 rpt with minor corrections 1971).
21. Quoted Joseph Anthony Wittreich Jr, ed. *The Romantics on Milton: Formal Essays and Critical Asides* (Cleveland and London: Case Western University Press, 1970), pp. 114–15.
22. Napoleon was not the only figure in the period to be Satanized. Catherine the Great (*CPW* 163), William Pitt and Robespierre were all subjected to the same treatment. On Pitt see Carl Woodring, *Politics in the Poetry of Coleridge*, p. 112. On Robespierre, see Brooke Hopkins, 'Representing Robespierre' in *History and Myth*, ed. Behrendt, pp. 116–26, and Nicholas Roe, 'Imagining Robespierre' in *Coleridge's Imagination: Essays in Memory of Pete Laver*, ed. Richard Gravil, Lucy Newlyn and Nicholas Roe (Cambridge University Press, 1985) pp. 161–78.
23. In *Shakespeare and the English Romantic Imagination* (Oxford: Clarendon Press, 1989) Jonathan Bate writes that 'the most effective appropriations of earlier works into later writings are usually those that invoke the full force of a passage's original context', p. 30. See also pp. 74–5, in which he writes

that in many of Wordsworth's poems 'a phrase is quoted from Milton or Shakespeare, and the reader is asked to bring the context of the original to bear on the passage that is appropriated'.

24. Wordsworth's transformation of Napoleon into the 'enemy of mankind' in the tract anticipates Coleridge's persistent representation of him as 'the enemy of the human race' (*F* II, 162; *EoT* II, 76), 'the enemy of human nature' (*EoT* II, 178), and 'the greatest enemy of [Great Britain], of mankind, nay of civilized society' (*EoT* II, 201).
25. On these sonnets see Gordon K. Thomas: 'Wordsworth's Iberian Sonnets: Turncoat's Creed?', *TWC* 13, 1 (Winter 1982), pp. 31–4.
26. Quoted Wittreich, ed. *The Romantics on Milton*, p. 116.
27. For an example of this type of conflation in Wordsworth's poetry, see Bate's analysis of the 1816 poem 'A little onward lend thy guiding hand' in which 'abrupt abyss' elides two separate lines of *Paradise Lost* (II, 405, 409), *Shakespeare and the English Romantic Imagination*, pp. 104–5.
28. Wittreich, ed. *The Romantics on Milton*, p. 117.
29. See *Shorter Poems, 1807–1820*, ed. Carl Ketcham (Ithaca and London: Cornell University Press, 1989), pp. 500–1, from which I take my text.
30. Ibid., p. 55.
31. Quoted Wittreich, ed. *The Romantics on Milton*, p. 116.
32. 'Byron and the Empire in the East' in *Byron: Augustan and Romantic*, ed. Andrew Rutherford (London: Macmillan, 1990), pp. 72.
33. *CoC* 214.
34. 'Prospectus' to 'The Excursion' line 23.
35. See *Shorter Poems*, ed. Carl Ketcham, pp. 8–11, for a discussion of these sonnets.
36. Curran, *Poetic Form and British Romanticism*, p. 135.
37. Butler, 'Byron and the Empire in the East', pp. 72.
38. In this projected poem that would become *Roderick, The Last of the Goths* Southey focused particularly on the process of the liberation of Spain (as did Scott in *The Vision of Don Roderick* and Landor in *Count Julian*. Wordsworth also wrote a fragmentary poem entitled *Pelayo* which he never published).
39. Kenneth Curry, *Southey*, Routledge Author Guides (London: Routledge and Kegan Paul, 1975), pp. 164–7.
40. See also xii, 1, 19–24; III, 58–61.
41. As Marilyn Butler has pointed out, however, the poem may also serve an imperialist function: 'The theme, the cruelty and anarchy of Hinduism, supported Southey's serious journalistic campaign to persuade the British public of the need to impose a strong Christian government on India.' 'Romanticism in England' in *Romanticism in National Context*, ed. Roy Porter and Mikulas Teich (Cambridge University Press, 1988), p. 58.
42. J. R. de J. Jackson, *Poetry of the Romantic Period* (London: Routledge, 1980), p. 280.

43. Victor Hugo, *Les Misérables*, trans. Norman Denny (Harmondsworth: Penguin, 1976), p. 542.
44. See also Wordsworth's sonnet XXXIII of 'Liberty and Independence':

    Never may from our souls one truth depart –
    That an accursed thing it is to gaze
    On prosperous tyrants with a dazzled eye (lines 7–9)

45. Elizabeth Longford, *Wellington, The Years of the Sword*, , pp. 256–63.
46. Ian R. Christie, *Wars and Revolution: Britain 1760–1815* (London: Edward Arnold, 1982), p. 317.
47. For examples of this catalogue see *EoT* II, 76–7, 194–5.
48. Hugo, *Les Misérables*, p. 542.
49. Paulson, *Representations of Revolution*, pp. 370, 187–9.
50. *CL* III, 828; see also *EoT* II, 271.
51. *EoT* II, 237; see also *EoT* II, 76, 14.
52. Paulson, *Representations of Revolution*, p. 370.
53. For Coleridge's notes for an essay in response to Ponsonby, see *CNB* III, 3845.
54. See also *CNB* III, 3845 and *EoT* II, 231.
55. Quoted in *Shakespearean Criticism*, 2 vols., ed. Thomas Middleton Raysor, Everyman's Library (London, Melbourne, Toronto; Dent, 1907, 2nd ed. 1960, rpt 1980), II, 209.
56. For example, *The Times* 12 November 1813.
57. See *LoL* II, 425.

4 STAGING HISTORY: BYRON AND NAPOLEON, 1813–1814

1. *Medwin's Conversations of Lord Byron*, ed. Ernest J. Lovell, Jr (Princeton University Press, 1966), pp. 184–5.
2. *Letters of John Keats*, ed. Gittings, p. 163.
3. *BLJ* III, 220.
4. *Don Juan*, ed. T. G. Steffan, E. Steffan and W. W. Pratt (Harmondsworth: Penguin 1973 rpt 1982), p. 699.
5. *Lady Blessington's Conversations of Lord Byron*, ed. Ernest J. Lovell, Jr (Princeton University Press, 1969), p. 183 – 'the laughing devils will return, and make a mockery of everything, as with me there is, as Napoleon said, but one step between the sublime and the ridiculous'.
6. *Byron*, The Oxford Authors (Oxford University Press, 1986) p. xii.
7. Behrendt, 'History, Mythmaking and the Romantic Artist', pp. 14–30.
8. See his comment of 25 December 1812, *BLJ* II, 261. For Byron's early comments on Napoleon from 1805–11, see *BLJ* I, 77, 118, 123, 206; II, 51.
9. Leslie Marchand, *Byron: A Biography*, I, 422.
10. See Marchand's note, *BLJ* III, 210.
11. Malcolm Kelsall, *Byron's Politics* (Sussex: Harvester Press, 1987), pp. 22–4, 29, 122.
12. Ibid., pp. 22–3.

13. Ibid., *passim.*
14. Marchand, *Byron: A Biography*, I, 139; Carl Woodring, *Politics in English Romantic Poetry*, p. 148.
15. Whately, *Historic Doubts*, pp. 20–1. On the Whig Party see John Derry, 'Opposition Whigs and the French Revolution, 1789–1815'. See also Anthony Burton and John Murdoch, *Byron: An Exhibition* (London: Victoria and Albert Museum, 1974) p.73. See also E. T. Lean, *The Napoleonists*, p. 92, and Marchand, *Byron: A Biography*, I, 351.
16. Marchand, *Byron: A Biography*, I, 351.
17. Quoted Lean, *The Napoleonists*, pp. 137–8.
18. Ibid., p. 140.
19. *Cobbett's Parliamentary Debates*, vol. XVII, London, 1810, p. 223.
20. See Derry, 'Opposition Whigs and the French Revolution', pp. 56–7.
21. Rowland E. Prothero, ed. *The Works of Lord Byron, Letters and Journals* (London: John Murray, 1898–1901), II, 323n.
22. *BLJ* II, 165.
23. Ernest J. Lovell Jr, *His Very Self and Voice*, p. 567.
24. Ibid., p. 31.
25. For the idea of *debellare superbos* see Kelsall, *Byron's Politics*, p. 69.
26. Frederick Raphael, *Byron* (London: Thames and Hudson, 1982), p. 29.
27. This paraphrase of what has been call Byron's 'need of fatality' is taken from McGann's introduction to *Byron*, p. xii.
28. Kelsall, *Byron's Politics*, p. 153.
29. *Medwin's Conversations of Lord Byron*, pp. 184–5.
30. Jerome Christensen, *Lord Byron's Strength: Romantic Writing and Commercial Society* (Baltimore and London: Johns Hopkins University Press, 1993), p. 129.
31. E. H. Coleridge, *The Works of Lord Byron: Poetry*, III, 303.
32. Quoted in J. M. Thompson, *Napoleon Bonaparte*, p. 358.
33. See the dedication to *The Corsair* and *BLJ* IV, 92.
34. Byron worked fervently on the 'Ode', which he expanded from ninety lines, on 10 April, to fifteen stanzas, when it was first published on 16 April (see *The Complete Poetical Works*, ed. Jerome J. McGann, III, 456 and Marchand, *Byron: A Biography*, I, 444). As E. H. Coleridge and Jerome McGann have both observed in their editions of the poetry, a second edition followed immediately after, but as publication of less than a sheet was liable to the stamp tax on newspapers, Byron added another stanza at Murray's request – the fifth – which was inserted in the third edition. By this means the pamphlet was extended to seventeen pages (E. H. Coleridge, *The Works of Lord Byron: Poetry*, III, 303–4; McGann, *The Complete Poetical Works*, III, 456). The concluding stanzas (17–19), were written with great reluctance by Byron seemingly for the same purpose, but he wrote to his publisher on 26 April that 'I don't like the additional stanzas *at all* – and they had better be left out' (*BLJ* IV,107). These stanzas were not printed in Byron's lifetime but were first included in a separate poem, in Murray's

edition of 1831, and were first appended to the 'Ode' in the seventeen-volume edition of 1832. As McGann observes, they introduce 'a new conclusion to the Ode' and 'injure the poem's accomplished pace' (*The Complete Poetical Works*, III, 456). Since they were written with such reluctance and relegated by Byron himself from the poem, I have concentrated on the sixteen-stanza version of the 'Ode' as printed by McGann in both *The Complete Poetical Works* and *Byron*, The Oxford Authors.

35. Robert Gleckner, *Byron and the Ruins of Paradise* (Westport, Conn.: Greenwood Press, 1967), p. 224.
36. E. H. Coleridge, *The Works of Lord Byron: Poetry*, III, 312.
37. Ibid., 313.
38. I am grateful to Timothy Webb for supplying me with a copy of the manuscript of this letter.
39. For the links between Byron's use of Prometheus and Shelley's *Prometheus Unbound*, see Stuart Curran, 'The Political Prometheus', 429–55.

5 WATERLOO: 'THE GREATEST EVENT OF MODERN TIMES'

1. Walter Scott, *Paul's Letters to his Kinfolk* (Edinburgh and London: Archibald Constable and Co, 1816), p. 194.
2. Full title 'Ode. The Morning of the Day Appointed for a General Thanksgiving. January 18, 1816.' I use Reading Text I in *Shorter Poems, 1807–1820*, ed. Carl H. Ketcham (Ithaca and London: Cornell University Press, 1989).
3. 'Thanksgiving Ode' line 166; *The Poet's Pilgrimage to Waterloo* I, i, 1. All quotations from Southey's poetry are taken from *Poems of Robert Southey*, ed. Fitzgerald, unless otherwise stated. References to *The Poet's Pilgrimage to Waterloo* are by part, section and stanza.
4. *Monthly Review*, quoted in *Robert Southey: The Critical Heritage* ed. Lionel Madden (London: Routledge, 1972), p. 207.
5. For contemporary reactions to the battle see esp. Antony Brett-James ed., *The Hundred Days: Napoleon's Last Campaign From Eye-Witness Accounts* (Cambridge: Ken Trotman, 1989) pp. 186–96, and Lean, *The Napoleonists*, p. 261.
6. Lean, *The Napoleonists*, p. 261.
7. Ibid., p. 261.
8. David Chandler, *Waterloo: The Hundred Days* (London: George Philip, 1980), pp. 10–11.
9. Ibid.
10. Lord Uxbridge's sister, Caroline Capel, called it 'odious'. See Elizabeth Longford, *Wellington: The Years of the Sword*, pp. 584–5.
11. Quoted in *Robert Southey: The Critical Heritage*, p. 207.
12. Francis Jeffrey, *The Edinburgh Review*, 54 (December 1816) p. 295.
13. Chandler, *Waterloo: The Hundred Days*, p. 11.
14. Betty Bennet, *British War Poetry in the Age of Romanticism*, p. 494.

15. Redpath, *The Young Romantics and Critical Opinion 1807–1824: Poetry of Byron, Shelley and Keats as seen by their Contemporary Critics*, (London: Harrap, 1973), p. 207.
16. Jeffrey, *The Edinburgh Review*, p. 295.
17. J. G. Lockhart, *The Life of Sir Walter Scott*, p. 314. For Scott's visits to Waterloo and Paris see pp. 314–29; also Edgar Johnson, *Sir Walter Scott: The Great Unknown*, 2 vols. (London: Hamish Hamilton, 1976) I, 495–513.
18. Lockhart, *The Life of Sir Walter Scott*, p. 316.
19. Lockhart details this debt in his edition of the poetry, *The Poetical Works of Sir Walter Scott*, 12 vols., 1833–4, xi, 263, 268, 277, 279.
20. Scott, *Paul's Letters to his Kinfolk*, p. 194.
21. Quoted by Carl Woodring, 'Three Poets on Waterloo', *TWC*, 18, 2 (Spring 1987), p. 56.
22. Marchand, *Byron: A Biography*, II, 611, and *The Complete Poetical Works*, ed. McGann, II, 297–9.
23. Gill, *William Wordsworth: A Life*, p. 338.
24. Madden, *Robert Southey: The Critical Heritage*, p. 208.
25. Scott, *Paul's Letters to his Kinfolk*, p. 194.
26. *Critical Review*, May 1816. Quoted Madden, *Robert Southey: The Critical Heritage*, p. 206.
27. Jeffrey, *The Edinburgh Review*, p. 295.
28. Bennett, *British War Poetry in the Age of Romanticism*, pp. 592–4.
29. John Keegan, *The Face of Battle* (Harmondsworth: Penguin, 1978), p. 117.
30. *The Poetical Works of Sir Walter Scott*, ed. J. Logie Robertson (London and Edinburgh: Henry Frowde, 1904), p. 619.
31. Fitzgerald similarly had written:

    His [Wellington's] eagle eye discerns from far
    That moment which decides the war (lines 58–9).

32. Walter Scott, *Quarterly Review*, 16 (October 1816), pp. 172–208.
33. Ibid., pp. 194, 196.
34. Ibid., p. 194.
35. Ibid., p. 191.
36. Ibid.
37. Southey, *The Poet's Pilgrimage to Waterloo*, I, iv, 2.
38. For a discussion of this poem, and of other literary responses to the Russian campaign, see Irene Collins, 'Variations on the Theme of Napoleon's Moscow Campaign', *History: The Journal of the Historical Association*, 71, 231 (Feb. 1986), 39–53.
39. See also his letter to Wynn, 15 December 1815: 'Do not suppose that I mean to rival Scott. My poem will be in a very different strain' (*SL* IV, 144).
40. Southey's use of Spenserian allegory has been noted before, by Woodring, 'Three Poets on Waterloo', p. 55, and by Carnall, *Robert Southey and his Age*, p. 210. Though Spenser was not in fact a Poet Laureate, Southey seems either to have believed that he was, or claimed him as such – as is revealed by the opening of *Carmen Triumphale*. Southey's use of 'blazon' in his stanza

on being laureate in *Poet's Pilgrimage* (I, i, 6) seems particularly to allude to Spenser's use of it in the first stanza of the 'Dedication' of *The Faerie Queene.*

41. For Milton's 'impious legions' see *Paradise Lost* VI, 64, 142, 206, 230, 232, 655.
42. See Isabel G. MacCaffrey, *Paradise Lost as 'Myth'* (Harvard University Press, 1959) pp. 84–5.
43. Kelsall, *Byron's Politics*, p. 79.
44. Quoted Carnall, *Robert Southey and his Age*, p. 210.
45. 'Thanksgiving Ode', line 166.
46. In Ketcham, *Shorter Poems*, pp. 533–4.
47. Ibid., pp. 533–4.
48. In 'Inscription', Wordsworth transforms Waterloo into a Miltonic war in heaven in which Britain defeats the 'impious crew' (line 8). Both these words have a Miltonic resonance and implication. Satan 'Raised impious war in Heaven' (*Paradise Lost*, I, 43), his 'impious' nature is criticized by Abdiel in Book V, 813 and 845, he has an 'impious crest', VI, 188. The rebel angels are the 'impious foes' of Christ (VI, 831), and are frequently referred to as Satan's 'crew' – I, 51, 688, 751, IV, 573, 952, 879, VI, 49, 277, 370, 806, xii, 38.) The phrase 'hideous rout' in 'Occasioned' again evokes the war of *Paradise Lost.* For Wordsworth's use of the word 'hideous', used by Milton for Satan's fall, to represent Napoleon's fall, see chapter 4. The defeat of the rebel angels is frequently described by Milton as a rout: *Paradise Lost* I, 747, II, 770, 995, IV, 3, VI, 387, 598, 873, VII, 34, X, 534. The 'choral shout' of the 'blest Angels' suggests that of *Paradise Lost* VI, 200 where it is a presage of the final victory over Satan, and of 1 Thessalonians 4, 16: 'The Lord himself shall descend from Heaven with a shout.' The Good Angels hymn Christ's victory in *Paradise Lost* VI, 882–92. In Revelations 12:9, immediately after the 'old serpent' Satan is cast out from heaven a loud voice is heard celebrating Christ's victory.
49. In 'February 1816' Wordsworth uses Filicaia's Canzone on John Sobieski's deliverance of Vienna from a seige by the Turks in 1683 as an analogy for Waterloo. Like Southey's parallel with Charles Martel's victory over the Moors this enables him to establish the battle as a great and decisive event, and to align it with the wars of Christianity against the infidel.
50. In 'February, 1816' Wordsworth draws this standard comparison in the opening line 'O, for a kindling touch of that pure flame' which obviously alludes to the opening line of *Henry V*, 'O, for a muse of fire . . .'.
51. There is no evidence that the sonnet was intended for an actual monument on the battlefield: Ketcham, *Shorter Poems*, p. 533.
52. *Chambers Twentieth Century Dictionary*, p. 853.
53. Ketcham is the only critic to have got to grips with the genre of the 'Thanksgiving Ode', *Shorter Poems*, p. 12. Paul H. Fry in *The Poet's Calling in the English Ode* (New Haven: Yale University Press, 1980) writes that 'I shall have nothing to say of the pseudo-laureate odes of 1814 that crow over the fall of Napoleon' in his chapter on Wordsworth (p. 307). Curran, similarly,

refuses to include the poem amongst Wordsworth's 'significant odes', *Poetic Form and British Romanticism*, p. 77.

54. The 'Thanksgiving Ode' is the principal poem of the volume *Thanksgiving Ode, January 18, 1816, with Other Short Pieces, Chiefly Referring to Recent Public Events.*
55. For the dating of this poem, see Ketcham, *Shorter Poems*, pp. 534–5.
56. Ibid., p. 12. On the encomiastic tradition of the Pindaric ode see M. H. Abrams, *A Glossary of Literary Terms*, 3rd ed. (New York: Holt, Rinehart and Winston, 1971), pp. 116–17, and Curran, *Poetic Form and British Romanticism*, pp. 63–84.
57. Quoted Ketcham, *Shorter Poems*, p. 180.
58. Gill, *William Wordsworth: A Life*, p. 319.
59. See Ketcham, *Shorter Poems*, p. 535.
60. Ibid., p. 180.
61. Gill, *William Wordsworth: A Life*, p. 319.
62. Ketcham, *Shorter Poems*, p. 16.
63. See *Peter Bell the Third* line 637 and the essay 'Coriolanus', *HCW* IV, 214.
64. *Poems of Robert Southey*, ed. Fitzgerald, p. 365, line 66.
65. In *Shorter Poems* Ketcham doesn't give a date for the publication of the 'Thanksgiving Ode' volume, and as late as 26 April 1816 Lamb wrote to Wordsworth that he had just finished the 'Revise' of the poem, p. 536.
66. F. De Hondt, *Promenade 1815: On Foot or by Bicycle around the Battlefields at Braine L'Alleud, Genappe, Lasne and Waterloo* (Brussels: Federation Touristique de la Province De Brabant, 1987), pp. 53, 50, 35.
67. 'Three Poets on Waterloo', p. 54.
68. See McGann's note, *Complete Poetical Works*, II, 301–2.
69. For commentaries on this passage see Kelsall, *Byron's Politics*, pp. 66–9 and Paulson, *Representations of Revolution*, pp. 275–80.
70. *Quarterly Review*, 16 (October 1816) p. 192.
71. Ibid., pp. 192–3.
72. Ibid., p. 194.
73. *The Complete Poetical Works*, II, 300.
74. *Byron*, The Oxford Authors, p. 1031.
75. Lean, *The Napoleonists*, pp. 82–6.
76. Marchand, *Byron: A Biography*, III, 971.
77. Marilyn Butler, *Romantics, Rebels and Reactionaries*, p. 118.
78. Jeffrey, *The Edinburgh Review*, p. 298.
79. Ibid.
80. Scott, *Quarterly Review*, p. 196.
81. Ibid., pp. 196–7.
82. See Marilyn Butler, *Peacock Displayed: A Satirist in his Context* (London: Routledge, 1979): 'There was nothing specifically observant between 1816 and 1818 in noticing the literary rage for indulging gloom and misanthropy: those who were not attacking it were generally busy imitating it. It was much more usual at that time, however, to blame Byron, and

especially the spectacular misanthropy of canto III of *Childe Harold* (1816)' (p. 119).

83. McGann, *Complete Poetical Works*, III, 492.

6 'A PROUD AND FULL ANSWER': HAZLITT'S NAPOLEONIC RIPOSTE

1. *HCW* xiii, ix.
2. Bracketed numerical references throughout this chapter are to *HCW*, cited by volume and page, unless otherwise stated.
3. Quoted by Stanley Jones, *Hazlitt: A Life, From Winterslow to Frith Street* (Oxford: Clarendon Press, 1989), p. 123.
4. *The Marriage of Heaven and Hell* in *Blake: Complete Writings*, ed. Geoffrey Keynes (Oxford University Press, 1969), p. 150.
5. For Coleridge's 'character of Caliban, as an original and caricature of Jacobinism' see *LoL* II, 24. For Hazlitt's reply, reading Caliban as the legitimate monarch of the island and Prospero as the Jacobin or Bonaparte, see xix, 207–8. For discussions of this debate, see David Bromwich, *Hazlitt: The Mind of a Critic* (Oxford University Press, 1983), pp. 270–4, and Jonathan Bate, *Shakespearean Constitutions: Politics, Theatre, Criticism 1730–1830* (Oxford: Clarendon Press, 1989), pp. 178–80.
6. *LoL* II, 13–14; *LS* I, 65, and see note 7 below.
7. Dorothy George, *English Political Caricature, 1793–1832: A Study of Opinion and Propaganda*, 2 vols. (Oxford: Clarendon Press, 1959), II, 167. George, *Catalogue of Political and Personal Satire*, number 12593.
8. There are two probable candidates for the 'noted political writer' of the following quotation, both of whom Hazlitt had attacked in his writing for their opinions on Napoleon and the Bourbons during the winter of 1813–14. Howe in his annotation suggests John Stoddard (v, 389), Hazlitt's brother-in-law, who referred to Napoleon by Satanic appellations such as 'the Rebel Chief' and the 'Arch-Rebel' in his editorials for *The Times*. (See, for example, the *Times*' report on the Battle of Waterloo, Thursday, 22 June, 1815). Just as likely seems Edward Sterling, 'Vetus', whose letters to *The Times* Hazlitt had attacked in his series 'Illustrations of Vetus' which ran from 2 December 1813 to 5 January 1814 (VII, 39–71). Indeed, in the third of his letters, 12 November 1813, to which Hazlitt replied publicly on 19 November, Vetus termed Napoleon 'the enemy of the peace of mankind' and quoted in full and applied to him the passage from *Paradise Lost* on the fall of Satan that Wordsworth had used (I, 38). Whether or not Hazlitt is replying directly to one of these two is not really important, for in the period before the first abdication the use of analogy was common. Coleridge seems likely to have made the analogy for the same purposes in his lecture of 9 April 1814 (*LoL* II, 13–14) and it was he who had first made frequent use of the 'enemy' tag. Hazlitt singled out Coleridge for his attacks on Napoleon, and his coining of the nickname 'The Corsican'. Hazlitt reviewed Coleridge's *Lay Sermon* for the *Edinburgh Review* of

December 1816 (XVI, 99–114) and in it comments on the Will, Reason, and Understanding passage that Coleridge had followed with his discussion of Satan and Napoleon (XVI, 100–1). He again refers to the *Lay Sermon* in an article of 1817 (VII, 146). It is possible, then, that Hazlitt was aware of Coleridge's use of the analogy. Similarly, Hazlitt may well have been aware of Southey's use of the Satanic character for Napoleon in the *Ode Written During the Negotiations with Buonaparte, In January, 1814*. Byron, of course, had used the Satan analogy at the time of the first abdication in his 'Ode to Napoleon Buonaparte' (lines 8–9) and in his description of Napoleon's fall in *Manfred*, written from summer 1816 to April 1817, he used again the Miltonic structure of Wordsworth's 'most wonderful sentence':

> The Captive Usurper,
> Hurl'd down from the throne,
> Lay buried in torpor,
> Forgotten and lone: . . . (II, iii, 16–20)

9. M. H. Abrams, *The Mirror and the Lamp*, p. 250.
10. Again here I am adopting Blake's formula from *The Marriage of Heaven and Hell, Blake: Complete Writings*, ed. Keynes, p. 150.
11. Robinson, *William Hazlitt's Life of Napoleon Buonaparte: Its Sources and Characteristics* (Geneva: Librairie E. Droz; Paris, Librairie Minard, 1959), p. 36. As Robinson has shown, Hazlitt has a preformulated view of Napoleon which he brings to bear on his various source material. He has a 'rigid pattern of conviction about . . . Napoleon himself which operated so constantly and so strongly that Hazlitt prejudged virtually all matters concerning [him]. In consequence . . . the work is never free from a powerful directing pressure of one kind or another' (p. 36). In my analysis of *The Life* I have concentrated on those passages which Robinson has identified as having been written by Hazlitt, rather than those he adapted from other sources.
12. IX, 112, 116, 143, 144, 145, 155.
13. Jones, *Hazlitt: A Life*, p. 172.
14. See John Whale, 'Hazlitt on Burke: The Ambivalent Position of a Radical Essayist', *SiR*, 25, 4 (Winter 1986), pp. 466–81.
15. For these terms see IV, 214–16.
16. John Kinnaird, *William Hazlitt: Critic of Power* (New York: Columbia University Press, 1978), p. 83.
17. Jones, *Hazlitt: A Life*, p. 178.
18. Ibid., p. 179.
19. Ibid.
20. Ibid., p. 138.
21. Ibid.
22. Kinnaird, *Hazlitt: Critic of Power*, p. 34.
23. See Jones, *Hazlitt: A Life*, pp. 2, 25–8, 217.
24. Ibid., p. 172.
25. Ibid.

26. See also VIII, 324; XVII, 22; XIV, 236.
27. *The Examiner*, 5 April 1817.
28. Review of *Christabel*, *Edinburgh Review*, 27 (Sept. 1816), p. 67.
29. Friedman, *Fabricating History*, pp. 70–1.
30. For Hazlitt on Napoleon's talent and genius see also XIII, 20, 176, 182, 226, 247, 282, 320; XIV, 7, 105; XV, 4, 6, 122, 196, 229-30, 269.
31. Kinnaird, *Hazlitt, Critic of Power*, p. 329.
32. See Howe's note, XIII, 361.
33. See also XIII, ix.
34. Bromwich, *Hazlitt: The Mind of a Critic*, pp. 293–4.
35. Ibid., p. 318.
36. John Whale, 'Hazlitt on Burke', *passim.* See also Bromwich, *Hazlitt: The Mind of a Critic*, pp. 288–99.
37. For example, Luke (1: 51–2): 'He hath shewed strength with his arm; he hath scattered the proud in the imagination of their hearts. He hath put down the mighty from their seats, and exalted them of low degree.'
38. Kinnaird, *Hazlitt: Critic of Power*, p. 326.
39. Joseph Anthony Wittreich Jr., *The Romantics on Milton*, p. 151, n. 23.
40. Edmund Burke, *A Philosophical Enquiry into the Origins of our Ideas of the Sublime and the Beautiful*, ed. Adam Phillips (Oxford University Press, 1990), p. 57.
41. Throughout *The Life* Hazlitt stresses Napoleon's 'will'. See XIV, 22, 99, 122, 126; XV, 12, 53, 72, 234.
42. For further examples, see XIV, 77, 92, 161, 176.
43. For example, by Jon Cook in his Introduction to *William Hazlitt: Selected Writing* (Oxford University Press, 1991).

CONCLUSION: *THE AGE OF BRONZE*

1. Quoted from *Poetical Works*, ed. Frederick Page, a new edition corrected by John Jump (Oxford University Press, 1970).
2. Ernest J. Lovell, *His Very Self and Voice*, p. 31.

Bibliography

PRIMARY SOURCES

Blake, William. *Complete Writings, with Variant Readings*. ed. Geoffrey Keynes. Oxford University Press, 1969.

Blessington, Lady. *Lady Blessington's Conversations of Lord Byron*. ed. Ernest J. Lovell, Jr. Princeton University Press, 1969.

Brontë, Charlotte. *Shirley*. ed. H. Rosengarten and M. Smith. Oxford: Clarendon Press, 1979.

Broughton, John Cam Hobhouse, Lord. *Recollections of a Long Life*. 2 vols. London: John Murray, 1910.

Burke, Edmund. *A Philosophical Enquiry into the Origins of our Ideas of the Sublime and Beautiful*. ed. Adam Phillips. Oxford University Press, 1990.

Reflections on the Revolution in France and on the proceedings in Certain Societies in London relative to that event. ed. Conor Cruise O'Brien. Harmondsworth: Penguin, 1968 rpt 1983.

Byron, George Gordon, Lord. *Byron*. ed. Jerome J. McGann. The Oxford Authors. Oxford University Press, 1986.

Byron's Letters and Journals. 12 vols. ed. Leslie Marchand. London: John Murray, 1973–82.

The Complete Poetical Works. 6 vols. ed. Jerome J. McGann. Oxford: Clarendon Press, 1980–91.

Don Juan. ed. T. G. Steffan, E. Steffan and W. W. Pratt. Harmondsworth: Penguin, 1973 rpt 1982.

Poetical Works. ed. Frederick Page. A new edition, corrected by John Jump. Oxford University Press, 1970.

The Works of Lord Byron: Letters and Journals. 6 vols. ed. Rowland E. Prothero. London: John Murray, 1898–1901.

The Works of Lord Byron: Poetry. 7 vols. ed. Ernest Hartley Coleridge. London: John Murray, 1898–1904.

Coleridge, Samuel Taylor. *Biographia Literaria or Biographical Sketches of my Literary Life and Opinions*. 2 vols. ed. James Engell and W. Jackson Bate. Bollingen Series. London: Routledge and Princeton University Press, 1983.

Coleridge's Verse: A Selection. ed. William Empson and David Pirie. London: Faber and Faber, 1972.

Collected Letters Of Samuel Taylor Coleridge. 6 vols. ed. E. L. Griggs. Oxford: Clarendon Press, 1956–71.

Essays On His Times – in The Morning Post and the Courier. 3 vols. ed David V. Erdman. Bollingen Series. London: Routledge and Princeton University Press, 1978.

The Friend. 2 vols. ed. Barbara E. Rooke. Bollingen Series. London: Routledge and Princeton University Press, 1969.

Lay Sermons. ed. R. J. White. Bollingen Series. London: Routledge and Princeton University Press, 1972.

Lectures 1808–1819 on Literature. 2 vols. ed. R. A. Foakes. Bollingen Series. London: Routledge and Princeton University Press, 1987.

The Notebooks of Samuel Taylor Coleridge. 6 vols. ed. Kathleen Coburn. New York: Pantheon Books, 1957–73.

Poems. ed. John Beer. Everyman's Library. London: Dent, 1963 rpt 1974.

The Poetical Works of Samuel Taylor Coleridge. 2 vols. ed. Ernest Hartley Coleridge. Oxford University Press, 1912 rpt 1983.

Samuel Taylor Coleridge. ed. H. J. Jackson. The Oxford Authors. Oxford University Press, 1985.

Shakespearean Criticism. 2 vols. ed. Thomas Middleton Raysor. Everyman's Library. London: Dent, 1907. 2nd ed. 1960.

Coleridge, Sara. *Memoirs and Letters of Sara Coleridge.* ed. Edith Coleridge. London: Henry S. King and Co., 1873.

Gance, Abel. *Napoleon.* trans. Moya Hassan, ed. Bambi Ballard. London, Boston: Faber and Faber, 1990.

Haydon, Benjamin Robert. *The Autobiography and Memoirs of Benjamin Robert Haydon (1786–1846).* 2 vols. ed. Aldous Huxley. London: Peter Davies, 1926.

Hazlitt, William. *The Complete Works of William Hazlitt.* 21 vols. ed. P. P. Howe. London: J. M.Dent, 1930–4.

The Letters of William Hazlitt. ed. Herschel Moreland Sikes, assisted by Willard Hallam Bonner and Gerald Lahey. New York University Press, 1978.

William Hazlitt: Selected Writing. ed. Jon Cook. Oxford University Press, 1991.

Hugo, Victor. *Les Misérables.* trans. Norman Denny. Harmondsworth: Penguin, 1976.

Hunt, Leigh. *Leigh Hunt's Political and Occasional Essays.* ed. Lawrence Huston Houtchens and Carolyn Washburn Houtchens, with an introduction by Carl Woodring. New York and London: Columbia University Press, 1962.

Jeffrey, Francis. Review of *Childe Harold's Pilgrimage III*, *Edinburgh Review*, 54, (Dec. 1816) 277–310, rpt in *The Young Romantics and Critical Opinion, 1807–1824.* ed. Theodore Redpath. London: Harrap, 1973, 217–22.

Johnson, Samuel. *The Complete English Poems.* Harmondsworth: Penguin, 1982.

Juvenal. *The Sixteen Satires.* trans. Peter Green. Harmondsworth: Penguin, 1967 rpt 1986.

Keats, John. *Letters of John Keats: A New Selection.* ed. Robert Gittings. Oxford University Press, 1970.

The Poems of John Keats. ed. Miriam Allott. London: Longman, 1970.

Landor, Walter Savage. *The Poetical Works of Walter Savage Landor.* 3 vols. ed. Stephen Wheeler. Oxford: Clarendon Press, 1937.

Selected Poetry and Prose ed. Keith Hanley. Manchester: Carcanet Press, 1981.

Medwin, Thomas. *Medwin's Conversations of Lord Byron.* ed. Ernest J. Lovell. Princeton University Press, 1966.

Milton, John. *Complete Shorter Poems.* ed. John Carey. London and New York: Longman, 1968 rpt with corrections 1981.

Paradise Lost. ed. Alastair Fowler. London: Longman, 1968 rpt with minor corrections 1971.

Ovid. *Metamorphoses.* trans. Mary M. Innes. Harmondsworth: Penguin, 1955.

Paine, Thomas. *Rights of Man.* ed. Eric Foner. Penguin, 1984 rpt 1987.

Pope, Alexander. *The Poems of Alexander Pope.* ed. John Butt. London: Methuen, 1963.

Scott, Sir Walter. *The Letters of Sir Walter Scott.* 12 vols. ed. H. J. C. Grierson. London: Constable, 1932–7.

The Life of Napoleon Buonaparte, Emperor of the French, with a Preliminary View of the French Revolution. Exeter: J. & B. Williams, 1843.

Paul's Letters to his Kinfolk. Edinburgh and London: Archibald Constable & Co, and John Murray, 1816.

The Poetical Works. ed. J. Logie Robertson. London and Edinburgh: Henry Frowde, 1904.

The Poetical Works of Sir Walter Scott. 12 vols. ed. J. G. Lockhart, 1833–4.

Review of *Childe Harold's Pilgrimage III, Quarterly Review,* 16 (October 1816), 172–208.

Shakespeare, William. *The Complete Poetical Works*, compact edition, general editors, Stanley Wells and Gary Taylor. Oxford: Clarendon Press, 1988.

Shelley, P. B. *Alastor and Other Poems: Prometheus Unbound with Other Poems: Adonais.* ed. P. H. Butler. Plymouth: Macdonald & Evans, 1970 rpt 1981.

The Letters Of Percy Bysshe Shelley. 2 vols, ed. Frederick L. Jones. Oxford: Clarendon Press, 1964.

Poetical Works. ed. Thomas Hutchinson. A new edition, corrected by G. M. Matthews. Oxford University Press, 1970.

Selected Poems. ed. Timothy Webb. Everyman's Library. London: J. M. Dent and Sons, 1977 rpt with corrections and minor revisions 1983 rpt 1988.

Southey, Robert. *The Life and Correspondence of the Late Robert Southey.* 6 vols. ed. Rev. Charles Cuthbert Southey. London: Longman, Brown, Green & Longmans, 1850.

New Letters of Robert Southey. 2 vols. ed. Kenneth Curry. New York and London: Columbia University Press, 1965.

Poems. ed. M. H. Fitzgerald. Oxford University Press, 1909.

Virgil. *The Eclogues, Georgics and Aeneid of Virgil.* trans. C. Day Lewis. Oxford University Press, 1966.

Whately, Richard. *Historic Doubts Relative to Napoleon Bonaparte.* ed. Ralph S. Pomeroy. Berkeley and London: Scolar Press, 1985.

Wordsworth, William. *Letters Of William and Dorothy Wordsworth, The Early Years,*

1787–1805. ed. E. de Selincourt, 2nd ed., revised Chester L. Shaver. Oxford: Clarendon Press, 1967.

The Letters of William and Dorothy Wordsworth: The Later Years, Part I 1821–1828. ed. E. de Selincourt, 2nd ed., revised by Alan G. Hill. Oxford: Clarendon, 1978.

Letters of William and Dorothy Wordsworth, The Middle Years, Part I, 1806–1811. ed. E de Selincourt, 2nd ed., revised by Mary Moorman. Oxford: Clarendon Press, 1967.

Letters of William and Dorothy Wordsworth, The Middle Years, Part II, 1812–1820. ed. E. de Selincourt, 2nd ed., revised by Mary Moorman and Alan G. Hill. Oxford: Clarendon Press, 1967.

Poems, in Two Volumes. ed. Jared Curtis. The Cornell Wordsworth. Ithaca and London: Cornell University Press, 1983.

The Poetical Works of William Wordsworth 5 vols. ed. E. de Selincourt and Helen Darbyshire. Oxford: Clarendon Press, 1947–54.

The Prelude: 1799, 1805, 1850. ed. Jonathan Wordsworth, M.H. Abrams, and Stephen Gill. New York, London: W. W. Norton & Company, 1979.

The Prelude; or, Growth of a Poet's Mind. ed E. de Selincourt, revised Helen Darbyshire. Oxford: Clarendon Press, 1959.

The Prose Works of William Wordsworth. ed. W. J. B. Owen and Jane Worthington Smyser. 3 vols. Oxford: Clarendon Press, 1974.

Shorter Poems, 1807–1820. ed. Carl Ketcham. The Cornell Wordsworth. Ithaca and London: Cornell University Press, 1989.

William Wordsworth. ed. Stephen Gill. The Oxford Authors. Oxford University Press, 1984 rpt with corrections 1986.

SECONDARY SOURCES

Abrams, M. H. 'Apocalypse: Theme and Romantic Variations' in *The Apocalypse in English Renaissance Literature*, ed. C. A. Patrides and Joseph Anthony Wittreich, Jr. Ithaca: Cornell University Press; Manchester: Manchester University Press, 1983. rpt in M. H. Abrams, *The Correspondent Breeze: Essays on English Romanticism.* New York and London: W. W. Norton & Co., 1984, 225–57.

'English Romanticism: The Spirit of the Age' in Romanticism Reconsidered: Selected Papers from the *English Institute*, ed. Northrop Frye. New York: Columbia University Press, 1963, 26–72. rpt in M. H. Abrams, *The Correspondent Breeze: Essays on English Romanticism.* New York and London: W. W. Norton & Co., 1984, 44–75.

(ed.). *English Romantic Poets: Modern Essays in Criticism.* 2nd. ed. Oxford University Press, 1975.

The Mirror and the Lamp: Romantic Theory and the Critical Tradition. Oxford University Press, 1953.

Natural Supernaturalism: Tradition and Revolution in Romantic Literature. New York and London: W. W. Norton & Co., 1971 rpt 1973.

'On Political Readings of Lyrical Ballads' in M.H.Abrams, *Doing Things with Texts: Essays in Criticism and Critical Theory*, ed. with a Foreword by Michael Fischer. New York and London: W. W. Norton & Co., 1989, 364–91.

'Structure and Style in the Greater Romantic Lyric' in *From Sensibility to Romanticism: Essays Presented to Frederick A. Pottle*, ed. Frederick W. Hilles and Harold Bloom. Oxford University Press, 1965, 527–60, rpt in M. H. Abrams, *The Correspondent Breeze: Essays on English Romanticism.* New York and London: W. W. Norton & Co., 1984, 76–108.

'Two Roads to Wordsworth' in *Wordsworth: A Collection of Critical Essays*, ed. M. H. Abrams. Englewood Cliffs, N. J.: Prentice-Hall inc., 1972, 1–11. rpt in M. H. Abrams, *The Correspondent Breeze: Essays on English Romanticism.* New York and London: W. W. Norton & Co., 1984, 145–58.

Aers, David, Cook, Jonathan, Punter, David. *Romanticism and Ideology: Studies in English Writing 1765–1830.* London: Routledge, 1981.

Albrecht, W. P. 'Hazlitt and the Romantic Sublime', *TWC*, 10 ,1 (Winter 1979), 59–68.

Arac, Jonathan. *Critical Genealogies.* New York: Columbia University Press, 1987.

Ashton, John. *English Caricature and Satire on Napoleon I.* London: Chatto and Windus, 1888.

Aspinall, Arthur. *Politics and the Press, 1780–1850.* Brighton: Harvester Press, 1973.

Bailey, John. *The Continuity of Letters.* Oxford: Clarendon Press, 1923.

Baker, Carlos. 'Sensation and Vision in Wordsworth' in *English Romantic Poets.* ed. M. H. Abrams. Oxford University Press, 1960 rpt 1973, 95–109.

Barbéis, Pierre. 'Napoléon: Structure et Signification d'un Mythe Litéraire', *Revue d'Histoire Litéraire de la France*, 70 (1970) 1031–58.

Barnard, John. *John Keats.* Cambridge University Press, 1990.

Barnet, Correlli. *Bonaparte.* London: George Allen and Unwin, 1978.

Barrell, John. *English Literature in History 1730–80: An Equal, Wide Survey.* London: Hutchinson Press, 1983.

Barton, Ann. *Byron and the Mythology of Fact.* Nottingham Byron Lecture: University of Nottingham, 1968.

Bate, Jonathan. *Romantic Ecology: Wordsworth and the Environmental Tradition.* London and New York: Routledge, 1991.

Shakespeare and the English Romantic Imagination. Oxford: Clarendon Press, 1989.

Shakespearean Constitutions: Politics, Theatre, Criticism 1730–1830. Oxford: Clarendon Press, 1989.

Beatty, Bernard. 'Continuity and Discontinuity in Language and Voice in Dryden, Pope and Byron' in *Byron: Augustan and Romantic* ed. Andrew Rutherford. Houndsmill, Basingstoke, Hampshire and London: Macmillan Press, 1990, 117–35.

Beer, John. *Coleridge The Visionary.* London: Chatto and Windus, 1959.

'The "Revolutionary Youth" of Wordsworth and Coleridge: another View', *Critical Quarterly*, 19 (1977), 79–87.

Behrendt, Stephen. (ed.). *History and Myth: Essays on English Romantic Literature.* Detroit: Wayne State University Press, 1990.

'History, Mythmaking and the Romantic Artist' in *History and Myth: Essays on English Romantic Literature* ed. Stephen Behrendt. Detroit: Wayne State University Press, 1990.

Bennett, Betty. *British War Poetry in the Age of Romanticism 1793–1815*. New York and London: Garland, 1976.

Bewell, Alan. 'The Political Implications of Keats's Classicist Aesthetics', *SiR*, 25, 2 (Summer 1986), 220–9.

Bloom, Harold. 'Napoleon and Prometheus: The Romantic Myth of Organic Energy', *Yale French Studies*, 26 (1969), 79–82.

The Ringers in the Tower. Chicago University Press, 1971.

Bostetter, Edward E. *The Romantic Ventriloquists*. Seattle: Washington University Press, 1963.

Bowle, John. *Napoleon*. London; George Weidenfeld and Nicolson, 1973.

Politics and Opinion in the Nineteenth Century, London: Cape, 1954.

Bradley, William. *The Early Poems of Walter Savage Landor: A Study of his Debt to Milton*. London: Bradley Agnew, 1914.

Brett-James, Antony (ed.). *The Hundred Days: Napoleon's Last Campaign From Eye-Witness Accounts*. Cambridge: Ken Trotman, 1989.

Brightfield, Myron F. 'Scott, Hazlitt and Napoleon', *Essays and Studies by the Members of the Department of English, University of California: Publications in Berkeley*. California University Press, 14, 181–98.

Brinton, Crane. *The Political Ideas of the English Romanticists*. Oxford University Press, 1926.

Broadley, A. M. *Napoleon in Caricature: 1795–1821*. 2 vols. London: The Bodley Head, 1911.

Bromwich, David. *Hazlitt: The Mind of a Critic*. Oxford University Press, 1983.

'Keats's Radicalism', *SiR*, 25, 2 (Summer 1986), 197–21.

Bronowski, Jacob. *William Blake and the Age of Revolution*. London: Routledge, 1972.

Bryant, Arthur. *The Age of Elegance, 1812–1822*. London: Collins, 1944 rpt 1975.

The Years of Endurance, 1793–1802. London: Collins, 1944 rpt 1975.

The Years of Victory, 1802–1812. London: Collins, 1944 rpt 1975.

Burnett, T. A. J. *The Rise and Fall of a Regency Dandy. The Life and Times of Scrope Berdmore Davies*. London: John Murray, 1981.

Burton, Anthony and Murdoch, John. *Byron: An Exhibition to Commemorate the 150th Anniversary of his Death in the Greek War of Liberation, 19 April 1824*. London: Victoria and Albert Museum, 1974.

Butler, Marilyn. 'Against Tradition: The Case for a Particularized Historical Method' in *Historical Studies and Literary Criticism*. ed. Jerome J. McGann. Madison: Wisconsin University Press, 1986, 25–47.

(ed.). *Burke, Paine, Godwin and the Revolution Controversy*. Cambridge University Press, 1984.

'Byron and the Empire in the East' in *Byron: Augustan and Romantic*. ed. Andrew Rutherford. London: Macmillan, 1990, 63–81.

Peacock Displayed: A Satirist in his Context. London: Routledge, 1979.

'Repossessing the Past: the Case for an Open Literary History' in *Rethinking Historicism: Critical Readings in English Romanticism*, Marjorie Levinson, Marilyn Butler, Jerome McGann, Paul Hamilton. Oxford and New York: Basil Blackwell, 1989, 64–84.

'Romanticism in England' in *Romanticism in National Context*. ed. Roy Porter and Mikulas Teich. Cambridge University Press, 1988, 37–67.

Romantics, Rebels and Reactionaries: English Literature and its Background, 1760–1830. Oxford University Press, 1981.

'Telling it Like a Story: The French Revolution as Narrative', *SiR*, 28, 3 (Fall 1989), 343–64.

Bygrave, Stephen. *Coleridge and the Self: Romantic Egotism*. New York: St Martin's Press, 1986.

Calleo, David. 'Coleridge on Napoleon', *Yale French Studies* 26 (1960–1), 83–93.

Carnall, Geoffrey. *Robert Southey and his Age: The Development of a Conservative Mind*. Oxford, Clarendon Press, 1960.

Chandler, David. *The Campaigns of Napoleon*. London: Weidenfeld and Nicolson, 1966.

Waterloo: The Hundred Days. London: George Philip, 1980.

Chandler, James. 'Wordsworth and Burke', *ELH*, 47, 4 (Winter 1980), 741–71.

Wordsworth's Second Nature: A Study of Poetry and Politics. Chicago University Press, 1984.

Chaplin, Chester F. *Personification in Eighteenth Century Poetry*. New York: Octagon Books, 1968.

Christensen, Jerome. *Lord Byron's Strength: Romantic Writing and Commercial Society*. Baltimore and London: The Johns Hopkins University Press, 1993.

Christie, Ian R. *Wars and Revolution: Britain 1760–1815*. London: Edward Arnold, 1982.

Cobban, Alfred. *Edmund Burke and the Revolt against the Eighteenth Century*. London : George Allen and Unwin, 1962.

Colley, Linda. *Britons: Forging the Nation 1707–1837*. New Haven and London: Yale University Press, 1992.

Collins, Irene. *Napoleon: First Consul and Emperor of the French*. London: The Historical Association, 1988.

'Variations on the Theme of Napoleon's Moscow Campaign', *History: The Journal of the Historical Association*. 71, 231 (February 1986) 39–53.

Colmer, John. *Coleridge: Critic of Society*. Oxford: Clarendon Press, 1959.

Cook, Jonathan. 'Hazlitt: Criticism and Ideology', in *Romanticism and Ideology: Studies in English Writing 1765–1830*. David Aers, Jonathan Cook, David Punter. London: Routledge, 1981.

Cooke, Katherine. *Coleridge*. London: Routledge, 1979.

Cooper, Andrew M. 'Chains, Pains, and Tentative Gains: The Byronic Prometheus in the Summer of 1816', *SiR*, 27, 4 (Winter 1988), 529–50.

Cronin, Vincent. *Napoleon*. London: The History Book Club by arrangement with William Collins, 1971.

Curran, Stuart. *Poetic Form and British Romanticism*. Oxford University Press, 1986.

'The Political Prometheus', *SiR*, 25, 3 (Fall 1986), 429–55.
Curry, Kenneth. *Southey*. London: Routledge, 1975.
Curtius, E. R. *European Literature and the Latin Middle Ages*. trans. Willard R. Trask. London: Routledge, 1953.
Darst, D. W. 'Napoleon in Romantic Thought ; A Study of Hazlitt, Stendhal and Scott'. Unpublished doctoral dissertation, Columbia University, 1976.
Davis, N. V. 'Five English Romantics And Napoleon'. Unpublished doctoral dissertation, Princeton University, 1957.
de Man, Paul. *The Rhetoric of Romanticism*. New York: Columbia University Press, 1984.
Deane, Seamus. *The French Revolution and the Enlightenment in England, 1789–1832*. Cambridge, Mass.: Harvard University Press, 1988.
Derry, John. 'Opposition Whigs and the French Revolution, 1789–1815' in *Britain and the French Revolution*, ed. H. T. Dickinson, London: Macmillan Education, 1989.
Dicey, A. V. *The Statesmanship of Wordsworth*. Oxford University Press, 1917.
Dowden, Edward. 'The French Revolution and English Literature' in *Studies in Literature, 1789–1877*. New York: Charles Scrivener and Sons, 1897.
Edwards, Thomas R. *Imagination and Power: A Study of Poetry on Public Themes*. London: Chatto and Windus, 1971.
Ellis, Geoffrey. *The Napoleonic Empire*. Studies in European History. London: Macmillan, 1991.
Emerson, Sheila. 'Byron's "one word": The Language of Self-Expression in *Childe Harold III*', *SiR*, 20, 3 (Fall 1981), 363–82.
Elwin, Malcolm. *Landor: A Replevin*. London: Macdonald, 1958.
Emsley, Clive. *British Society and the French Wars, 1793–1815*. London: Macmillan, 1979.
Erdman, David V. *Blake, Prophet against Empire: A Poet's Interpretation of the History of his own Times*. Princeton University Press, 1984.
'Coleridge as Editorial Writer' in *Power and Consciousness*, ed. Conor Cruise O'Brien and Willian Dean Vanech. London University Press, 1969.
'The Man who was not Napoleon', *TWC*, 12, 1 (Winter 1981), 92–6.
'Milton! Thou should'st be living', *TWC*, 19 (1988), 2–8.
Europe Special issue: 'Napoleon et la littérature', 47 (April–May 1969).
Everest, Kelvin. *English Romantic Poetry: an Introduction to the Historical Context and the Literary Scene*. Milton Keynes: Open University Press, 1990.
(ed.). *Revolution in Writing*. Buckingham: Open University Press, 1991.
Fink, Zera. 'Wordsworth and the English Republican Tradition', *Journal of English and German Philology* (1948), 107–26.
Foot, Michael. *The Politics of Paradise: A Vindication of Byron*. London: William Collins & Co., 1988.
Friedman, Barton R. *Fabricating History: English Writers on the French Revolution*. Princeton University Press, 1988.
Fry, Paul. *The Poet's Calling in the English Ode*. New Haven: Yale University Press, 1980.

Frye, Northrop. *Fables of Identity: Studies in Poetic Mythology*. New York: Harbinger, 1963.

(ed.). *Romanticism Reconsidered: Selected Papers from the English Institute.* New York and London: Columbia University Press, 1968.

A Study of English Romanticism. Brighton: Harvester Press, 1983.

Furst, Lillian R. *The Contours of European Romanticism.* London: Macmillan, 1979.

Fussell, Paul. *The Great War and Modern Memory*. Oxford University Press, 1975.

Wartime: Understanding and Behaviour in the Second World War. Oxford University Press, 1989.

Garrison, James D. *Dryden and the Tradition of Panegyric.* California University Press, 1975.

George, Eric. *The Life and Death of Benjamin Robert Haydon, Historical Painter, 1786–1846.* 2nd. ed. with additions by Dorothy George. Oxford: Clarendon Press, 1976.

George, Mary Dorothy. *Catalogue of Political and Personal Satires Preserved in the Department of Prints and Drawings in the British Museum.* Vols VII–X, 1793–1827. London: The British Museum, 1942–52.

English Political Caricature, 1793–1832: A Study of Opinion and Propaganda. 2 vols. Oxford: Clarendon Press, 1959.

Geyl, Pieter. *Napoleon: For and Against.* London: Penguin in association with Jonathan Cape, 1949 rpt 1965.

Gill, Stephen. *William Wordsworth: A Life.* Oxford Lives. Oxford University Press, 1989.

Gittings, Robert and Manton, Jo. *Dorothy Wordsworth.* Oxford Lives. Oxford University Press, 1988.

Gleckner, Robert F. *Byron and the Ruins of Paradise.* Westport, Conn.: Greenwood Press, 1967.

Goldstein, Lawrence. *Ruins and Empire – The Evolution of a Theme in Augustan and Romantic Literature.* Pittsburgh: University Press, 1977.

Grace, William J. *Ideas in Milton.* London: Notre Dame University Press, 1968.

Guerard, Albert Leon. *Reflections on the Napoleonic Legend.* London: T. Fisher Unwin, 1924.

Hagin, Peter. *The Epic Hero and the Decline of Heroic Poetry.* Bern: Franke Verlag, 1964.

Halsted, John B (ed). *Romanticism.* New York: Walker and Co., 1969.

Hamilton, Paul. *Wordsworth.* Harvester New Readings. Brighton, Sussex: Harvester Press, 1986.

Hancock, Albert Elmer. *The French Revolution and the English Poets: A Study in Historical Criticism.* New York: Henry Holt, 1899.

Horward, D. 'Napoleon, His Legend and Sir Walter Scott', *Southern Humanities Review*, 16, 1 (Winter 1982), 1–13.

Harris, R. W. *Romanticism and the Social Order, 1780–1830.* London: Blandford Press, 1969.

Hartman, Geoffrey. *Wordsworth's Poetry: 1787–1814.* New Haven: Yale University Press, 1964.

Harvey, A. D. *English Literature and the Great War with France: An Anthology and Commentary*. London: Nold Jonson Books, 1981.

Havens, Raymond Dexter. *The Influence of Milton on English Poetry*. New York: Russell and Russell, 1961.

Haydon, John O. Review of Alan Liu's *Wordsworth: The Sense of History, Nineteenth Century Literature*, 45, 2 (Sept. 1990), 245–9.

Haythornwaite, Philip J. *The Napoleonic Source Book*. London: Arms and Armour, 1990.

Hemmings, F. W. J. *Culture and Society in France 1789–1849*. Leicester University Press, 1987.

Hill, James L. 'Experiments in the Narrative of Consciousness: Byron, Wordsworth and *Childe Harold*, Cantos 3 and 4', *ELH*, 35 (1986), 121–40.

Hirst, Wolf. 'Lord Byron Cuts a Figure: The Keatsian View', *The Byron Journal*, 13 (1985), 36–51.

Herold, J. Christopher. *The Age of Napoleon*. London: Weidenfeld and Nicolson, 1963.

Hobsbawm, E. J. *The Age of Revolution: Europe 1789–1848*. London: Abacus, 1972.

Hodgson, John A. 'The Structures of *Childe Harold III*', *SiR*, 18, 3 (Fall 1979), 363–82.

Holmes, Richard. *Coleridge*. Past Masters. Oxford University Press, 1982.

Coleridge, Early Visions. Harmondsworth: Penguin, 1990.

Hondt, F. De. *Promenade 1815: On Foot or by Bicycle around the Battlefield at Braine L'Alleud, Genappe, Lasne and Waterloo*. Brussells: Federation Touristique de la Province De Brabant, 1987.

Hopkins, Brooke. 'Representing Robespierre' in *History and Myth: Essays on English Romantic Literature*. ed. Stephen Behrendt. Detroit: Wayne State University Press, 1990.

Horsman, E. A. 'The Design of Wordsworth's *Prelude*' in *Wordsworth's Mind and Art*. ed. A. W. Thomson. Edinburgh: Oliver & Boyd, 1969, 95–110.

Horward, Donald. 'Napoleon, his Legend, and Sir Walter Scott', *Southern Humanities Review*, 16 (Winter 1982), 1–13.

Howarth, David. *Waterloo: A Near Run Thing*. Glasgow: Collins and Fontana Books, 1968 rpt 1972.

Jackson, J. R. de J. *Poetry of the Romantic Period*. London: Routledge, 1980.

Jacobus, Mary. *Romanticism, Writing and Sexual Difference: Essays on 'The Prelude'*. Oxford: Clarendon Press, 1989.

Jamil, Tahir. *Trancendentalism in English Romantic Poetry*. New York: Vantage Press, 1989.

Johnson, Edgar. *Sir Walter Scott: The Great Unknown*. 2 vols. London: Hamish Hamilton, 1976.

Jones, R. Ben. *Napoleon: Man and Myth*. New York: Holmes and Meyer, 1972.

Jones, Stanley. *Hazlitt: A Life, From Winterslow to Frith Street*. Oxford: Clarendon Press, 1989.

Jump, John D. (ed.). *Byron: A Symposium*. London: Macmillan, 1975.

Keegan, John. *The Face of Battle: A Study of Agincourt, Waterloo and the Somme.* Harmondsworth: Penguin, 1978.

Kelley, Theresa M. 'J. M. W. Turner, Napoleonic Caricature, and Romantic Allegory', *ELH*, 58 (Summer 1991), 351–82.

Wordsworth's Revisionary Aesthetics. Cambridge University Press, 1989.

Kelsall, Malcolm. *Byron's Politics.* Sussex: Harvester Press, 1987.

Kestner, Joseph. 'The Genre of Landor's *Gebir*: "Eminences Excessively Bright"', *TWC*, 5 (1974), 41–9.

Kinnaird, John. *William Hazlitt Critic of Power.* New York: Columbia University Press, 1978.

Klancher, Jon. 'English Romanticism and Cultural Production', in *The New Historicism*, ed. Aram Veeser. London: Routledge, 1989, 77–88.

'Romantic Criticism and the Meaning of the French Revolution', *SiR*, 28, 3 (Fall 1989), 463–91.

Knight, G. Wilson. *Byron and Shakespeare.* London: Routledge, 1966.

Lord Byron Christian Virtues. London: Routledge, 1952.

Lord Byron's Marriage, The Evidence of Asterisks. London: Routledge, 1957.

Poets of Action. London: Methuen, 1968.

Kroeber, Carl. *Romantic Landscape Vision.* Madison: University of Wisconsin Press, 1975.

Lean, E. Tangye. *The Napoleonists: A Study in Political Disaffection, 1760–1960.* Oxford University Press, 1970.

Lefebvre, George. *Napoleon.* 2 vols. New York: Columbia University Press, 1969.

Legois, Emile. *The Early Life of William Wordsworth.* New York: 1918.

Lerner, Lawrence. *The Uses of Nostalgia: Studies in Pastoral Poetry.* London: Chatto and Windus, 1972.

Lévi-Strauss, Claude. *The Savage Mind.* University of Chicago Press, 1966.

Levinson, Marjorie. *Keats's Life of Allegory: The Origins of a Style.* Oxford: Basil Blackwell, 1988.

Rethinking Historicism: Critical Readings in Romantic History. With Marilyn Butler, Jerome McGann, Paul Hamilton. Oxford: Basil Blackwell, 1989.

Wordsworth's Great Period Poems: Four Essays. Cambridge University Press, 1986.

Liu, Alan. 'The Power of Formalism: The New Historicism', *ELH*, 56 (1989), 721–71.

Review of David Simpson's *Wordsworth's Historical Imagination: The Poetry of Displacement*, *TWC*, 19, 4 (Autumn 1988), 172–81.

'Wordsworth: The History in "Imagination"', *ELH*, 51 (Fall 1984), 504–48.

Wordsworth: The Sense of History. Stanford University Press, 1989.

Lockhart, John Gibson. *The Life of Sir Walter Scott, Bart.* London: Adam and Charles Black, 1893.

Longford, Elizabeth. *Byron.* London: Hutchinson, 1976.

Wellington: The Years of the Sword. London: Weidenfeld and Nicolson, 1969 rpt Panther, 1972.

Lovell, Ernest J. Jr. *His Very Self and Voice: Collected Conversations of Lord Byron.* New York: Octagon Books, 1980.

Lutzeler, Paul Michael. 'The Image of Napoleon in European Romanticism' in *European Romanticism: Literary Currents, Modes and Models*, ed. Gehart Hoffmeister. Detroit: Wayne State University Press, 1990, 211–28.

MacCaffrey, Isabel G. *Paradise Lost as 'Myth'*. Cambridge, Mass.: Harvard University Press, 1959.

MacCunn, F. J. *The Contemporary English View of Napoleon*. London: G. Bell and Sons, 1914.

McGann, Jerome J. *Don Juan in Context*. London: John Murray, 1976.

Fiery Dust: Byron's Poetic Development. Chicago University Press, 1968.

The Romantic Ideology: A Critical Investigation. Chicago University Press, 1983.

Maclean, Catherine Macdonald. *Born under Saturn: A Biography of William Hazlitt*. London: Collins, 1943.

Madden, Lionel. *Robert Southey: The Critical Heritage*. London: Routledge, 1972.

Maniquis, Robert M. 'Holy Savagery and Wild Justice: English Romanticism and the Terror', *SiR*, 28, 3 (Fall 1989), 365–95.

Manning, Peter J. *Reading Romantics; Texts and Contexts*. Oxford University Press, 1990.

Review of Alan Liu's *Wordsworth: The Sense of History*, *SiR*, 28, 3 (Fall 1989), 414–22.

Marchand, Leslie A. *Byron: A Biography*. 3 vols. London: John Murray, 1957.

Markham, Felix. *Napoleon*. London: Weidenfeld and Nicolson, 1963.

Martin, Philip W. 'Romanticism, History, Historicism' in *Revolution in Writing*, ed. Kelvin Everest. Buckingham: Open University Press, 1991.

Matthews, G. M. 'A Volcano's Voice in Shelley'. *ELH*, 24, 3 (September 1957), 191–228.

Maurois, André. *Byron*. London: The Bodley Head, 1950.

Napoleon: A Pictorial Biography. London: Thames and Hudson, 1963.

Maxwell, J. C. 'Wordsworth and the Subjugation of Switzerland', *MLR*, 65, 1 (January 1970), 16–18.

Mellor, Anne K. *English Romantic Irony*. Cambridge, Mass.: Harvard University Press, 1980.

Mitchell, Leslie. *Holland House*. London: Duckworth, 1980.

Monk, Samuel H. *The Sublime, A Study of Critical Theories in XVIII Century England*. Michigan: Ann Arbor Paperbacks, 1960.

Moorman, Mary. *William Wordsworth: A Biography; The Early Years; 1770–1803*. Oxford University Press, 1957 rpt 1968.

William Wordsworth: A Biography; The Later Years; 1803–1850. Oxford University Press, 1965.

Nicholson, Andrew. 'Form and Content in Byron's Poetry and Prose', *The Byron Journal*, 13 (1985), 52–60.

Oman, Carola. *Britain Against Napoleon*. London: Faber and Faber, 1942.

Page, Norman. (ed.). *Byron: Interviews and Recollections*. London: Macmillan, 1985.

Paulson, Ronald. *Representations of Revolution (1780–1820)*. New Haven: Yale University Press, 1983.

Pedley, Colin. 'Anticipating Invasion: Some Wordsworthian Contexts', *TWC*, 21, 2 (Spring 1990), 64–75.

Porter, Roy and Teich, Mikulas. (eds.). *Romanticism in National Context*. Cambridge University Press, 1988.

Prickett, Stephen (ed.). *England and the French Revolution*. Houndsmill, Basingstoke, Hampshire and London: Macmillan Education, 1989.

Purkis, John. *The World of the English Romantic Poets: A Visual Approach*. London: Heinemann, 1982.

Putnam, M. C. J. *Virgil's Pastoral Art: Studies in the Eclogues*. Princeton University Press, 1970.

Quennell, Peter. *Byron: The Years of Fame; Byron in Italy*. London: Collins, 1974.

Raphael, Frederick. *Byron*. London: Thames and Hudson, 1982.

Reitz, Bernard. '"To die as honour dies" – Politics of the Day and the Romantic understanding of History in Southey's, Shelley's and Byron's Poems on Napoleon' in *The Hanover Byron Symposium: 1979*. ed. James Hogg. Salzburg: University of Salzburg, 1981.

Redpath, Theodore. *The Young Romantics and Critical Opinion, 1807–1824: Poetry of Byron, Shelley and Keats as seen by their Contemporary Critics*. London: Harrap, 1973.

Renwick, W. L. *English Literature 1789–1815*. Oxford: Clarendon Press, 1963.

Robinson, Charles E. *Shelley and Byron: The Snake and Eagle Wreathed in Fight*. Baltimore and London: Johns Hopkins University Press, 1976.

Robinson, Robert E. *William Hazlitt's Life of Napoleon Buonaparte; Its Sources and Characteristics*. Geneva: Librairie E. Droz; Paris: Librairie Minard, 1959.

Roe, Nicholas. 'Imagining Robespierre' in *Coleridge's Imagination: Essays in Memory of Pete Laver*. ed. Richard Gravil, Lucy Newlyn and Nicholas Roe. Cambridge University Press, 1985, 161–70.

Wordsworth and Coleridge: The Radical Years. Oxford: Clarendon Press, 1988.

Root, Christina M. 'History as Character: Byron and the Myth of Napoleon' in *History and Myth: Essays on English Romantic Literature*. ed. Stephen C. Behrendt. Detroit: Wayne State University Press, 1990, 149–65.

Rudé, George. *Revolutionary Europe 1783–1815*. London: Fontana, 1986.

Rudich, Norman. '"Kubla Khan": A Political Poem', *Romanticisme*, 8 (1974), 36–53.

Russell, Bertrand. *History of Western Philosophy and its Connection with Political and Social Circumstances from the Earliest Times to the Present Day*. London: George Allen and Unwin, 1946.

Rutherford, Andrew. (ed.). *Byron: Augustan and Romantic*. London: Macmillan in association with The British Council, 1990.

(ed.). *Byron: The Critical Heritage*. London: Routledge, 1970.

Said, Edward. *Orientalism*. London: Routledge, 1978.

Scott, Gordon C. 'Scott among the Partisans: A Significant Bias in his *Life of Napoleon Buonaparte*', *Scott Bicentenary Essays*. ed. Allen Bell. Edinburgh: Scottish Academic Press, 1973.

Scott, Ian Robertson. 'From Radicalism to Conservatism: The Politics of

Wordsworth and Coleridge, 1787–1818'. Unpublished doctoral dissertation, Edinburgh, 1987.

'"Things as They Are": The Literary Response to the French Revolution' in *Britain and the French Revolution, 1789–1815*. ed. H.T. Dickinson. London: Macmillan, 1989, 229–49.

Shilstone, Frederick W. *Byron and the Myth of Tradition*. Nebraska University Press, 1988.

Simpson, David. 'Recent Studies in the Nineteenth Century', *Studies in English Literature, 1500–1900*, 30, 4 (Winter 1990), 715–48.

Wordsworth's Historical Imagination: The Poetry of Displacement. London: Methuen, 1987.

Smith, L. P. *Four Words, Romantic, Originality, Creative, Genius*. Oxford: Clarendon Press, 1924.

Spater, George. *William Cobbett: The Poor Man's Friend*. 2 vols. Cambridge University Press, 1982.

Spiegelman, Wilfred. *Wordsworth's Heroes*. Berkeley, Los Angeles and London: California University Press, 1985.

Super, R. H. *Walter Savage Landor: A Biography*. London: John Calder, 1957.

Thomas, Gordon Kent. *Wordsworth's Dirge and Promise*. Nebraska University Press, 1971.

'Wordsworth's Iberian Sonnets: Turncoat's Creed?', *TWC*, 13, 1 (Winter 1982), 31–4.

Thompson, E. P. 'Disenchantment or Default? A Lay Sermon' in *Power and Consciousness*, ed. Conor Cruise O'Brien and William Dean Vanech. London University Press, 1969, 149–82.

Thompson, J. M. *Napoleon Bonaparte: His Rise and Fall*. Oxford: Basil Blackwell, 1952 rpt 1988.

Thorslev, Peter L. Jr. *The Byronic Hero: Types and Prototypes*. Minnesota University Press, 1962.

'Post Waterloo Liberalism: The Second Generation', *SiR*, 28, 3 (Fall 1989), 437–61.

Todd, F. M. *Politics and the Poet: A Study of Wordsworth*. London: Methuen & Co., 1957.

Tripp, Edward. *Dictionary of Classical Mythology*. London: Collins, 1970.

Trueblood, Paul Graham (ed.). *Byron's Political and Cultural Influence in Nineteenth Century Europe: A Symposium*. Atlantic Highlands, New Jersey: Humanities Press, 1981.

Tulard, Jean. *Le Myth de Napoléon*. Paris: Armand Collins, 1971.

Napoleon: The Myth of the Saviour. trans. Teresa Waugh. London, Methuen & Co., 1985.

Turner, John. *Wordsworth: Play and Politics*. London: Macmillan, 1986.

Vitoux, Pierre. '*Gebir* as an Heroic Poem', *TWC*, 7, 1 (Winter, 1976), 51–7.

Wakefield, David. *Stendhal: The Promise of Happiness*. Bedford: The Newstead Press, 1984.

Walker, Eric C. 'Wordsworth, Warriors and Naming', *SiR*, 29, 2 (Summer 1990), 224–40.

Wardle, Ralph M. *Hazlitt*. Nebraska University Press, 1971.

Watson, G. 'The Revolutionary Youth of Wordsworth and Coleridge', *Critical Quarterly*, 18 (1976), 49–66.

Watson, J. R. *English Poetry of the Romantic Period: 1780–1830*. London and New York: Longman, 1985.

Watson, J. Steven. *The Reign of George III 1760–1815*. Oxford: Clarendon Press, 1960.

Webb, Timothy. 'Byron and the Heroic Syllables', *Keats–Shelley Review*, 5 (Autumn 1990), 41–74.

Weinbrot, Howard D. *Augustus Caesar in 'Augustan' England – The Decline of a Classical Norm*. Princeton University Press, 1978.

Weinstein, Mark A. 'Sir Walter Scott's French Revolution: The British Conservative View', *Scottish Literary Journal*, 7, 1 (May 1980), 31–40.

Whale, John. 'Hazlitt on Burke: The Ambivalent Position of a Radical Essayist', *SiR*, 25, 4 (Winter 1986), 466–81.

White, Hayden. *The Tropics of Discourse*. Baltimore: Johns Hopkins University Press, 1978.

White, R. J. *Political Tracts of Wordsworth, Coleridge and Shelley*. Cambridge University Press, 1953.

White, Terence DeVere. *Tom Moore*. London: Hamish Hamilton, 1977.

Wichert, R. A. 'Napoleon and the English Romantic Poets'. Unpublished doctoral dissertation, Cornell University, 1948.

Wilkie, Brian. *Romantic Poets and Epic Tradition*. Wisconsin University Press, 1965.

Williams, John. *Wordsworth: Romantic Poetry and Revolutionary Politics*. Manchester University Press, 1989.

Winbolt, S. E. (ed.). *England and Napoleon (1801–1815)*. 2nd ed., London: G. Bells and Sons, 1915.

Wingarten, Renee. *Writers and Revolution: The Fatal Lure Of Action*. Wisconsin University Press, 1965.

Wittreich, Joseph Anthony Jr. (ed.). *The Romantics On Milton: Formal Essays and Critical Asides*. Case Western Reserve University Press, 1970.

Woodring, Carl R. 'On Liberty in the Poetry of Wordsworth', *PMLA*, 70 (1955) 1033–48.

Politics in English Romantic Poetry. Cambridge, Mass.: Harvard University Press, 1970.

Politics in the Poetry of Coleridge. Wisconsin University Press, 1961.

'Three Poets on Waterloo', *TWC*, 18, 2 (Spring 1987) 54–6.

Wordsworth, Jonathan. *William Wordsworth and the Age of English Romanticism*. With Michael C. Jaye and Robert Woof, with the assistance of Peter Funnell. New Brunswick & London: Rutgers University Press; Dove Cottage, Grasmere: The Wordsworth Trust, 1988.

Wright, D. G. *Napoleon and Europe*. Seminar Studies in History. London and New York, 1984.

Yale French Studies. Special Issue: The Myth Of Napoleon. 26 (1960–1).

Index

CAMBRIDGE STUDIES IN ROMANTICISM
TITLES PUBLISHED

1. *Romantic Correspondence*
Women, Politics and the Fiction of Letters
MARY A. FAVRET

2. *British Romantic Writers and the East: Anxieties of Empire*
NIGEL LEASK

3. *Edmund Burke's Aesthetic Ideology*
Language, Gender and Political Economy in Revolution
TOM FURNISS

4. *Poetry as an Occupation and an Art in Britain, 1760–1830*
PETER MURPHY

5. *In the Theatre of Romanticism: Coleridge, Nationalism, Women*
JULIE A. CARLSON

6. *Keats, Narrative and Audience*
ANDREW BENNETT

7. *Romance and Revolution: Shelley and the Politics of a Genre*
DAVID DUFF

8. *Literature, Education, and Romanticism*
Reading as a Social Practice, 1780–1832
ALAN RICHARDSON

9. *Women Writing About Money*
Women's Fiction in England, 1790–1820
EDWARD COPELAND

10. *Shelley and the Revolution in Taste*
The Body and the Natural World
TIMOTHY MORTON

11. *William Cobbett: The Politics of Style*
LEONORA NATTRASS

12. *The Rise of Supernatural Fiction, 1762–1800*
E. J. CLERY

13. *Women Travel Writers and the Language of Aesthetics, 1716–1818*
ELIZABETH A. BOHLS

14. *Napoleon and English Romanticism*
SIMON BAINBRIDGE

15. *Romantic Vagrancy*
CELESTE LANGAN